IMAGES
of America

BLOOMFIELD HILLS
HOME OF CRANBROOK

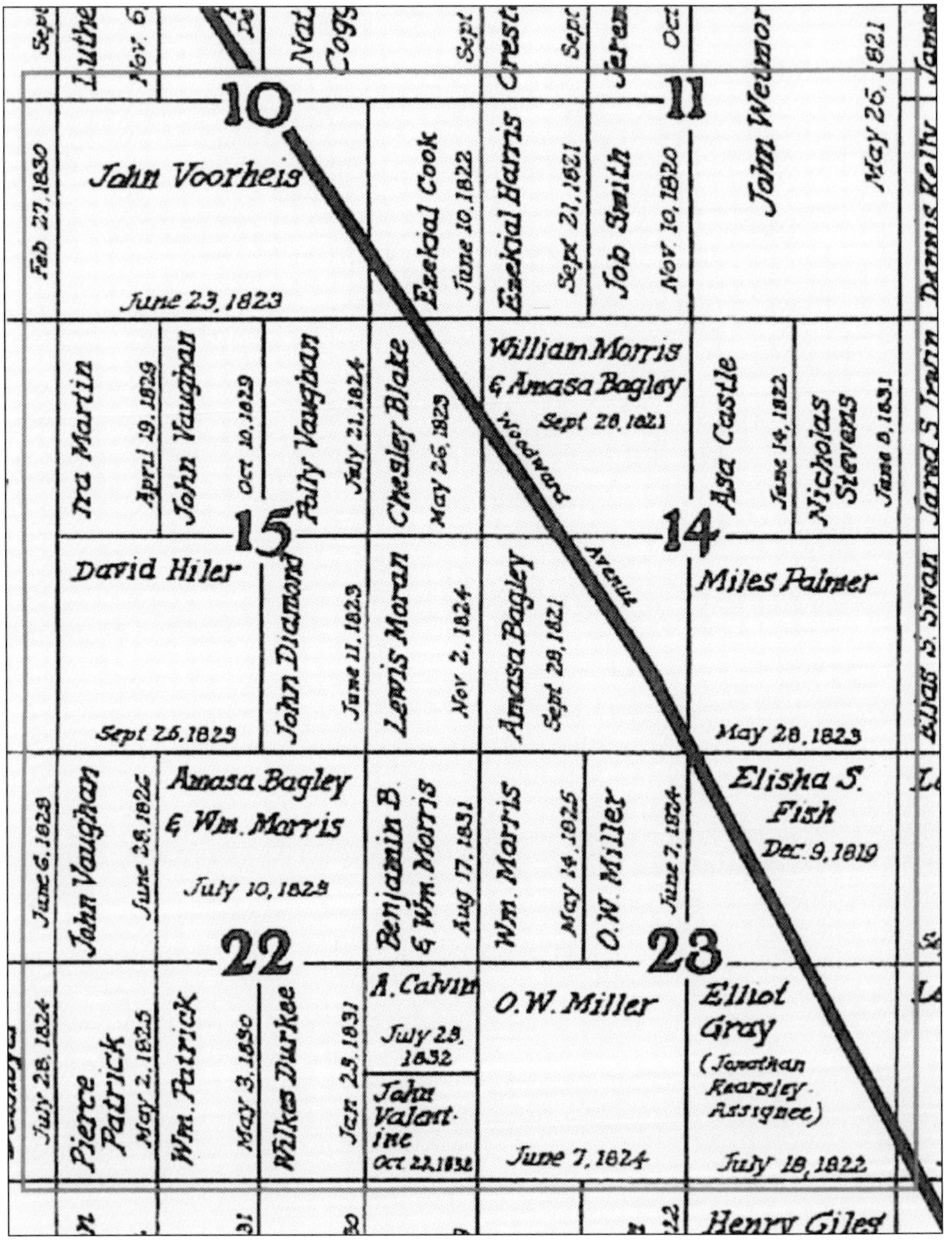

This map detail shows the earliest landowners in the area that is now Bloomfield Hills. The slanting vertical line from the top left to the bottom right is Woodward Avenue (then the Saginaw Trail). The bottom horizontal line represents today's Quarton Road. The top horizontal line represents today's Hickory Grove Road, while the horizontal line bisected by the numbers 14 and 15 approximates today's Long Lake Road. (Courtesy of John Marshall.)

On the Cover: The Booths' touring car sits in front of the recently completed Cranbrook House around 1910. Warren Booth is seated in the front with Parks Walter, the Booth family's first chauffeur, while Grace Booth sits in the backseat. The house, designed by Albert Kahn, was the first major building completed in what would eventually become Cranbrook Educational Community. (Courtesy of Cranbrook Archives.)

IMAGES
of America

Bloomfield Hills
Home of Cranbrook

Christine Blackwell

ARCADIA
PUBLISHING

ISBN 978-1-4671-1655-8

Published by Arcadia Publishing
Charleston, South Carolina

Printed in the United States of America

Library of Congress Control Number: 2015959729

For all general information, please contact Arcadia Publishing:
Telephone 843-853-2070
Fax 843-853-0044
E-mail sales@arcadiapublishing.com
For customer service and orders:
Toll-Free 1-888-313-2665

Visit us on the Internet at www.arcadiapublishing.com

Dedicated in loving memory of Gladys and Edward Blackwell,
who lived in Bloomfield Hills from 1972 to 1984

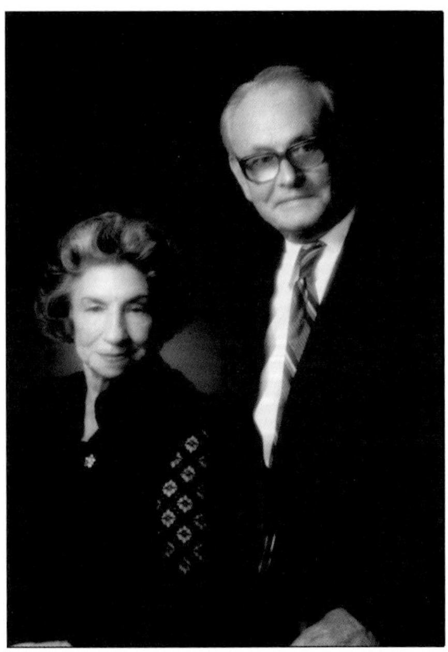

CONTENTS

Acknowledgments

The process of writing a book "takes a village," and I have been fortunate to work with a very intelligent and generous village of people interested in helping to create an accurate record of Bloomfield Hills history. I am grateful to many people, but foremost to my title manager, Sarah Gottlieb, and to my reviewers—Pat Hardy, former Bloomfield Hills mayor and city commissioner; Leslie Edwards, head archivist of the Cranbrook Archives; John Marshall, Bloomfield historian; and Tera Moon, assistant library director at Bloomfield Township Public Library. Additionally, I would like to thank the following people who have helped to make this book possible: Gina Tecos, archivist for the Cranbrook Archives; Dawn Eurich and Romie Minor of the Burton Historical Collection at the Detroit Public Library; Dana Bellant and Victor G. Martin of Kingsley Inn; Paul A. DePorre, attorney-at-law; Diane K. Bert; Kathleen Tillson of Next; Nicholas E. Graczyk of Bloomfield Hills Country Club; Mark Wood; Candy Geeter; Msgr. Anthony Tocco of St. Hugo of the Hills; Richard Orton; Kim Hoxworth of Dittrich Furs; Craig Arnold; Marcia Ruff, school historian, the Roeper School; Camelia Lewis of the Roeper School; Zoe Lewis; Maria Mainville of Taubman; Jim Shettel and Lisa Crawford of Birmingham Unitarian Church; Richard Smith of Woodward Hills Nursing Center; Barbara Frye and Breanna Koehler of Oakland County Pioneer and Historical Society; Brenda McKeen; Al Kaline; Barbara Broock Bini; Louise Simpson and Gary Hendrickson of the Village Club; Commissioner Michael Dul; Harry C. Walsh; the Women's Spirituality Group of Christ Church Cranbrook, especially Leslie McNamara; Bee Engelhart, Sue Nine, and the rest of the Friends of Preservation Bloomfield; Deborah A. Stevens; my brother and sister-in-law, Norm and Laurie Blackwell; Greg Kowalski; Scott Romney; Bruce Annett and Anne Adamus of Lawrence Technological University; Susan Kehoe; Dana Bachman at the Bentley Historical Library, University of Michigan; Deborah Rice, audiovisual archivist at the Walter P. Reuther Library, Wayne State University; Carol DeWeese; Anthony Pordon of Penske Automotive; Nancy Hague; Dave and Kathleen Royer; Niki Gallaudet of Stonycroft Hills Club; the Detroit Historical Society; Sean Southers and Dawn Zsalako of Premier Health Care Management; Nancy Magnus; Caitlin Lapratt of Bloomfield Open Hunt Club; Nicole Pielecha of Academy of the Sacred Heart; Fr. Peter Fennessy of Manresa Jesuit Retreat House; Amy Burton; John Kroell; John Zawiskie of Cranbrook Institute of Science; and Kris McDonagh.

Introduction

This book presents a visual history of Bloomfield Hills from its earliest days to the mid-1990s. Its scope is limited by the photographs that could be obtained to tell its story as well as the number of images that could fit between this book's covers. Bloomfield Hills' history as a city is quite short; the city has been incorporated only since 1932. Its physical size is equally limited: its boundaries encompass an area of only 5.04 square miles. However, the city's size and short history belie the disproportionate number of contributions that its residents have made not only to Detroit and Michigan, but also to the nation and the world in almost every area of the arts and sciences, as well as in philanthropy. In this regard, the city's history is quite unique.

Today, Bloomfield Hills is an affluent suburban city located 20 miles north of downtown Detroit with a population that hovers just under 4,000 people. Most of its residents are well educated, work in professional fields, and enjoy the privilege of living among the city's rolling, tranquil hills in homes ranging from upscale condominiums to grand estates worth millions of dollars. However, the city did not start out this way, and its past was at times as rocky as its original landscape. As you read through this book, you will discover that Bloomfield Hills has been a city of many contrasts. It was shaped and built over the decades by residents who had varying visions of what it could become. Indeed, it was built with money but also with hard physical work that took decades to complete.

Above all else, the city of Bloomfield Hills is the home of Cranbrook, the internationally renowned educational community created by George Gough Booth and his wife, Ellen Scripps Booth. That community is now a National Historic Landmark. Its private schools and institutions are considered to be among the best in the nation. In 1904, the Booths purchased the first 175 acres of land that they would begin transforming at first into their country home and later into the now-famous educational community. The Booths are highlighted within this city's history because their contributions touched almost every aspect of this city's development in one way or another.

Prior to its becoming a village in 1927 and then a city in 1932, Bloomfield Hills was mostly farms and fruit orchards and was devoid of the many mature tall trees it is known for today. However, the history of its landscape actually began 13,000 years ago. As the Huron and Erie glacial lobes collided and retreated across this area, they carved out the hills but also dragged and left behind large rocks and boulders from other regions. When settlers first started moving to this area in the early 1800s, they found the rocky soil difficult to cultivate and spent much time and energy removing the rocks. Today, remnants of that difficult period appear in the long, beautiful fieldstone walls that were built near many of the city's roads. Also ubiquitous throughout the city are the many tributaries and branches of the Rouge River. These depressions were formed by the meltwaters as the glaciers retreated.

As the climate warmed, various plants grew and animals began to inhabit the area. Evidence of Native American life in the form of arrowheads has been discovered near streams and rivers in several parts of the city, suggesting hunting as well as skirmishes, but the land does not show evidence of being permanently inhabited until settlers arrived.

The first Europeans arrived in the Detroit area between 1660 and 1760, and they were mostly French, but the area north of Detroit that was to become Bloomfield Hills remained unsettled.

Part of the reason for this is that initially there were very few settlers in all of Michigan. Federal surveyors had declared much of Michigan uninhabitable because of its swampland, and the entire region was bypassed by settlers who instead headed west to Illinois and Missouri.

For a long time, the Saginaw Trail, which was the footpath used by Native Americans to travel from their settlement in Saginaw to Detroit, was also considered nearly impassable by surveyors. That was until 1817, when Col. Henry Leavenworth established a military road along it, and by 1824, the soggy route had been partially transformed into a plank road from Detroit to Pontiac, complete with tollbooths.

Following treaties with Native American tribes between 1819 and 1821, property rights began to be recognized and new settlers from the East began moving into Michigan. According to *The History of Oakland Country, 1817–1877*, published by L.H. Everts and Co., the first settlers to the area included Elijah Fish, Amasa Bagley, and William Morris. You will read more about each of these settlers and their contributions in the pages of this book.

By 1820, Bloomfield was established as a township. In 1825, after the completion of the Erie Canal and with government incentives to purchase land at $2 an acre, the area's population began to surge. The surge was relative, however, because the census of 1830 showed that only 30 families lived within the 36 square miles of the township.

By the late 1800s, the area was replete with farms, as can be seen in the maps on several pages within this book. Then, in 1897, the Interurban, or "Oakland Railway," electric trolley was extended from Detroit to Pontiac, connecting the farming community to the main centers of population and ensuring delivery of the farms' produce at the best rates. The Interurban also made it possible for residents to begin traveling between the cities of Detroit and Pontiac.

With the advent of the automobile at the turn of the century, the migration of Detroit's wealthiest citizens to the area began, at first to establish summer and weekend homes in the country, as well as to practice a bit of farming, which was in vogue then as a gentleman's pastime. Soon, large homes began to dot the hills along Woodward Avenue and Bloomfield's other main roads. Many of the earlier homes reflected a New England style, sometimes reminiscent of the owners' former homes on the East Coast. Examples of these homes include Deepdale and Uplands, which you will find pictured in the pages of this book.

However, more changes were soon to come. A booming economy and excursions abroad by Bloomfield's wealthy new residents influenced tastes, and the new homeowners began to build large English-style manor homes on the hills, mimicking those they had visited in England and the rest of Europe. Prominent builders and developers during this time included Manley Davis and Judson Bradway. Davis built the Fox and Hounds Inn in Bloomfield Hills after visiting inns and taverns around Oxford, England. Bradway developed Trowbridge Farms, Country Club Estates, and several other subdivisions in the area after a successful career developing real estate in downtown Detroit. Davis, along with Edward J. Butler and William Barbour, began to transform the intersection at Long Lake Road and Woodward Avenue into a microcosm of old England. All of their buildings had a distinct Tudor Revival design. However, their efforts to complete a city center of English-style businesses were thwarted when the Great Depression began.

Davis, Bradway, and Butler were not the only people who had a vision of what Bloomfield Hills could become. A sampling of the city's other movers and shakers and their dreams for this city are also included in this book. As an example, the various contributions made by William Barbour, George Booth, Edwin George, and Charles Stinchfield are prominently featured within these pages because they, along with William Chittenden, established the Bloomfield Hills Country Club.

The history of Bloomfield Hills towards the end of the 20th century is of a place more settled and diverse. With the next generation came new landowners and ideas. For a variety of reasons, including taxes and inflation as well as the post–World War II growth of the suburbs, many of the former estate properties were sold or torn down and the land subdivided. By 1990, condominiums began dotting the terrain along Woodward Avenue. Nonetheless, even the smallest homes in the city would be considered elegant by most people's standards, and you can still find the names of the grand estates on many of the city's street signs.

One

THE EARLY YEARS

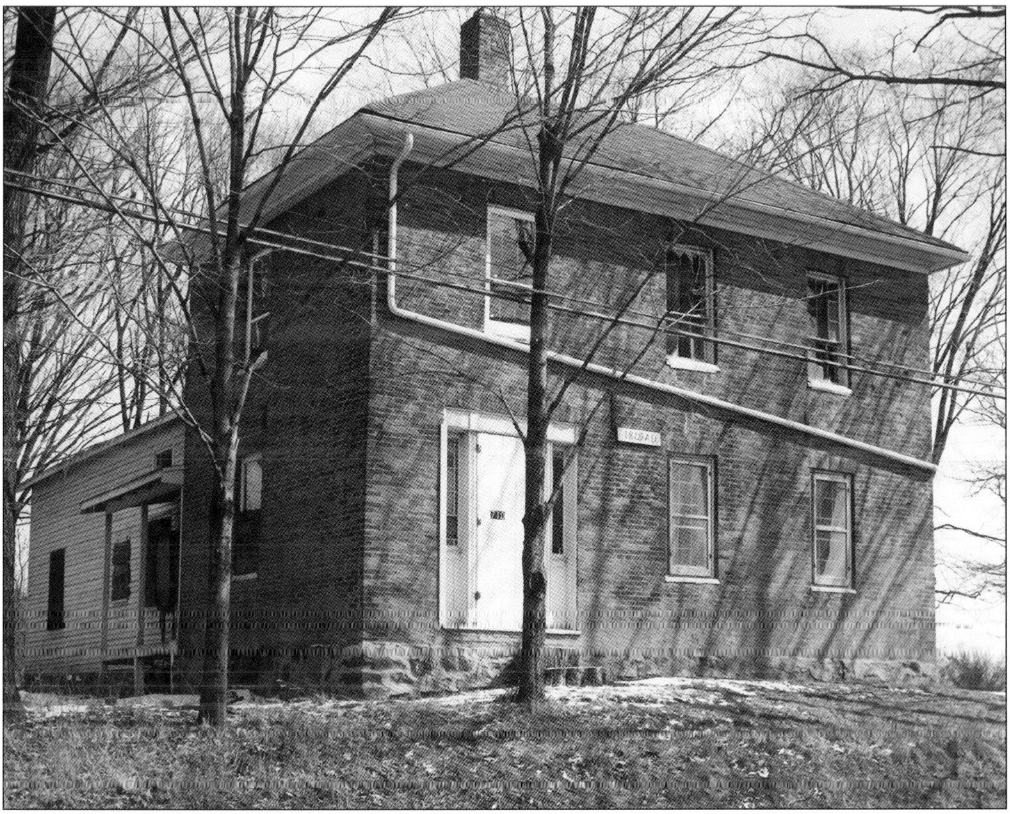

The Fish-Benedict House was Oakland County's oldest brick and wood home. It was built by Deacon Elija S. Fish, one of the area's first settlers. In 1819, Fish purchased 80 acres just north of present-day Lone Pine Road and Woodward Avenue, and he later conducted the area's first Presbyterian meetings in his barn. In 1857, he sold the house to Eri Benedict. The house was demolished in the 1970s. (Courtesy of Birmingham Historical Museum and Park.)

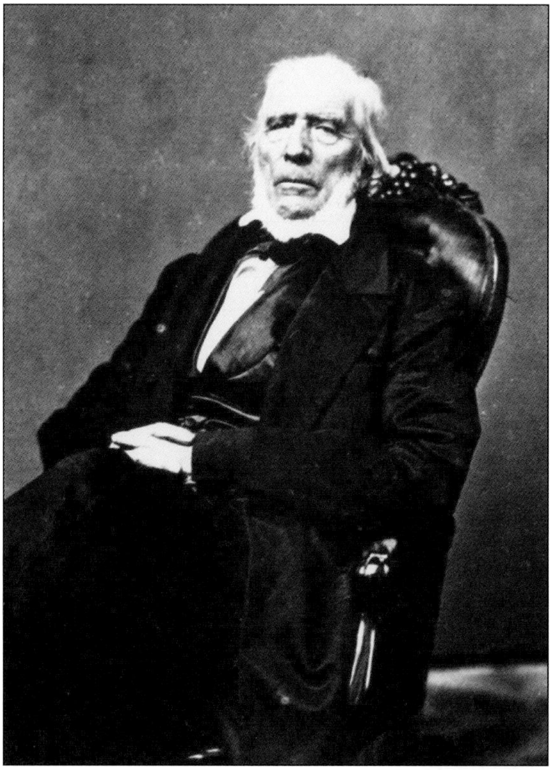

Amasa Bagley (1778–1863) and Nancy Brown Bagley (1786–1866) were two of the earliest settlers to the area. They came by sleigh in 1817–1818 to what was then a territory. In 1819, the Bagleys and their five daughters built a log home in the area that later became Bloomfield Hills. A community leader, Amasa was appointed the first judge of Oakland County. In 1832, the Bagleys built and lived in a frame house with several rooms, which they turned into a tavern. The tavern was a popular gathering place for town meetings, and its use led to the area being called Bagley's Corners. One of the daughters, Nancy Davis, later recalled seeing hundreds of Indians pass their house daily. She also recalled a visit to their tavern by Alexis de Tocqueville. (Both, courtesy of Cranbrook Archives.)

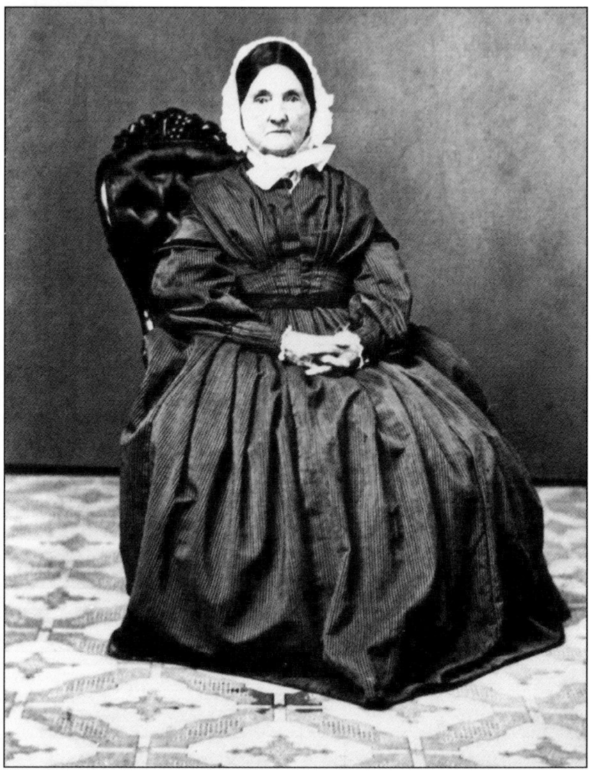

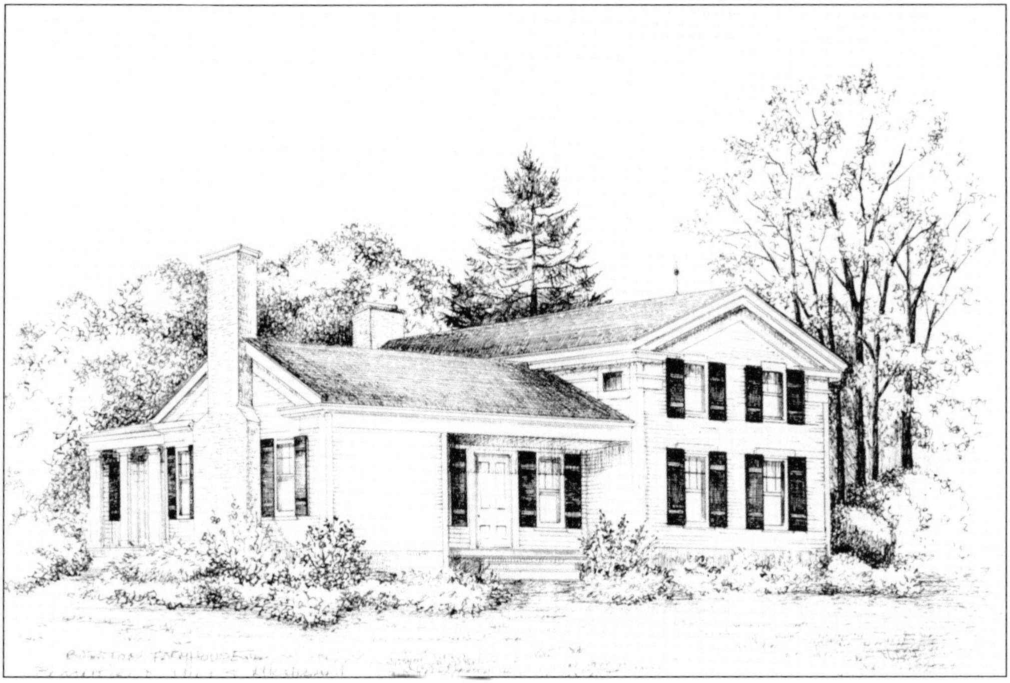

The Barton Farmhouse is estimated to have been built between 1832 and 1845 on property located on the south side of East Long Lake Road between the Bloomfield Open Hunt Club and Eastways Road. The Benjamin family lived there from 1844 to 1895. After several changes in ownership, Carl Barton bought the property in 1937, and he sold it to a developer in 2006. The house was moved in 2008 to Bowers School Farm. (Courtesy of Pat Hardy.)

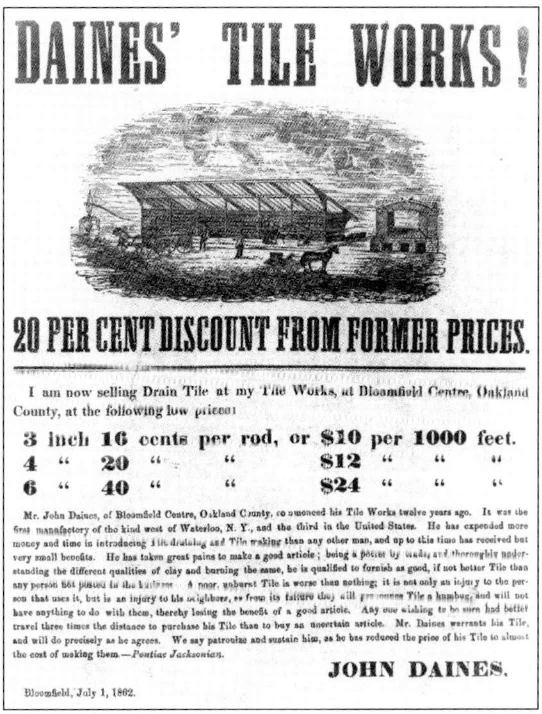

This advertisement for Daines Tile Works is from 1862. J. Daines was the owner of property on both sides of what is now Woodward Avenue at Long Lake Road. By 1872, the area would be called Bloomfield Centre, and A. Pearsall would own the business that formerly operated on the Daines property. Pearsall named his company Bloomfield Tile Works and Pottery. (Courtesy of Cranbrook Archives.)

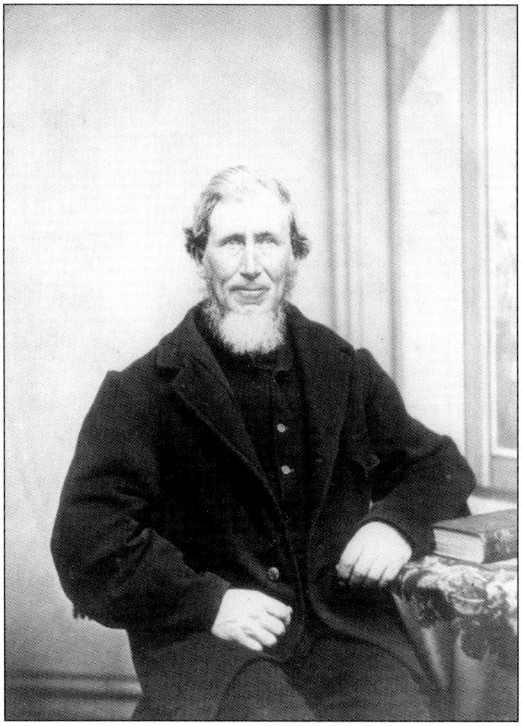

Benjamin Morris (1809–1881) was the first cousin once removed of William Morris, one of the original settlers of Bloomfield Hills and the namesake of the Morris Mill, which was rebuilt and still exists today. Benjamin co-owned land with William that would later become part of the Cranbrook property. (Courtesy of Cranbrook Archives.)

Benita Alexander Dyer, daughter of Samuel and Kezia Alexander, drew this 1889 sketch of the Morris Grist Mill. For many years, William Morris used his mill to grind the grain of local farmers. By 1900, the first Morris Mill had burned to the ground. Benita's father, Samuel Alexander, would later sell his farm to George Booth. (Courtesy of Cranbrook Archives.)

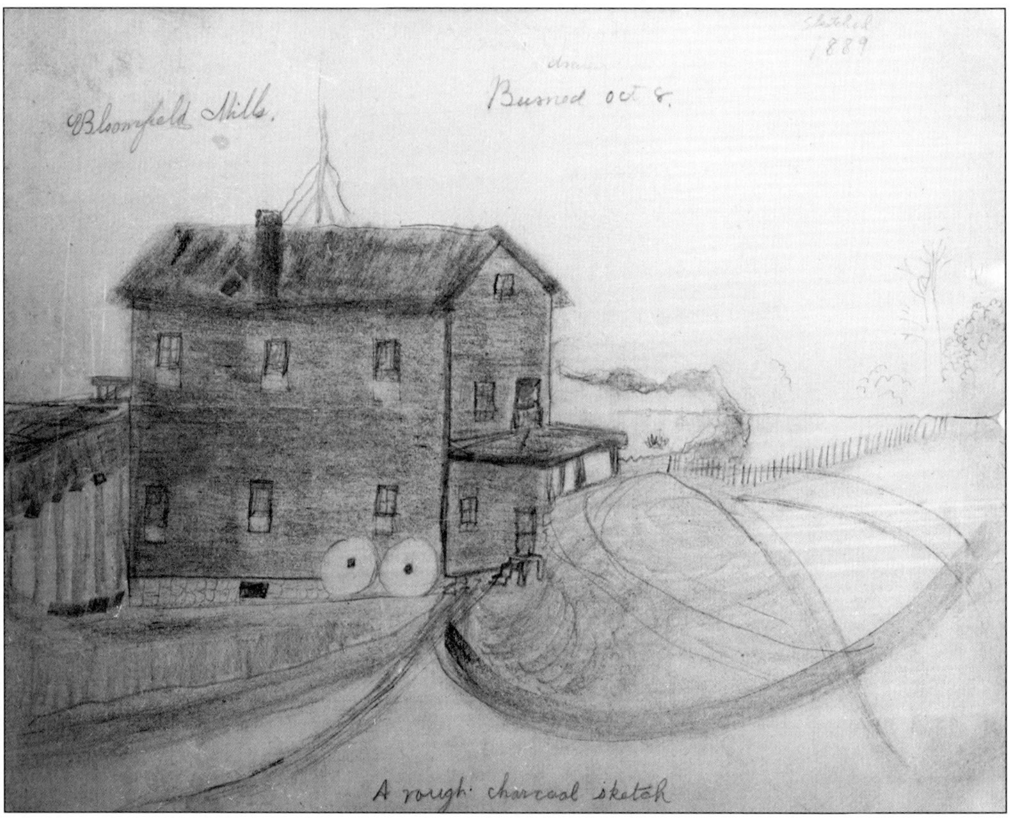

William DeWing (1839–1906) was a first cousin twice removed of William Morris, one of Bloomfield's earliest settlers. DeWing lived in the area of Bloomfield Centre that is now Long Lake Road and Woodward Avenue. A copy of DeWing's diary, which includes his experiences in the Civil War, is in the Cranbrook Archives. (Courtesy of Cranbrook Archives.)

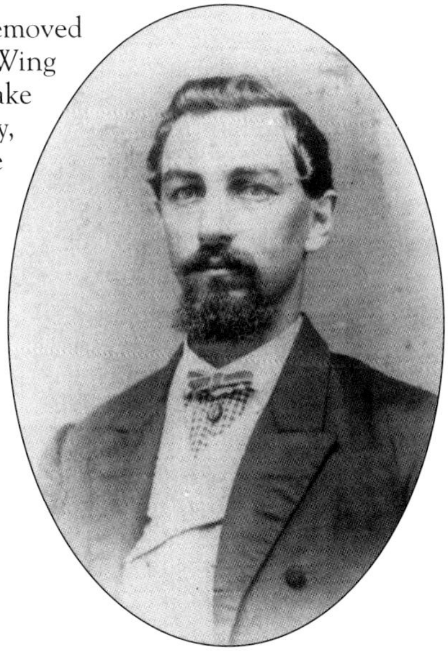

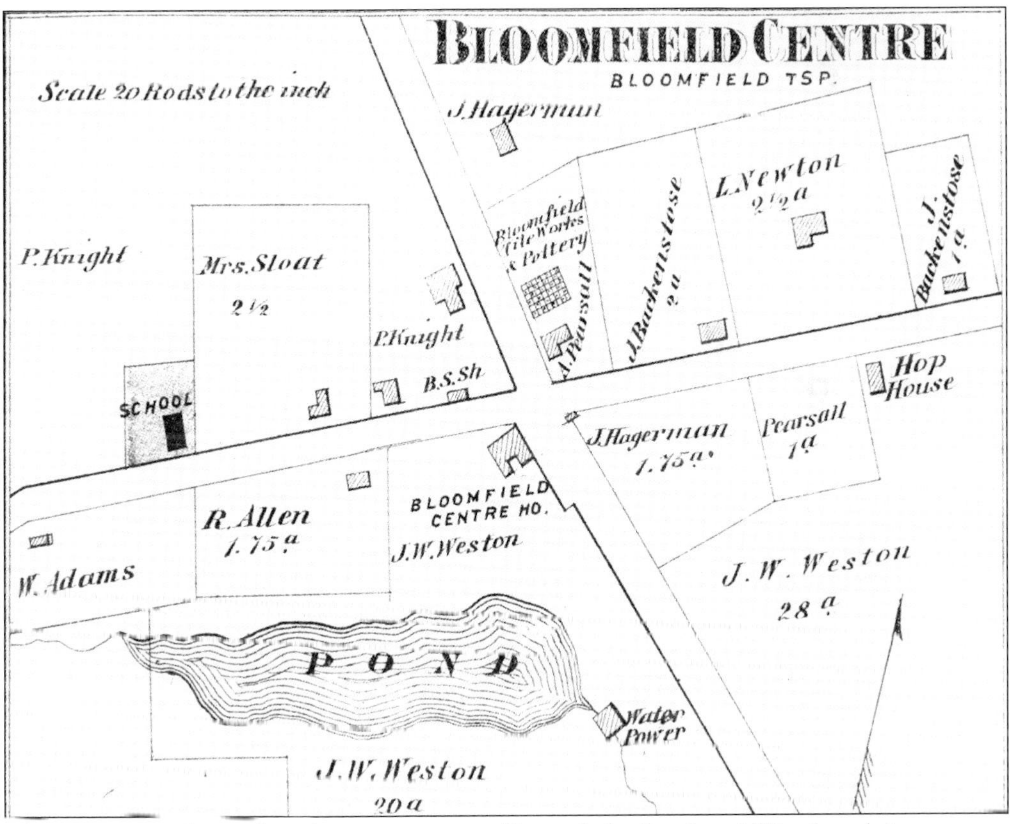

This 1872 map shows that the intersection of Long Lake Road and Woodward Avenue was being called Bloomfield Centre (or sometimes Center) rather than Bagley's Corners. At this point, Bloomfield Centre was still part of Bloomfield Township. The ownership of the land and businesses had completely turned over in 50 years, with most of the land owned by J.W. Weston. (Courtesy of Pat Hardy.)

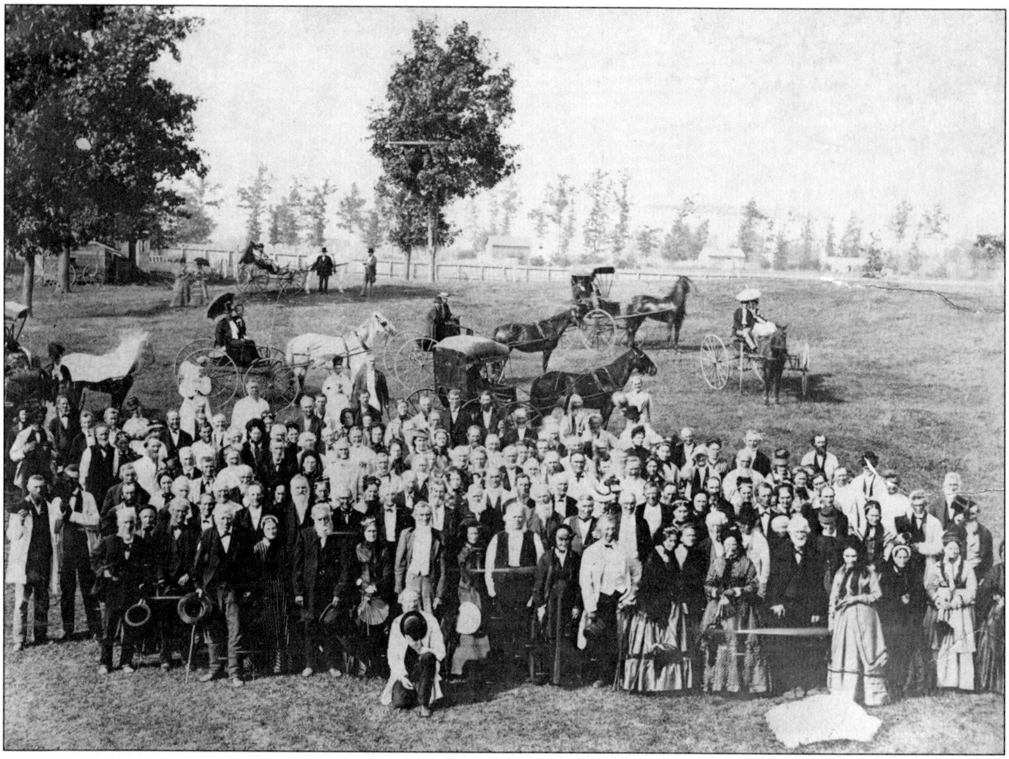

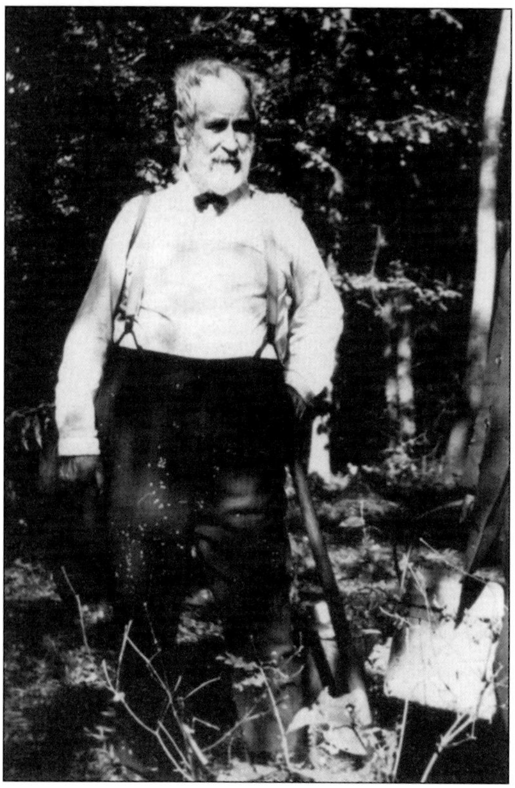

In 1874, the first semiannual meeting and picnic was held by some of Oakland County's first settlers. That year, they had organized themselves into the Pioneer Society of Oakland County. Initial members were required to be residents prior to 1840. Early Bloomfield settler family names such as Fish and Hendrickson (née Bagley) are on the membership list. (Oakland County Pioneer and Historical Society.)

Samuel Alexander, shown here around 1900, would sell his run-down farm to George Gough Booth in 1904. Booth paid $120 an acre for the 100-acre property, which included apple, pear, and peach trees as well as a dilapidated 17-year-old farmhouse. Booth remodeled the farmhouse and used it as his family's summer home from 1904 to 1908. (Courtesy of Cranbrook Archives.)

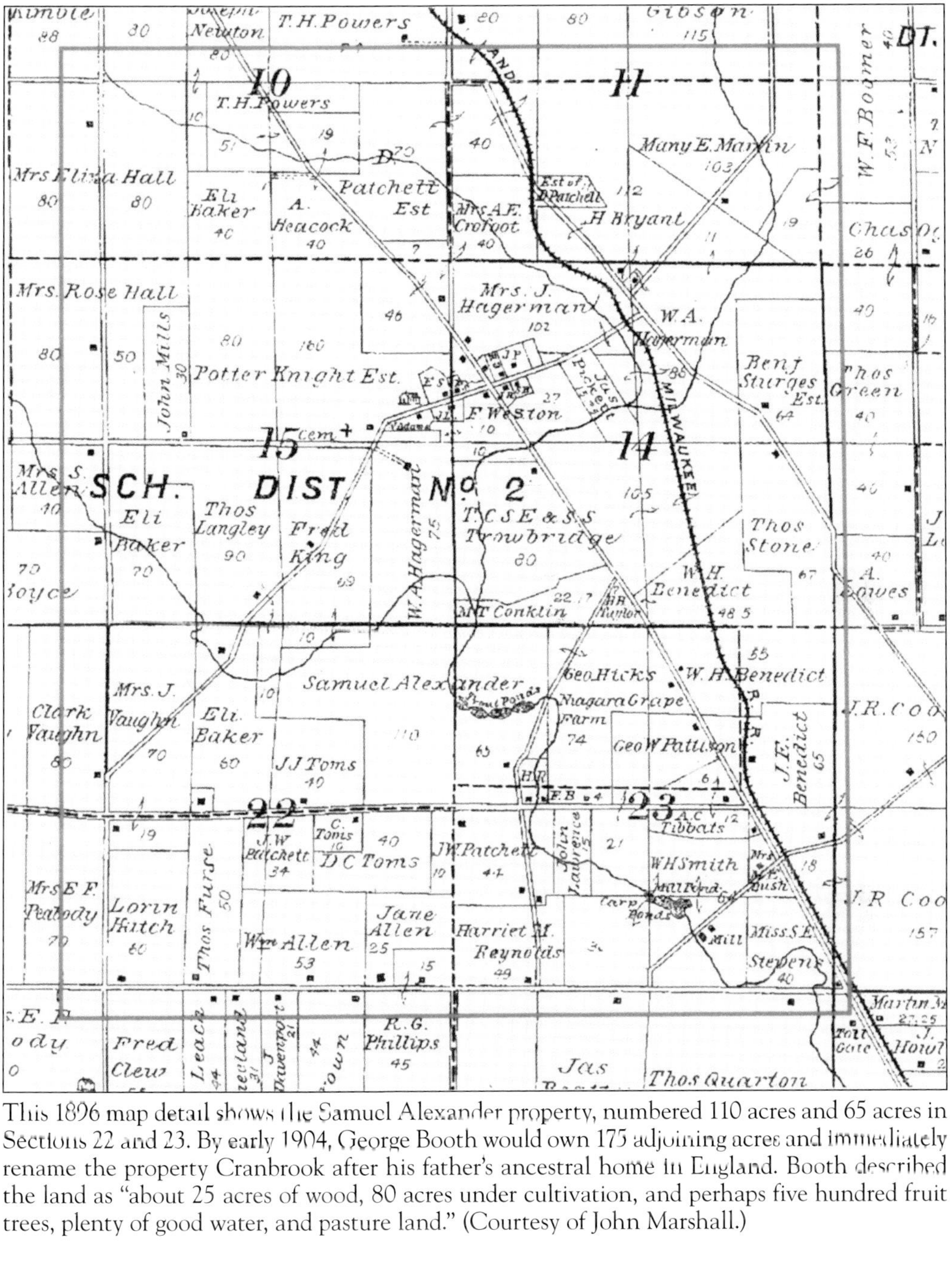

This 1896 map detail shows the Samuel Alexander property, numbered 110 acres and 65 acres in Sections 22 and 23. By early 1904, George Booth would own 175 adjoining acres and immediately rename the property Cranbrook after his father's ancestral home in England. Booth described the land as "about 25 acres of wood, 80 acres under cultivation, and perhaps five hundred fruit trees, plenty of good water, and pasture land." (Courtesy of John Marshall.)

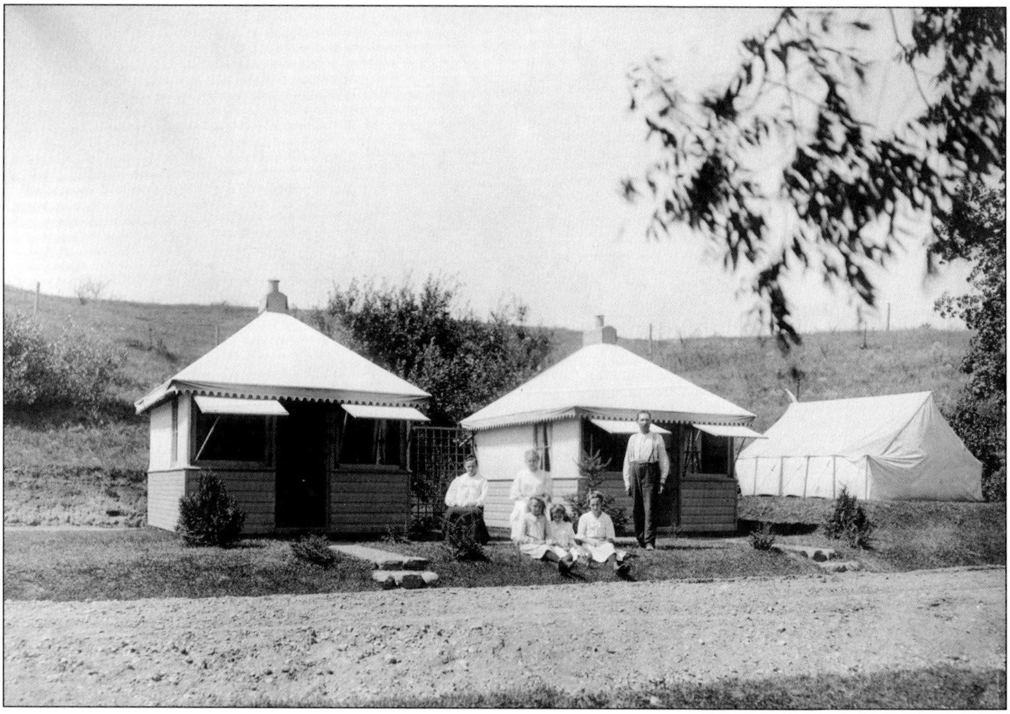

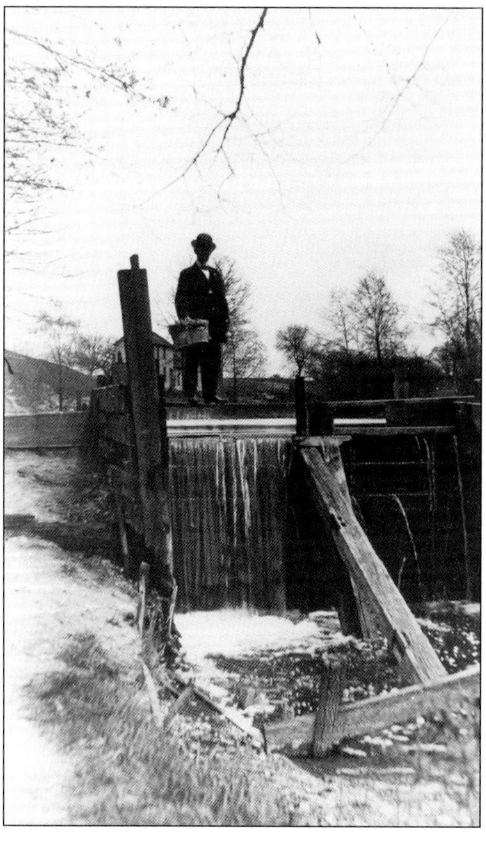

This c. 1906 photograph shows "the Camp" on the grounds of Cranbrook. In 1906, Booth's *Detroit News* competitor, the *Detroit Free Press*, began sponsoring the largest fresh-air camp in the Detroit area to give underprivileged and handicapped city children the opportunity to experience fresh air and sunshine in the country. (Courtesy of Cranbrook Archives.)

An unidentified man overlooks the original millpond dam on the Cranbrook property. On the back of this photograph, Henry Booth wrote notes questioning whether the former Alexander farmhouse or the poorhouse is shown in the background. Before Alexander owned the farm, it was owned by William Morris, who was also the area's sheriff and responsible for the care of the poor. (Courtesy of Cranbrook Archives.)

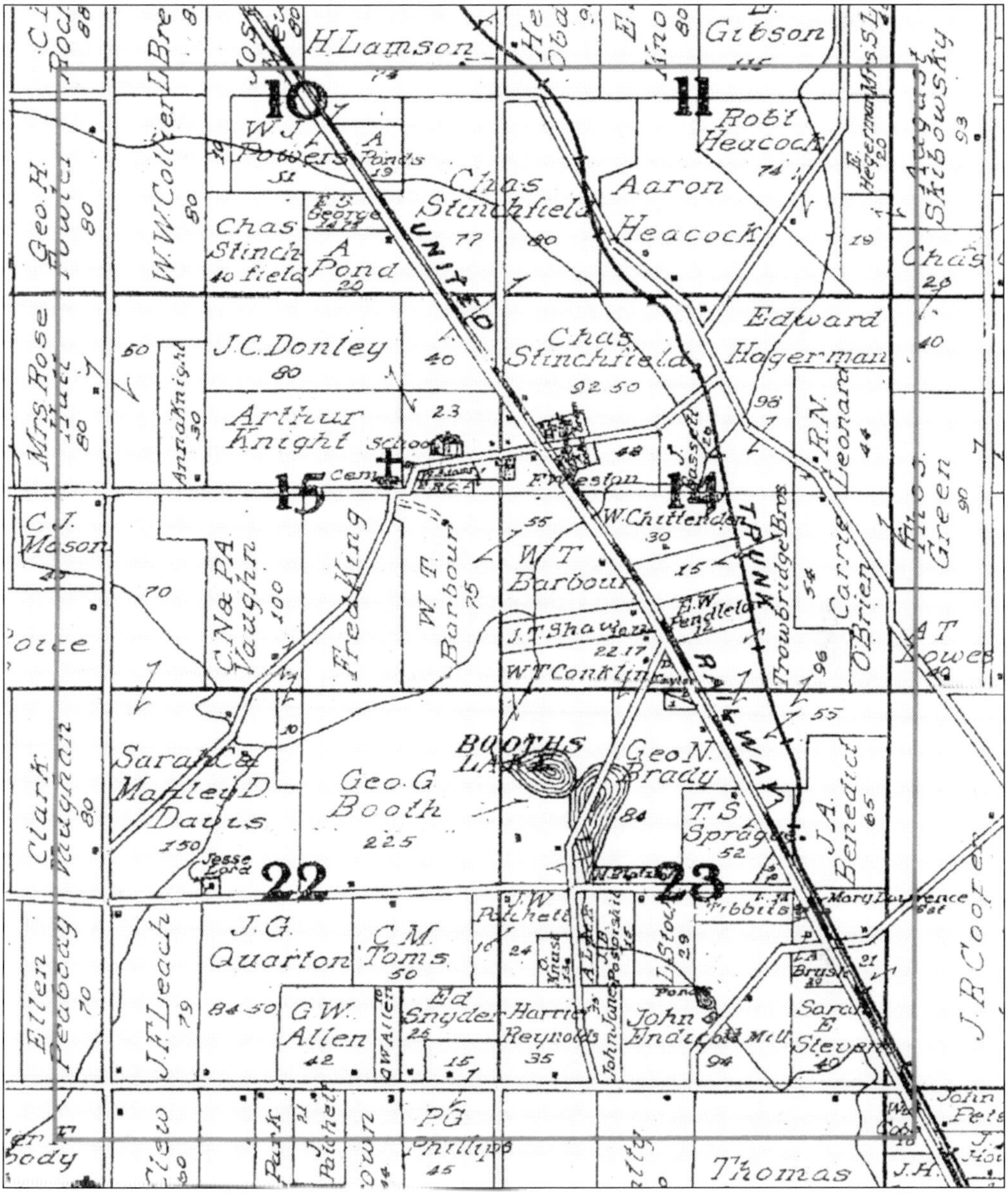

This map shows the 1908 ownership of land within the future boundaries of the city of Bloomfield Hills. Lining Woodward Avenue are the names of many of the new estate builders. The two largest landowners closest to Woodward Avenue at Long Lake Road are Charles Stinchfield and William Barbour. The cross in Section 15 indicates a cemetery northwest of Vaughan and Long Lake Roads. The cemetery would later be moved to Pontiac. To the right of the cemetery is Circle School. George Booth owns acreage in Sections 22 and 23 and has altered the former millponds to form a lake, which will later be named Kingswood Lake. A section of the Rouge River crosses Cranbrook Road onto the Brady property. (Courtesy of John Marshall.)

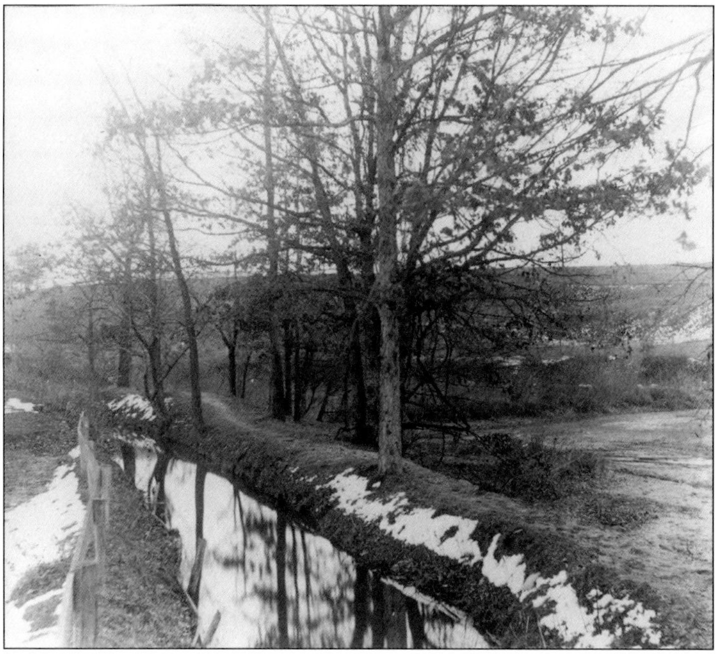

Today, plenty of trees and a stone wall hide the view of the old millrace that runs along Cranbrook Road. But this northward view shows what it looked like when the Booths purchased the property at the beginning of the 20th century. This is just north of where the Morris Grist Mill stood. (Courtesy of Cranbrook Archives.)

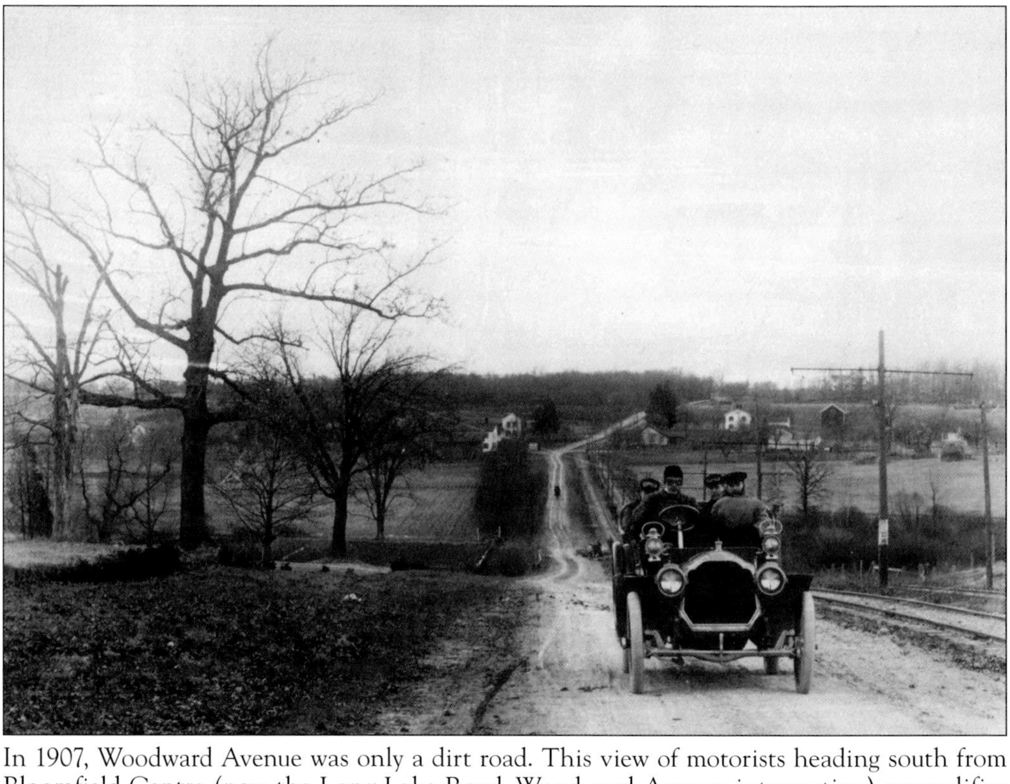

In 1907, Woodward Avenue was only a dirt road. This view of motorists heading south from Bloomfield Centre (now the Long Lake Road–Woodward Avenue intersection) exemplifies residents who typically belonged to the early auto clubs. Often, the residents drove the models of the Detroit companies they worked for. The Bagley Inn can be seen on the far left. (Courtesy of Cranbrook Archives.)

Bloomfield Hills City Hall was previously the Bloomfield Township Garage. The garage was completed in 1927 in an English style that the *Birmingham Eccentric* called "in keeping with the homes and other buildings in Bloomfield Hills Village." The township used the garage primarily for the storage and repair of its trucks. It gifted the building to Bloomfield Hills when the village incorporated as a city in 1932. (Courtesy of Pat Hardy.)

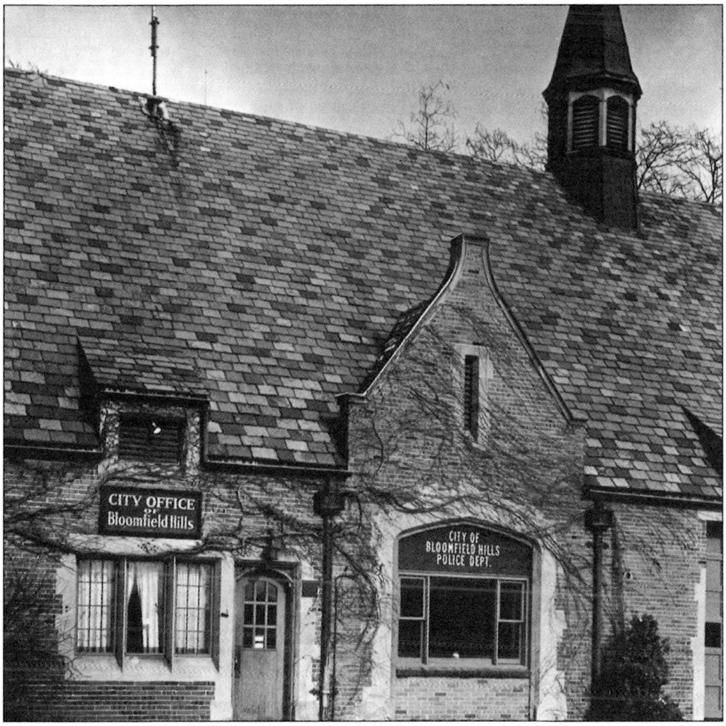

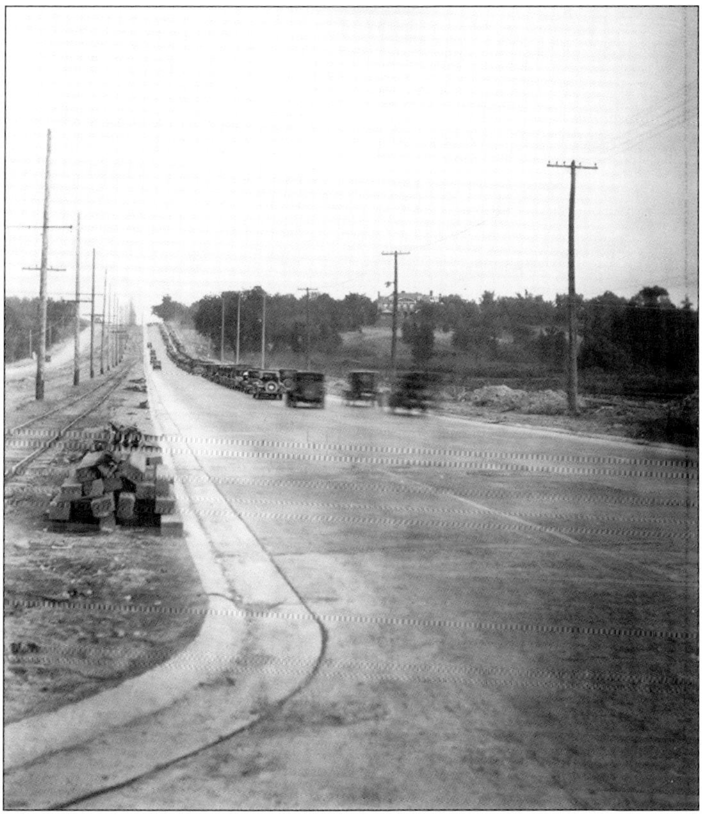

This c. 1920 photograph shows backed-up traffic heading south from Woodward Avenue and Long Lake Road to Birmingham. More lanes were desperately needed, even with the Interurban and the Grand Trunk Western Railroad also operating, as seen by the tracks on the left. In 1923, the state legislature passed a bill to widen Woodward Avenue to four lanes going each way. (Courtesy of Birmingham Historical Museum and Park.)

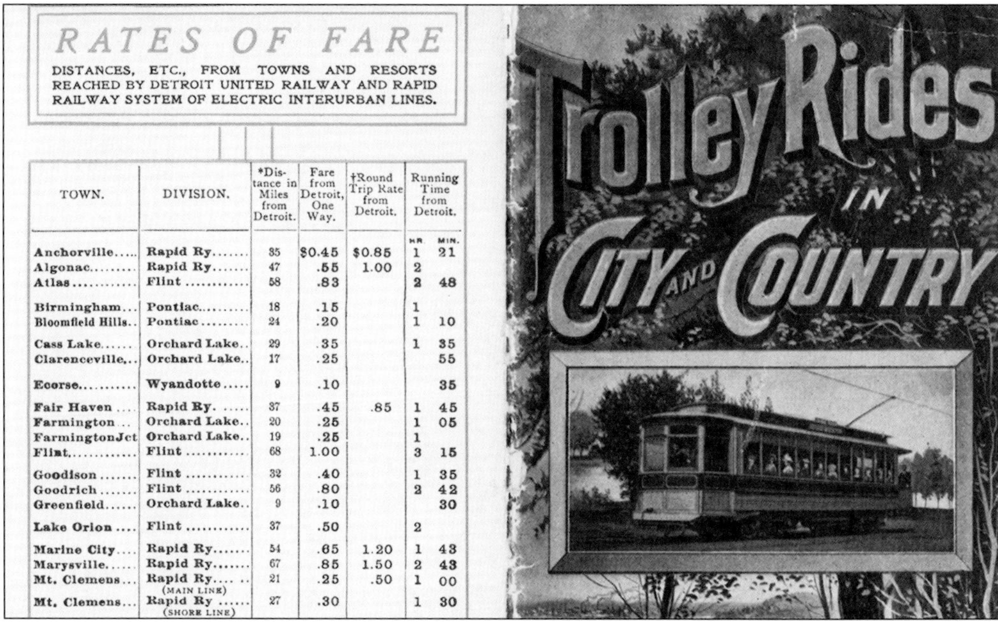

RATES OF FARE

DISTANCES, ETC., FROM TOWNS AND RESORTS REACHED BY DETROIT UNITED RAILWAY AND RAPID RAILWAY SYSTEM OF ELECTRIC INTERURBAN LINES.

TOWN.	DIVISION.	*Distance in Miles from Detroit.	Fare from Detroit, One Way.	†Round Trip Rate from Detroit.	Running Time from Detroit. HR.	MIN.
Anchorville.....	Rapid Ry.......	35	$0.45	$0.85	1	21
Algonac.........	Rapid Ry.......	47	.55	1.00	2	
Atlas...........	Flint...........	58	.83		2	48
Birmingham...	Pontiac.........	18	.15		1	
Bloomfield Hills..	Pontiac.........	24	.20		1	10
Cass Lake......	Orchard Lake..	29	.35		1	35
Clarenceville,..	Orchard Lake..	17	.25			55
Ecorse..........	Wyandotte.....	9	.10			35
Fair Haven	Rapid Ry.	37	.45	.85	1	45
Farmington ...	Orchard Lake..	20	.25		1	05
FarmingtonJct	Orchard Lake..	19	.25		1	
Flint............	Flint...........	68	1.00		3	15
Goodison	Flint...........	32	.40		1	35
Goodrich	Flint...........	56	.80		2	42
Greenfield......	Orchard Lake..	9	.10			30
Lake Orion	Flint...........	37	.50		2	
Marine City....	Rapid Ry.......	54	.65	1.20	1	43
Marysville......	Rapid Ry.......	67	.85	1.50	2	43
Mt. Clemens...	Rapid Ry..... .. (MAIN LINE)	21	.25	.50	1	00
Mt. Clemens...	Rapid Ry ...... (SHORE LINE)	27	.30		1	30

Trolley Rides in City and Country

This c. 1910 Detroit United Railway Brochure cites the fare from Detroit to Bloomfield Hills as 20¢, with a scheduled traveling time of one hour and 10 minutes. This trolley line, nicknamed the Interurban, was officially called the Detroit United Railway and Rapid Railway System of Electric Interurban Lines. (Courtesy of Birmingham Historical Museum and Park.)

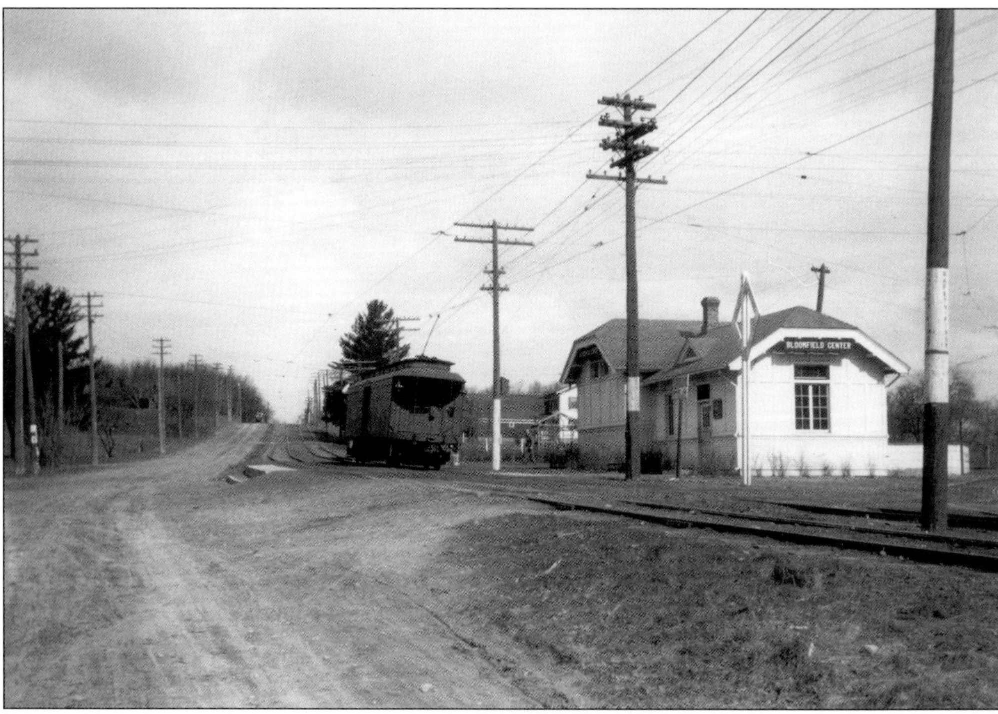

Around 1915, a spiderweb of electric lines crisscrosses over the Bloomfield Center Interurban station that was located at Woodward Avenue and Long Lake Road. Woodward Avenue, pictured on the left, was still a dirt road. (Courtesy of Cranbrook Archives.)

Two

HOMES OF DISTINCTION

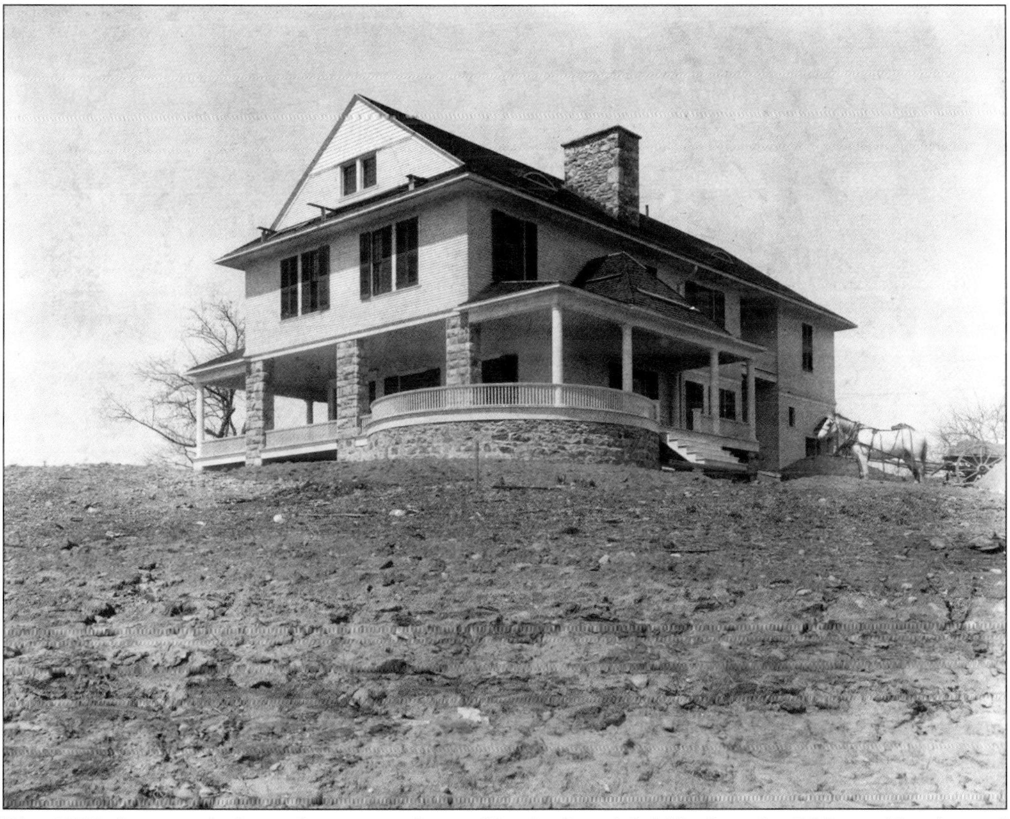

This 1897 photograph shows the summer home Charles Stinchfield built on his 286-acre Tanglewood Farm in the area that now extends north at Opdyke Road and Woodward Avenue. Tanglewood Farm was originally the Patchett, Crofoot, and Hagerman farms. Stinchfield greatly improved the property, which included a small lake and an icehouse. (Courtesy of the Burton Historical Collection, Detroit Public Library.)

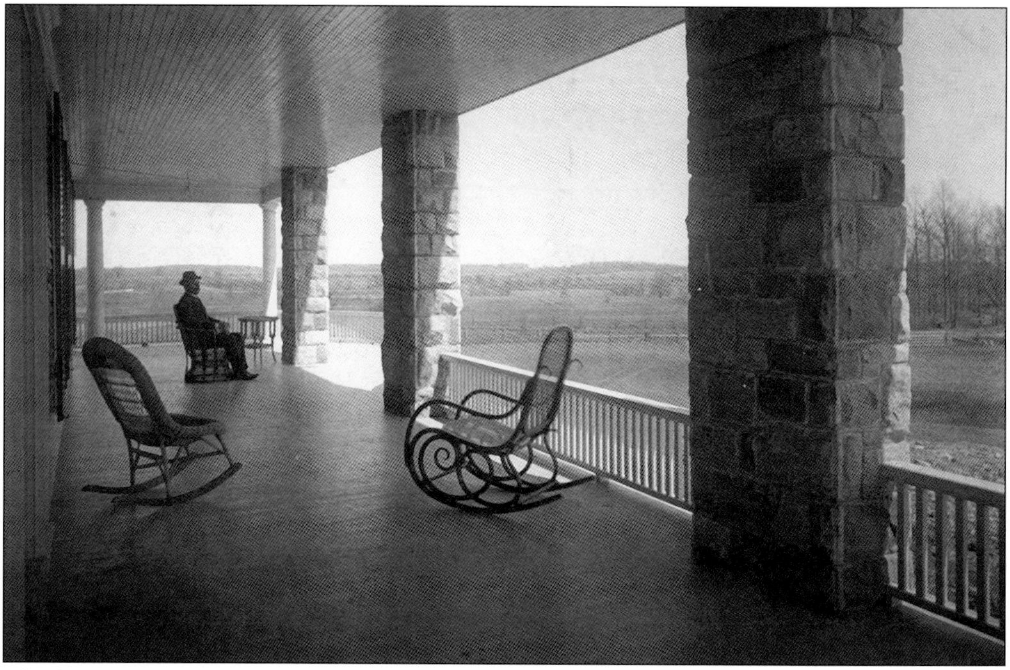

Charles Stinchfield, who made his fortune in lumber, saw this view as he looked out from his porch in 1897. Bloomfield Hills was still mostly farmland and devoid of the tall trees for which it is now known. The rolling land of his Tanglewood Farm included several barns and houses, a water tank, a mill, and a blacksmith shop. (Courtesy of the Burton Historical Collection, Detroit Public Library.)

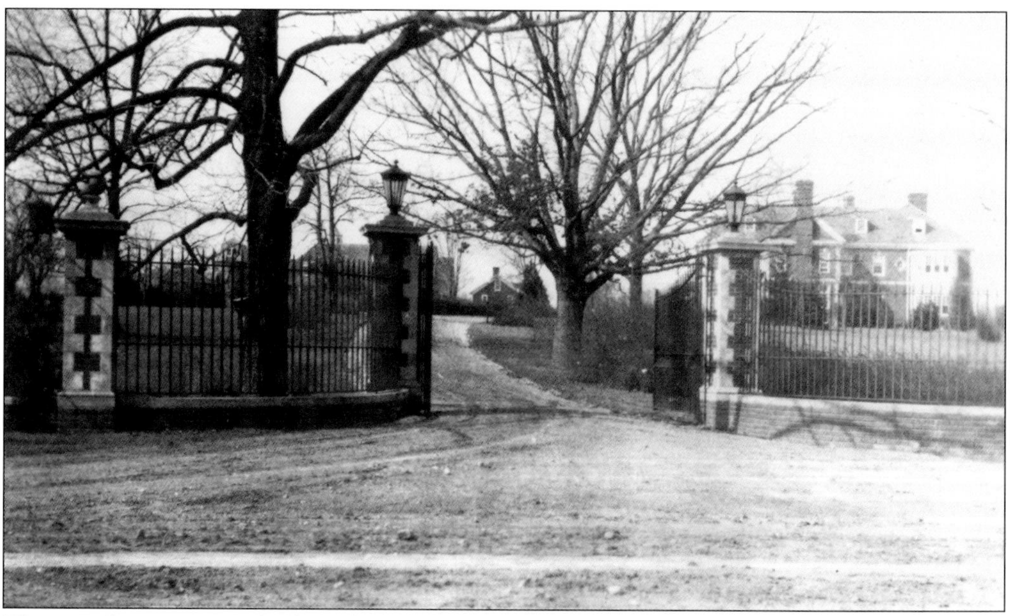

This grand entranceway leads to the summer home of William T. Barbour and his family. Barbour had purchased the property from the Trowbridge family. The pillars, built around 1904, are still standing today, although the entranceway is surrounded by tall trees. (Courtesy of the Burton Historical Collection, Detroit Public Library.)

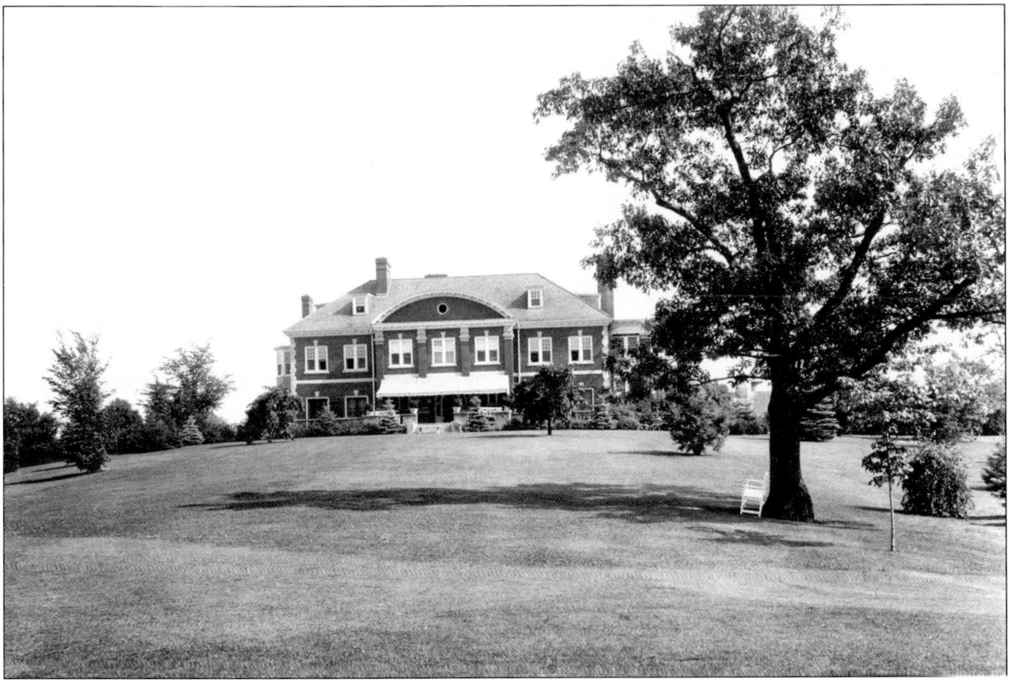

This 1904 photograph shows a closer view of the home of William T. Barbour, who was president of Detroit Stove Works. The Barbour family called their Georgian-style house Briar Bank. In 1943, the Daughters of Divine Charity acquired the home, which is now St. Elizabeth Briarbank, an assisted-living facility. (Courtesy of the Burton Historical Collection, Detroit Public Library.)

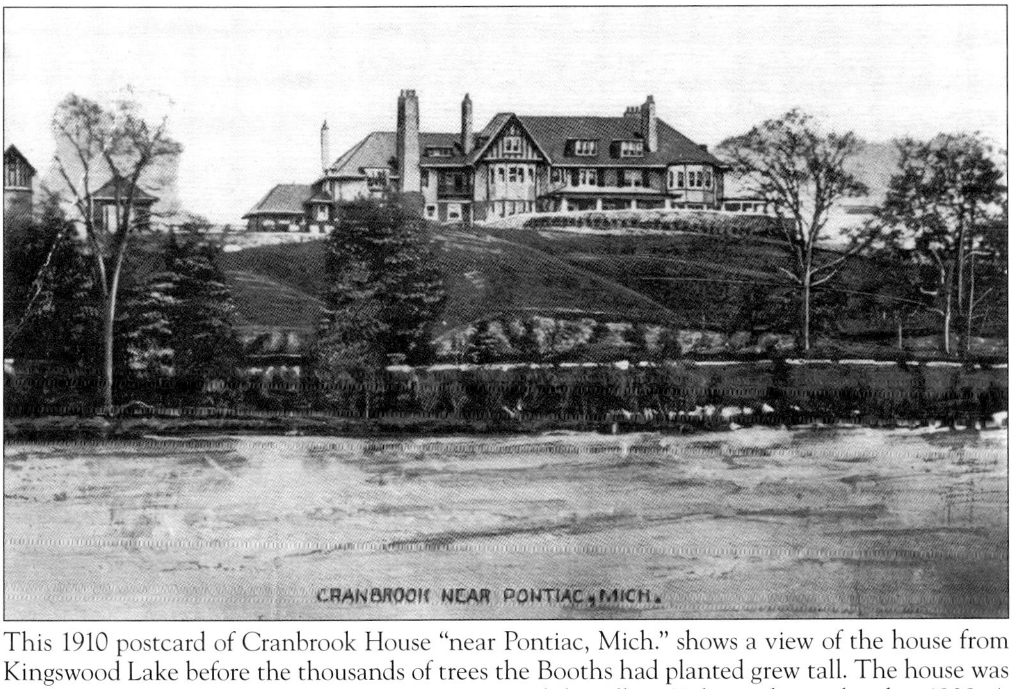

This 1910 postcard of Cranbrook House "near Pontiac, Mich." shows a view of the house from Kingswood Lake before the thousands of trees the Booths had planted grew tall. The house was designed for George Gough and Ellen Scripps Booth by Albert Kahn and completed in 1908. A small portion of Tower Cottage can be seen on the far left. (Author's collection.)

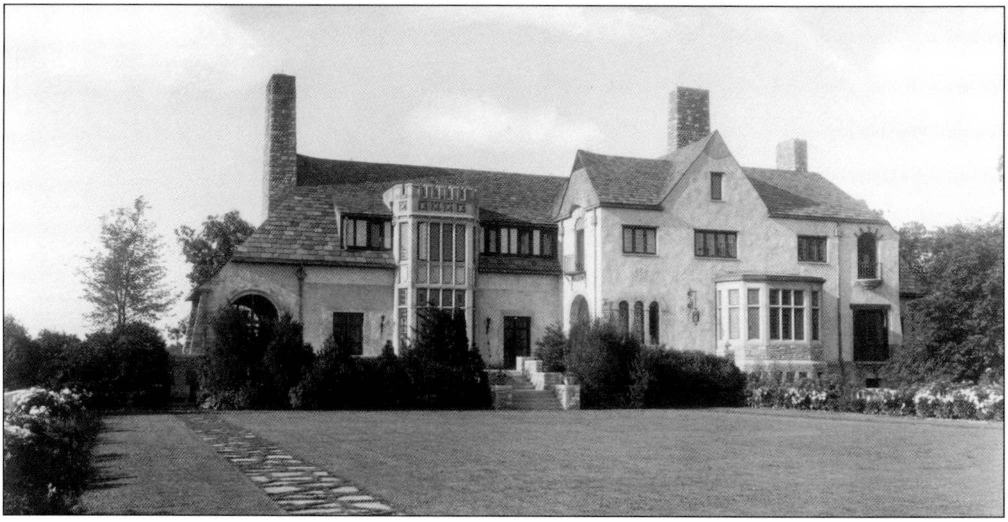

Cedarholm, shown in 1925, was the 40-acre estate of Col. Edwin S. George that he donated in 1947 to the Presbytery of Detroit. The presbytery built Kirk in the Hills there. George is important to the history of the city of Bloomfield Hills because he was also one of the founders of the Bloomfield Hills Country Club. (Courtesy of the Burton Historical Collection, Detroit Public Library.)

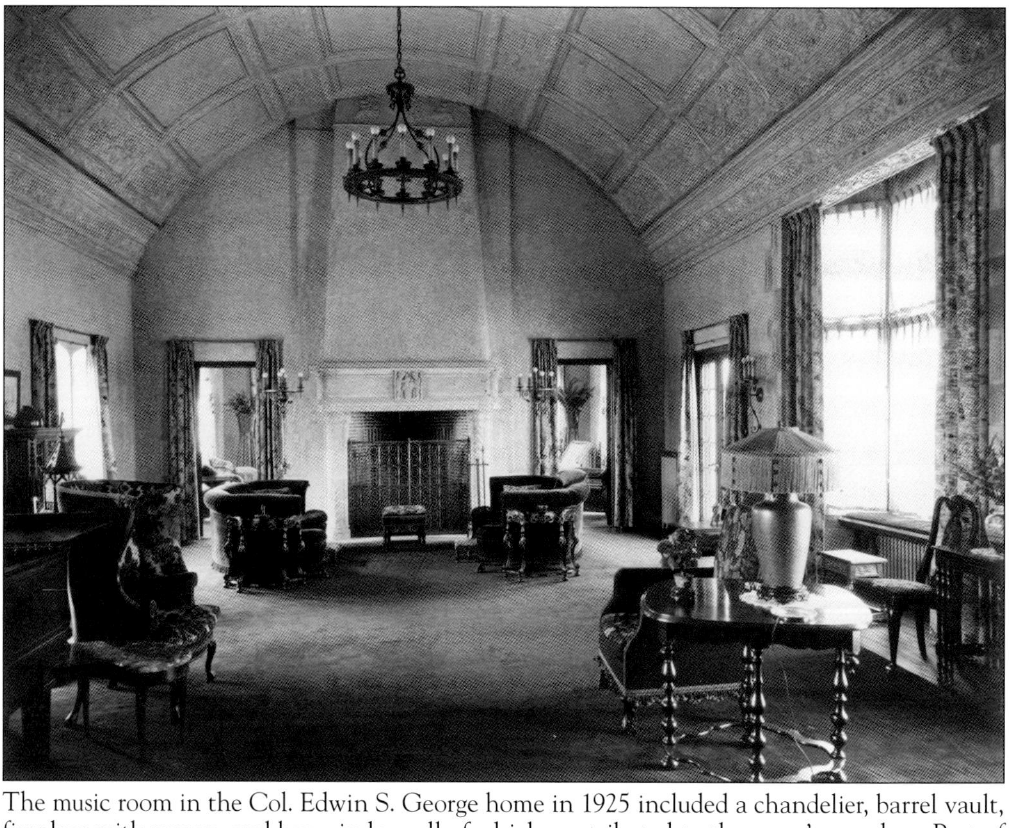

The music room in the Col. Edwin S. George home in 1925 included a chandelier, barrel vault, fireplace with screen, and bay window, all of which contributed to the room's grandeur. Part of the George house remains, having been incorporated into Kirk in the Hills. (Courtesy of the Burton Historical Collection, Detroit Public Library.)

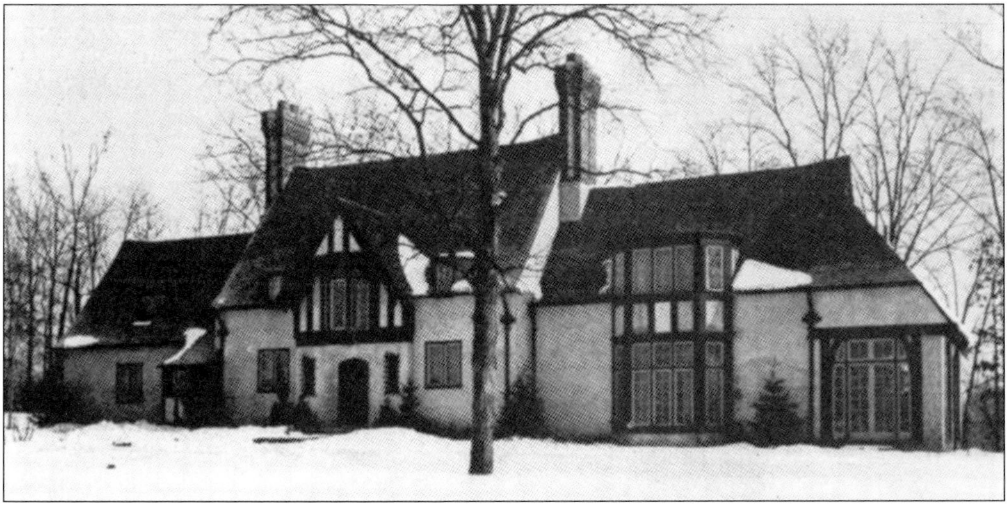

This c. 1962 photograph shows the Tudor Revival manor house of A.C. Born, which was designed by architect J. Ivan Dise and built in the 1920s. Born called his home Nestledown. The home was located on Burnham Road and was one of the first two estate houses built in the Trowbridge Farms subdivision. (Courtesy of the Burton Historical Collection, Detroit Public Library.)

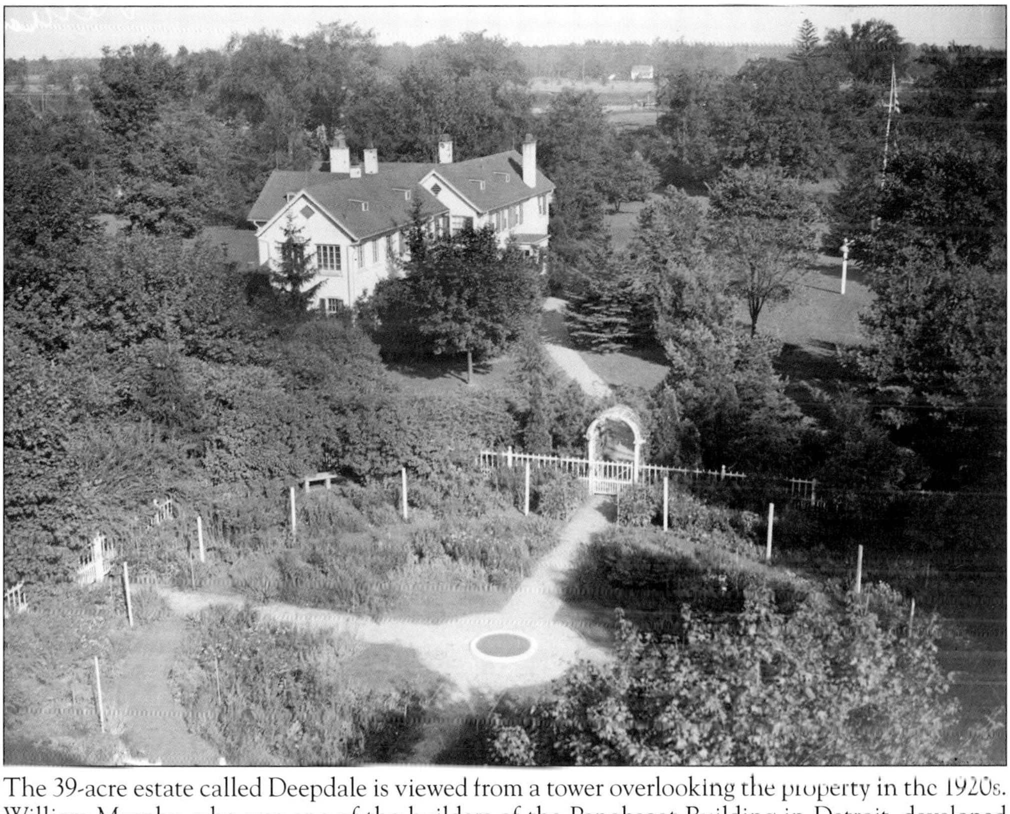

The 39-acre estate called Deepdale is viewed from a tower overlooking the property in the 1920s. William Murphy, who was one of the builders of the Penobscot Building in Detroit, developed the property to include a tile barn for milk cows and a pump house. In 1926, he sold the property, which became Manresa Jesuit Retreat House. (Walter P. Reuther Library, Archives of Labor and Urban Affairs, Wayne State University.)

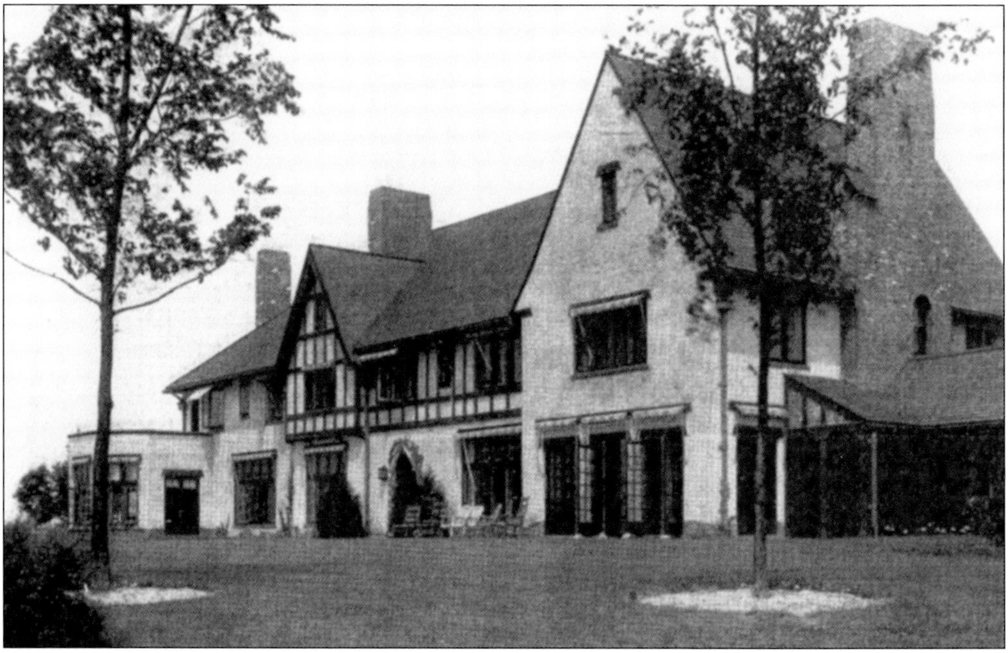

Edward Hammond built this half-timbered stucco manor house on 82 acres that he purchased in 1921. The house was called Hillwood and was used only as a summer residence. Hammond and his family lived in Grosse Pointe the rest of the year. The property bordered Vhay Lake south of Bloomfield Center Road (now Long Lake Road) and was east of Kensington Road. Hammond also built stables and three buildings to house staff. (*Afterglow*.)

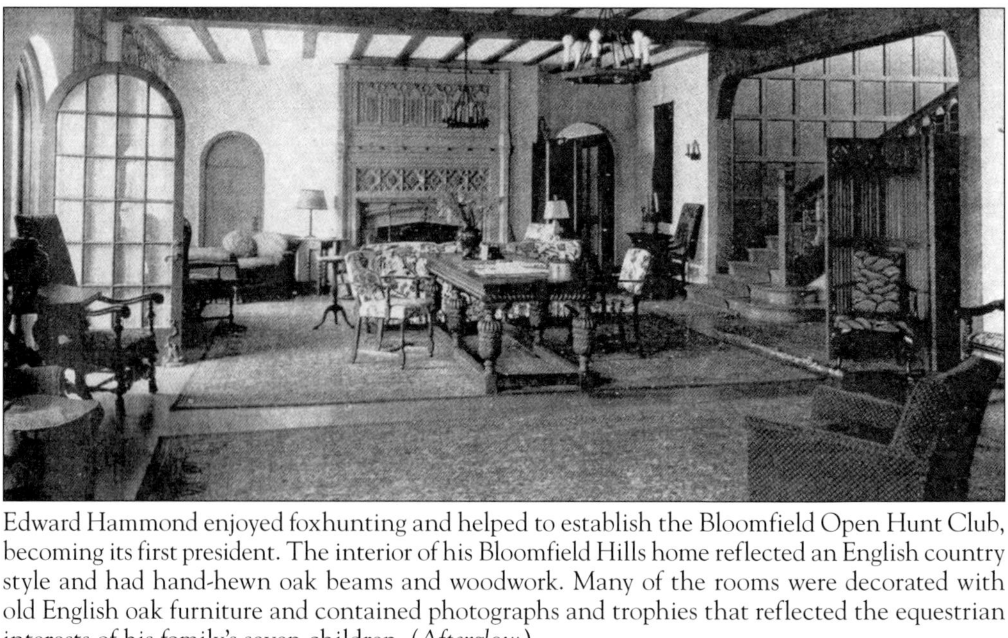

Edward Hammond enjoyed foxhunting and helped to establish the Bloomfield Open Hunt Club, becoming its first president. The interior of his Bloomfield Hills home reflected an English country style and had hand-hewn oak beams and woodwork. Many of the rooms were decorated with old English oak furniture and contained photographs and trophies that reflected the equestrian interests of his family's seven children. (*Afterglow*.)

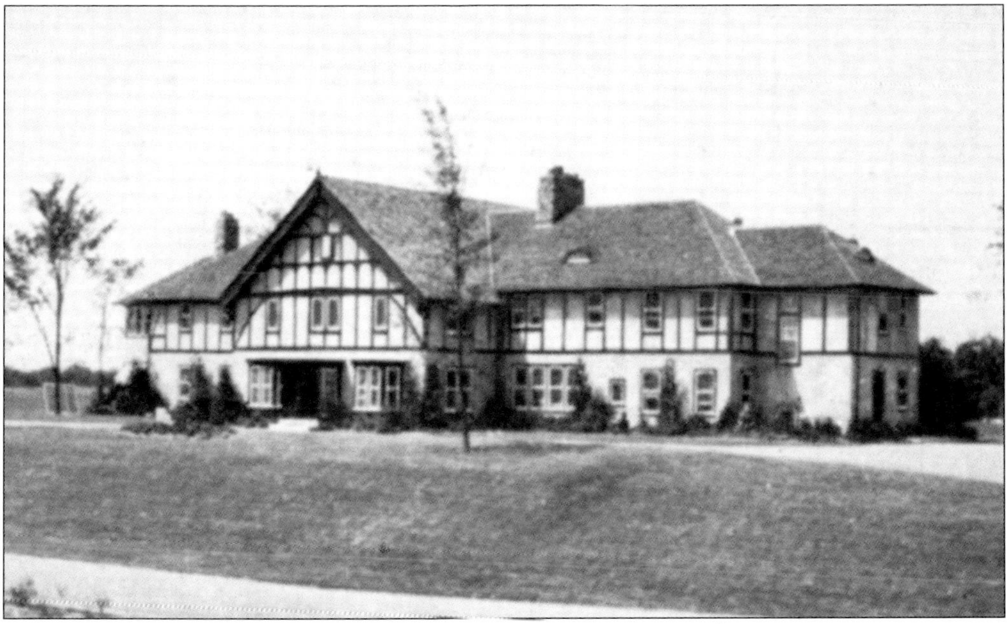

Walbri was the 147-acre estate of Walter O. Briggs, who owned both the Detroit Tigers and Briggs Stadium, which later became Tiger Stadium. Built in 1925, the summer home served as a hunting lodge and had several outbuildings that still exist today as private homes and can be seen on both sides of Long Lake Road west of Squirrel Road. (Courtesy of Cranbrook Archives.)

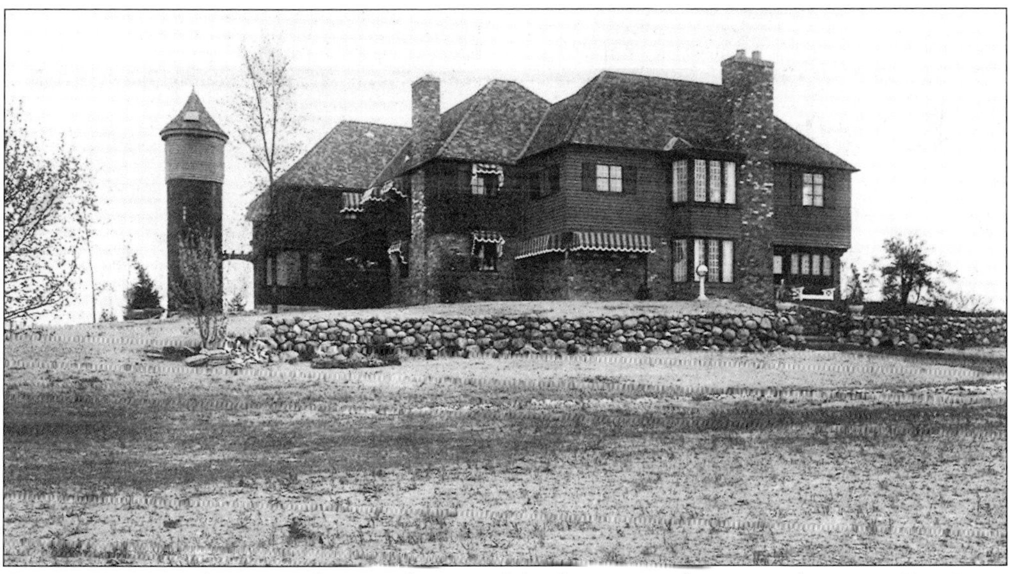

Quartermore was the name that Gordon Mendelssohn gave to his manor house on East Long Lake Road. The name was a play on words and meant that the house, being within a stone's throw of the Bloomfield Open Hunt Club, gave Mendelssohn a quarter of an hour more to sleep on mornings of early hunts. This 1924 photograph shows the home before a fire resulted in the house being divided into two residences. (Courtesy of Cranbrook Archives.)

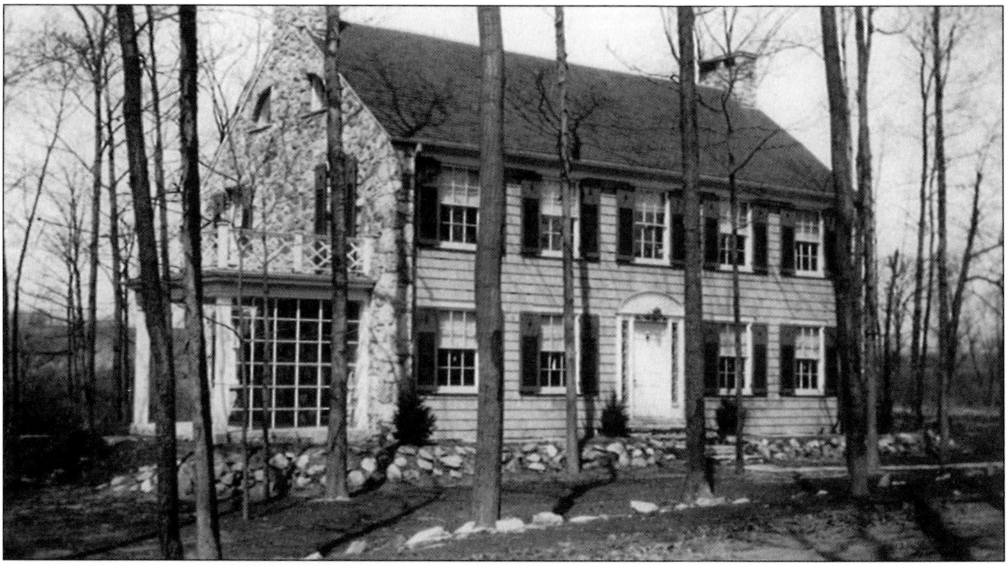

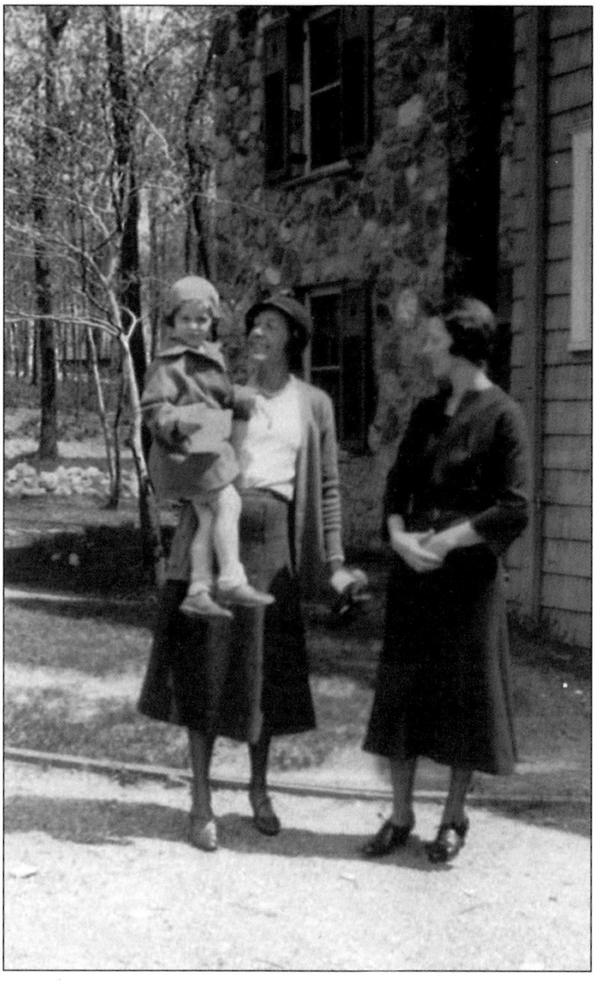

Builder Harold Broock, son of Max Broock, built this house on Lone Pine Court in 1929. Broock built other homes on Lone Pine Court as well as on Woodward Avenue and Vaughan Road, but only the Lone Pine Court houses remain. For projects requiring modern design, he commissioned architect J. Robert F. Swanson. When building materials became scarce during World War II, Broock switched to marine design. (Courtesy of Barbara Broock Bini.)

In 1932, Barbara Broock, age three, her aunt Katherine Rice Broock, and her mother, Bernice (right), are in front of the house that her father built for them on Lone Pine Court. She remembers attending Vaughan School, playing at Cranbrook House, visiting the Cranbrook weaving studios and Loja Saarinen, and watching Eero Saarinen build models in the basement of the Circle School. (Courtesy of Barbara Broock Bini.)

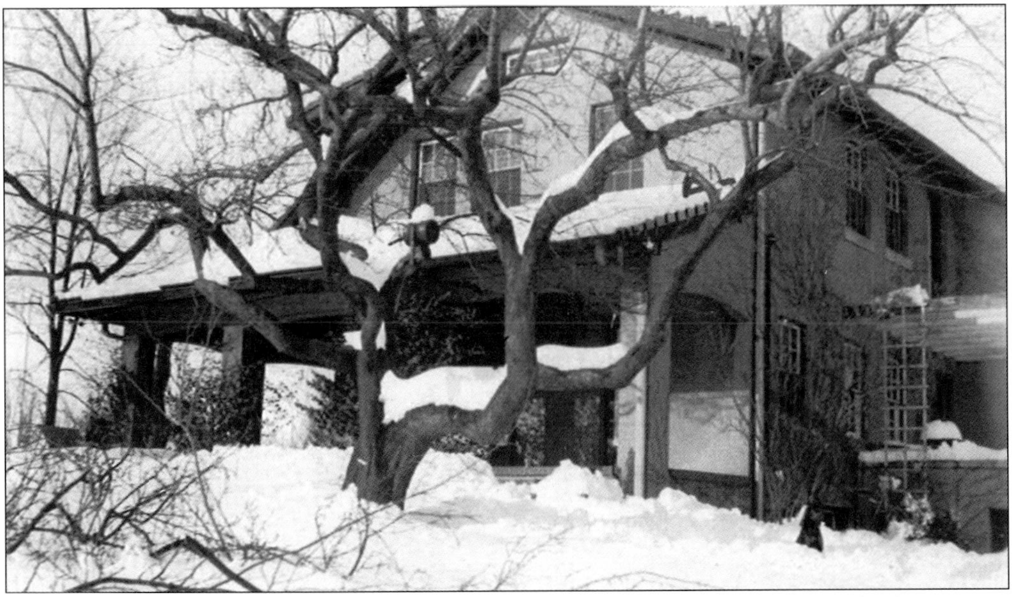

Snow Apple was built by Harold Broock around 1934. It stood on 24 acres just north of Lone Pine Road where Arbor Court now meets Woodward Avenue. Barbara Broock Bini remembers sitting on the hill watching automobiles go by. Two of her childhood friends were Patricia Sanderson, whose grandparents were the Uplands Bromleys, and Margaret Barton, who lived in the Barton Farmhouse. (Courtesy of Barbara Broock Bini.)

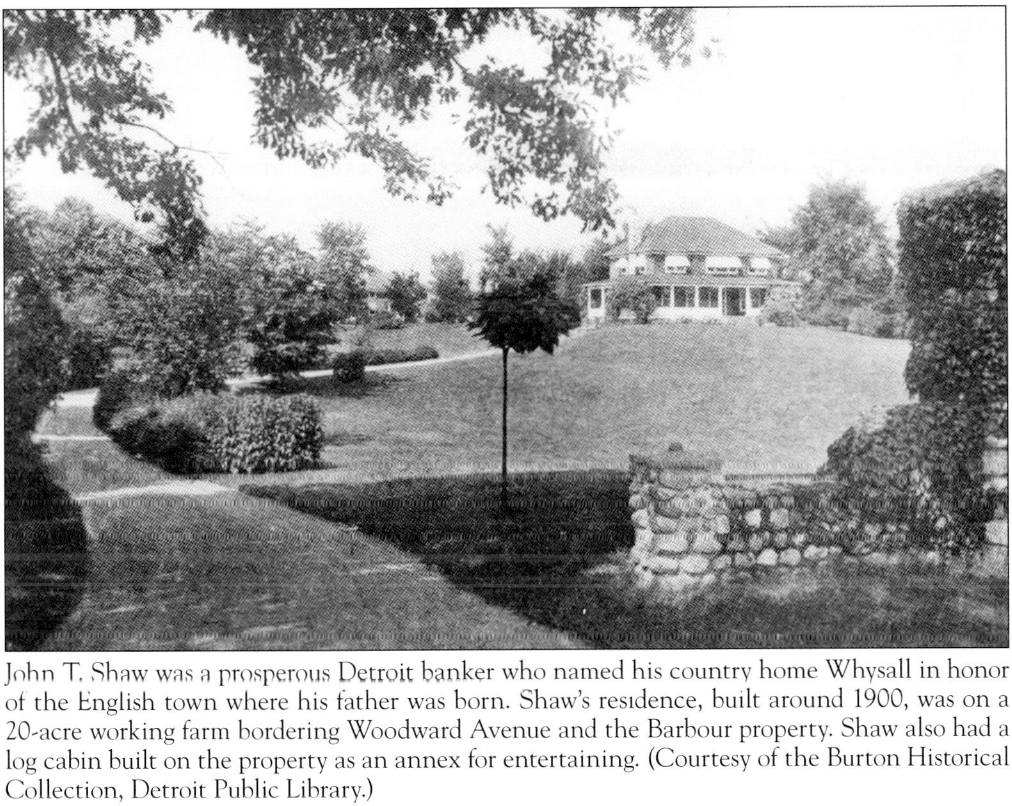

John T. Shaw was a prosperous Detroit banker who named his country home Whysall in honor of the English town where his father was born. Shaw's residence, built around 1900, was on a 20-acre working farm bordering Woodward Avenue and the Barbour property. Shaw also had a log cabin built on the property as an annex for entertaining. (Courtesy of the Burton Historical Collection, Detroit Public Library.)

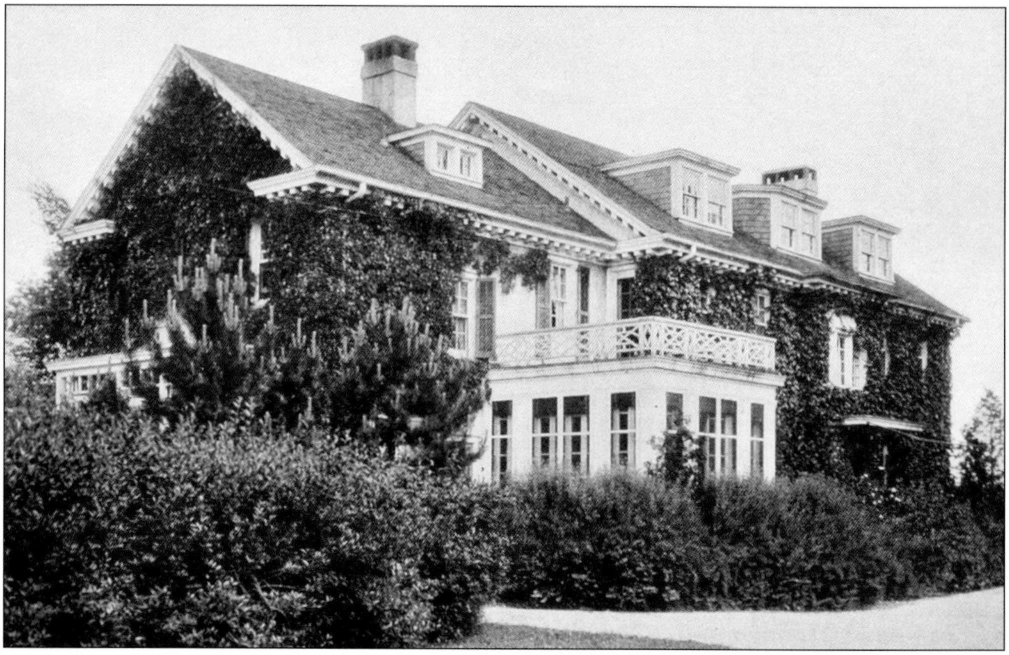

Uplands was the large country home of Frank Bromley. The house, shown here in 1927, was designed and built by Albert Kahn for its original owner, Edward Pendleton, and reflected a New England design. Features of the home included a Pewabic-tiled fireplace, exquisite woodwork, and floor-to-ceiling French doors. The building was demolished, and the property is now the site of the Congregational Church of Birmingham. (Courtesy of Cranbrook Archives.)

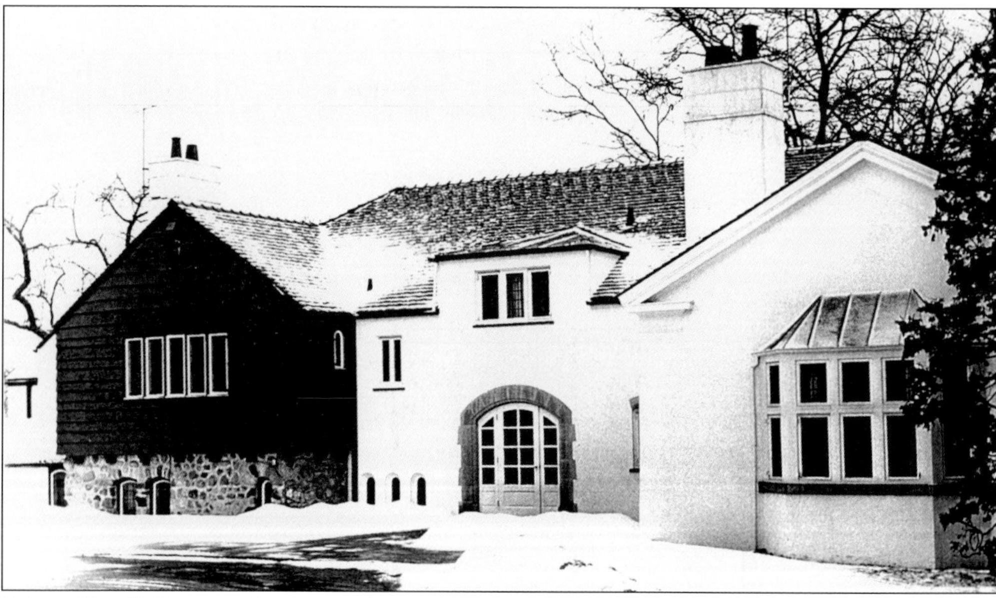

Robin Hood's Barn is the name that C.C. Winningham gave to the home he purchased in 1919 from the Vhays, who had purchased the property from J. Bassett, a farmer. Mrs. Vhay had converted the large barn and its attached wooden schoolhouse into a residence. Winningham further converted the structure into a stately home that included wall paintings of Robin Hood. The building is now the Village Club. (Courtesy of the Village Club.)

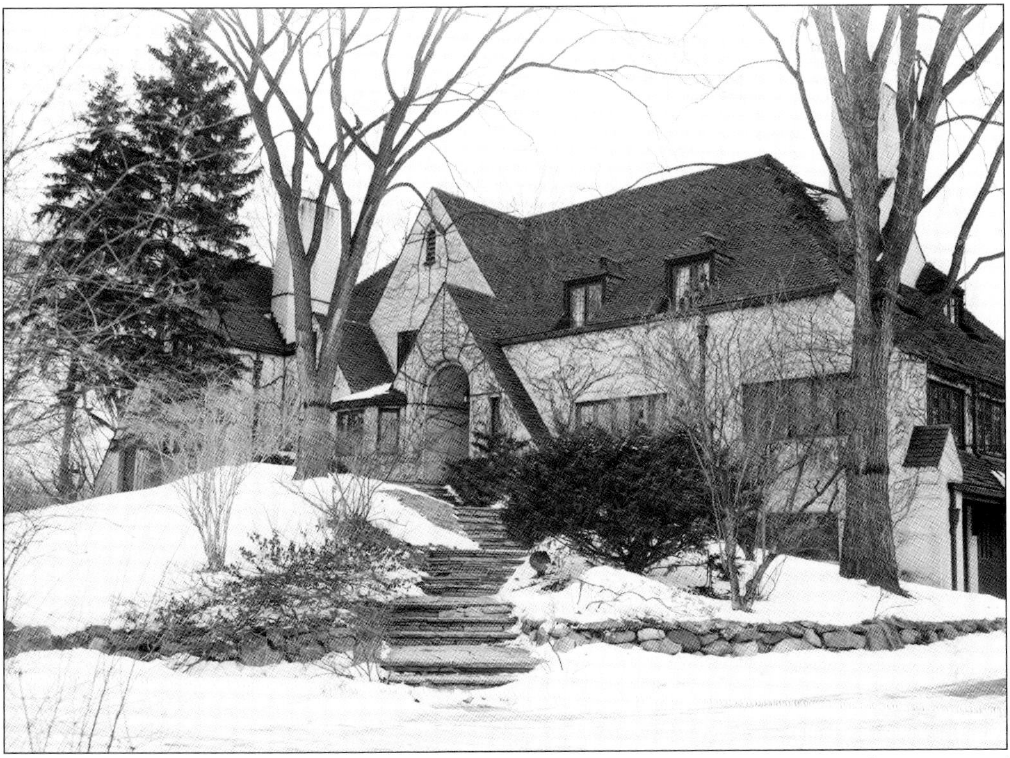

This large manor home was built by J. Howard Muzzy in 1927. Muzzy was cofounder in 1899 of the Muzzy Lyon Company, which manufactured mill supplies and rubber products. That company expanded over time to become the Federal-Mogul Corporation. A tributary of the Rouge River runs through the property, which includes other buildings. (Courtesy of Walter P. Reuther Library, Archives of Labor and Urban Affairs, Wayne State University.)

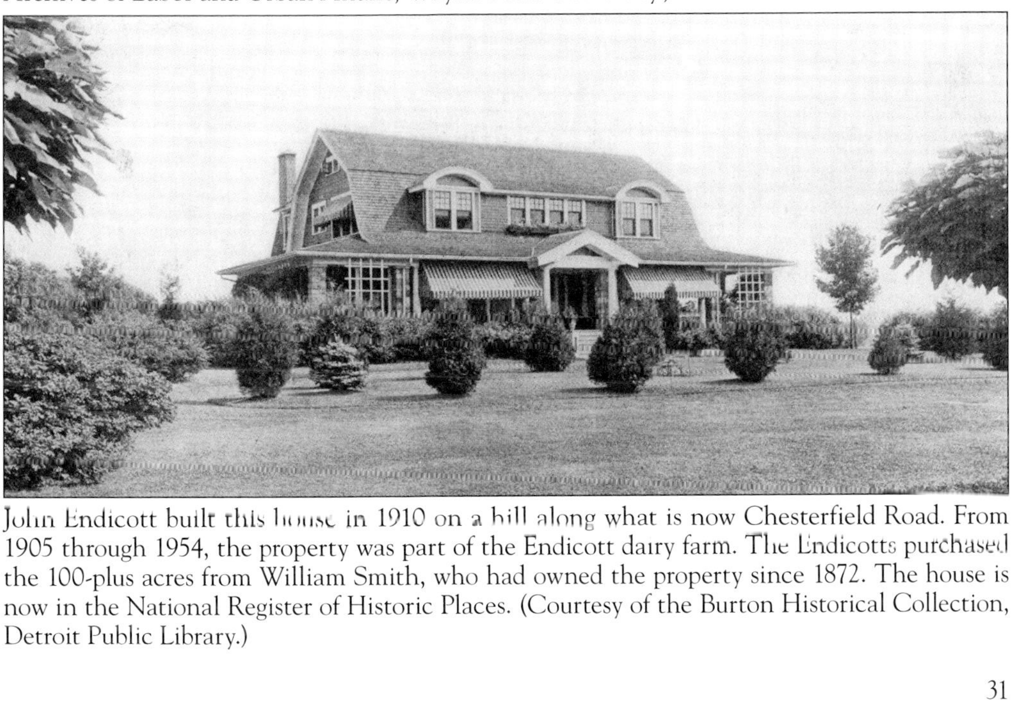

John Endicott built this house in 1910 on a hill along what is now Chesterfield Road. From 1905 through 1954, the property was part of the Endicott dairy farm. The Endicotts purchased the 100-plus acres from William Smith, who had owned the property since 1872. The house is now in the National Register of Historic Places. (Courtesy of the Burton Historical Collection, Detroit Public Library.)

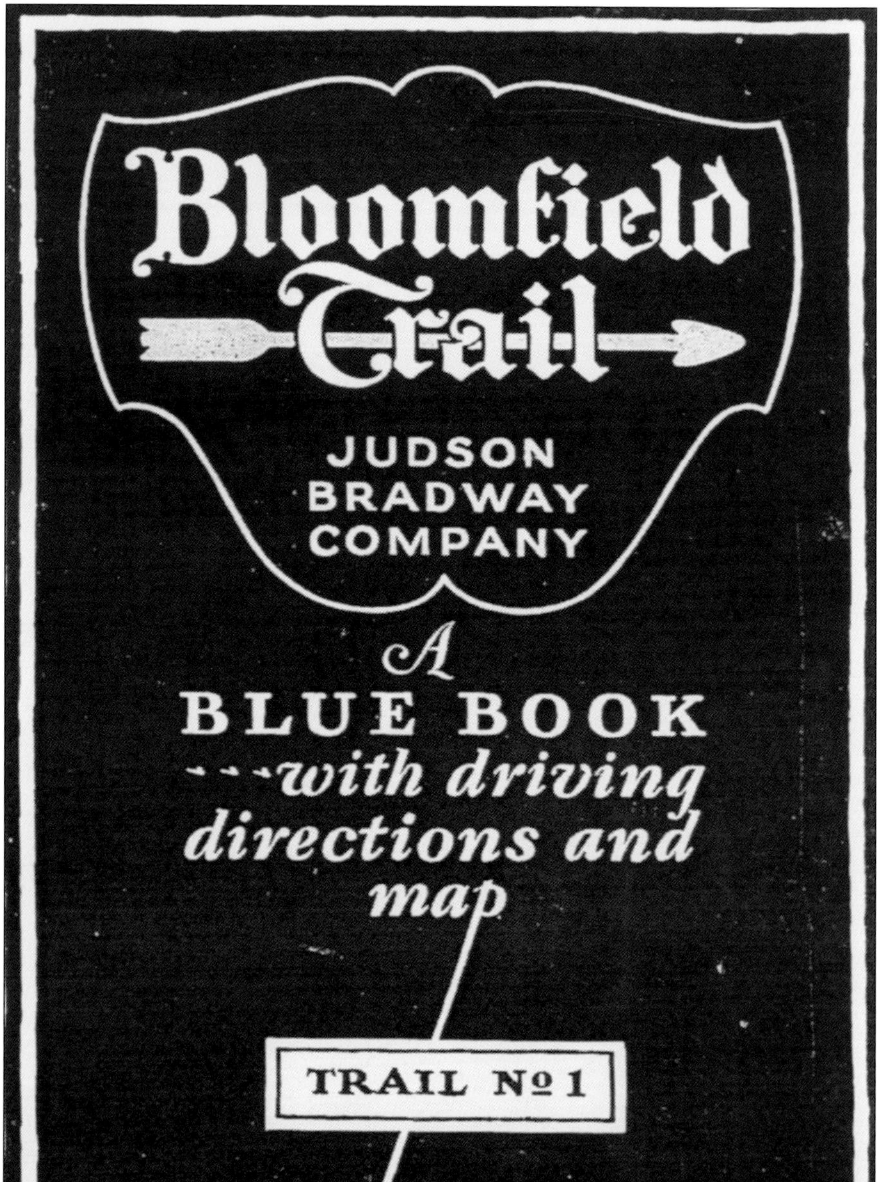

Judson Bradway was one of the most prolific developers in the Bloomfield area between 1910 and 1930. Today, he is perhaps best remembered for his development of Bloomfield Village just to the west of the city limits of Birmingham. In 1927, to promote sales within his developments, which included the Trowbridge Farms and Country Club Estates subdivisions in Bloomfield Hills, he created two *Bloomfield Trail Blue Books*, each with detailed driving directions and map. Drivers were asked to open their booklets, set their odometers at zero, and drive northward on Woodward Avenue, watching for roadside direction signs. The signs and map would lead the drivers past stately manor homes, the kind that they themselves could have if they bought property from Bradway. Each *Blue Book* contained photographs of many of the homes as well as prominent amenities, such as the Bloomfield Hills Country Club. (Courtesy of John Marshall.)

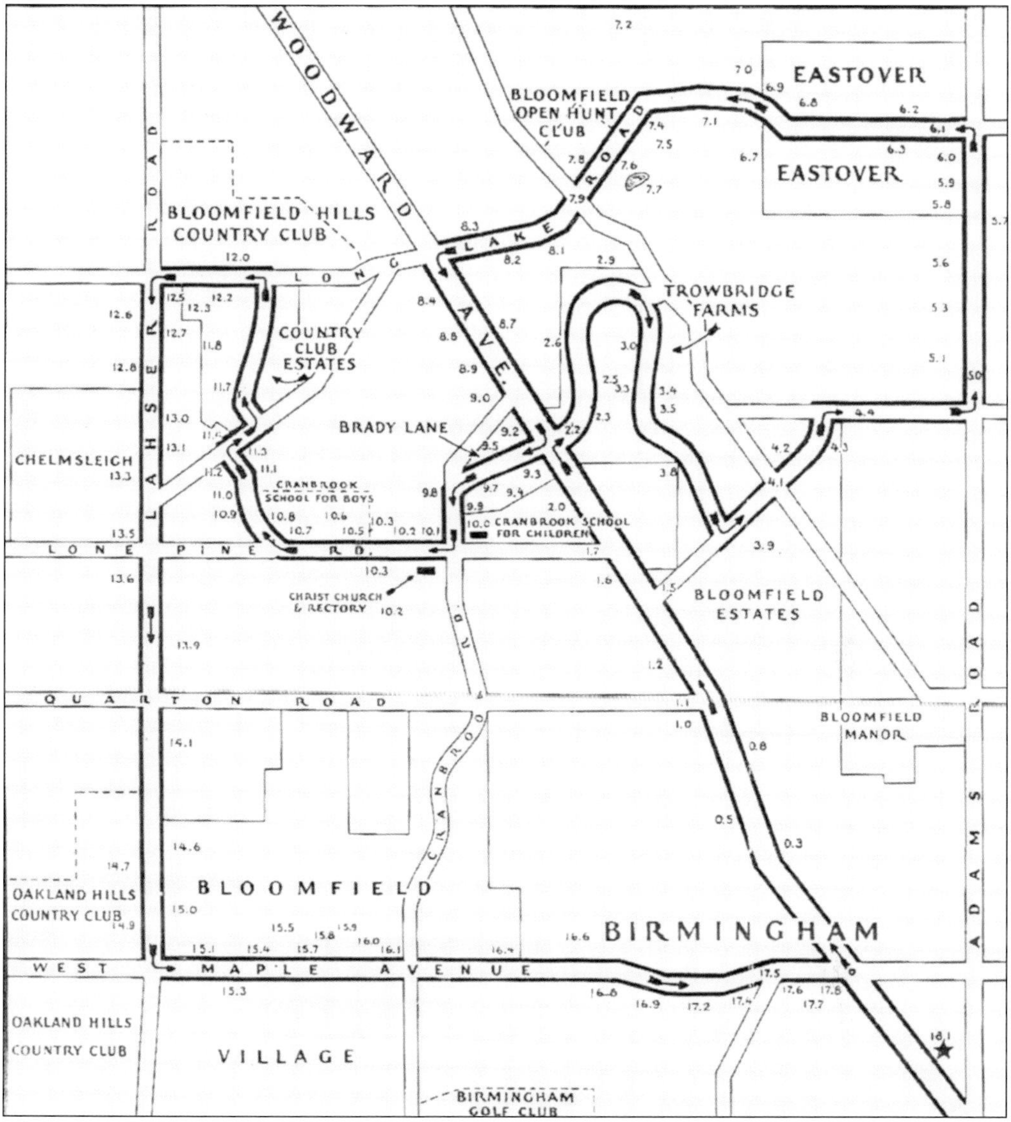

This map was printed in the Trail No. 1 *Bloomfield Trail Blue Book*. The starting point was the Judson Bradway Co. office at 315 South Woodward Avenue near Adams Road. Arrows indicate the path that drivers, and thus potential buyers, were asked to follow north along Woodward Avenue until they reached Trowbridge Road at the 2.2-mile mark. At that point, drivers would turn right and begin their tour past some of Bloomfield Hills' largest manor homes on one- to six-acre estates. Within the 200-acre Trowbridge Farms development alone, drivers would pass by or could view T.W. Taliaferro's Hilltop mansion; Hillwood, the home of E.P. Hammond; and Nestledown, the home of A.C. Born. Outlining an affluent area, this map created by Judson Bradway is one of the best records of Bloomfield Hills' early mansion-building period. With the advent of the Great Depression, Bradway's career as a major developer slowed considerably. (Courtesy of John Marshall.)

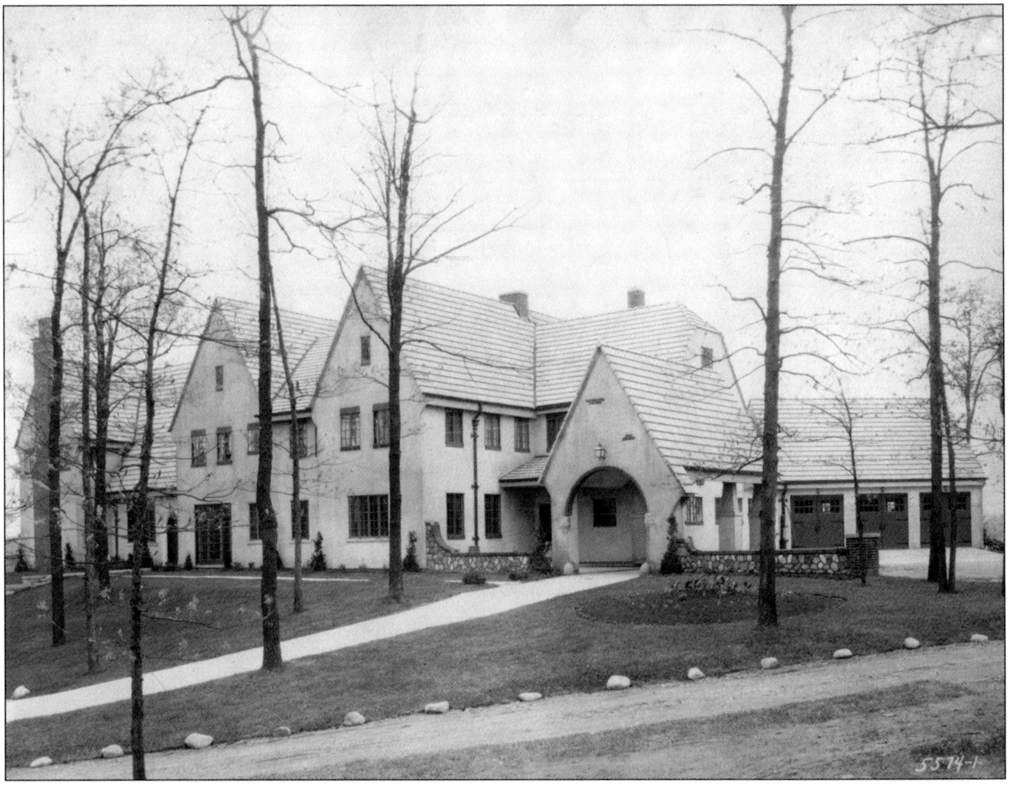

This 1946 photograph shows Coventry Crest, the 20-room white-stucco mansion built by Albert Foster Stephens and his wife, Zillah, on the hilltop along Woodward Avenue that now houses the Roeper School administrative offices. Before building this house in 1927, the Stephenses had suffered two catastrophic fires, so they had this one built with a steel frame and concrete. (Courtesy of the Roeper School Archive, Roeper City and Country School, Inc.)

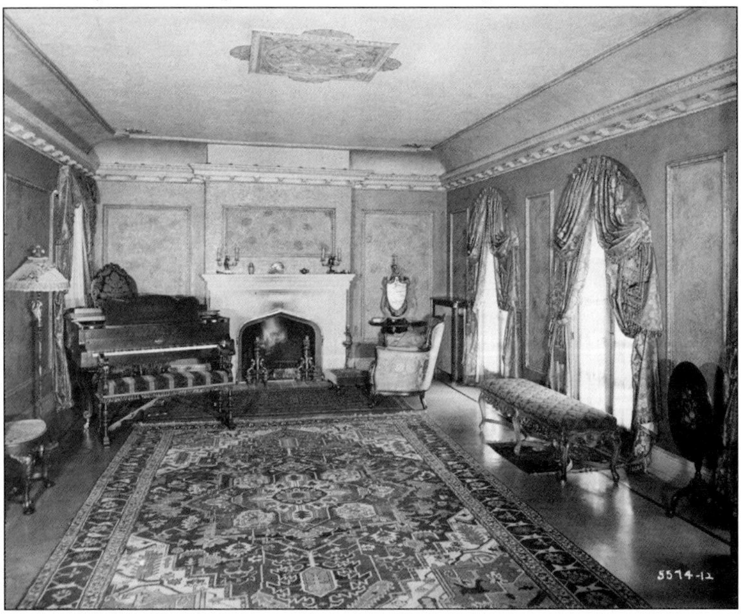

The music room in Coventry Crest, the Stephenses' mansion, shows the type of elegant furnishings the family of four enjoyed. Pewabic tile was used throughout the house, which also had a marble kitchen. The Roepers purchased the home, which is now called Hill House, in 1946. (Courtesy of the Roeper School Archive, Roeper City and Country School, Inc.)

In 1927, developer and builder Edward J. Butler promoted Bloomfield Downs, a village of English-style houses congruent with nearby buildings such as the Fox and Hounds south of Long Lake Road and east of Woodward Avenue. Only a few of these village homes remain. (Author's collection.)

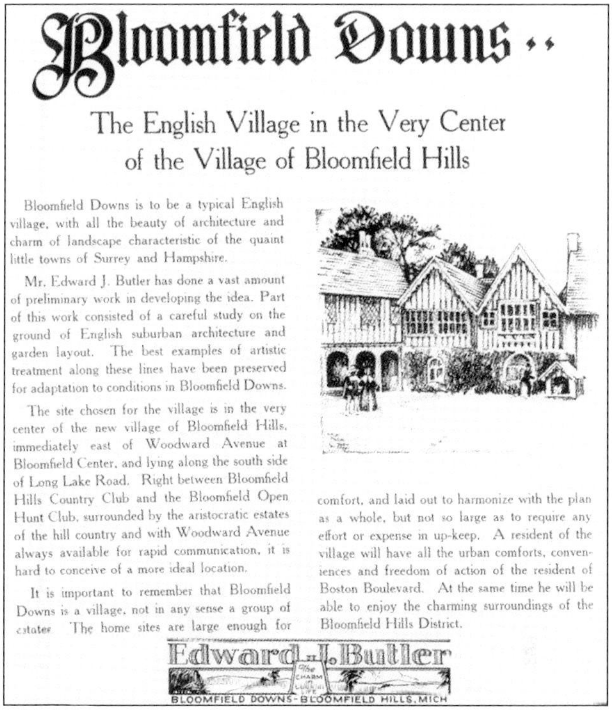

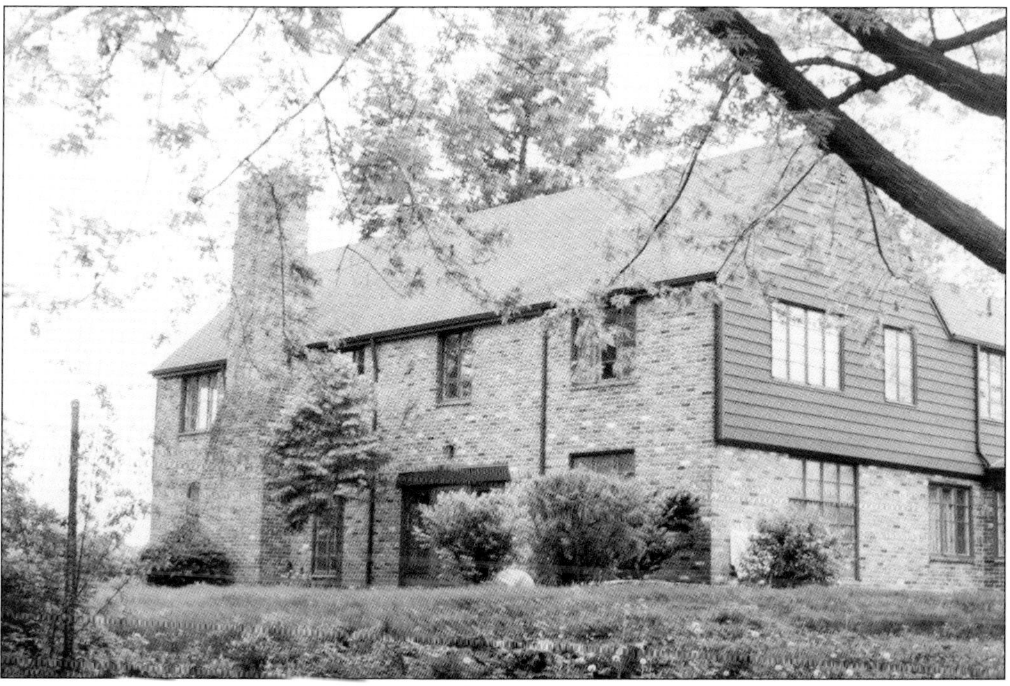

The George A. Bee house on Opdyke Road was built prior to 1931 for Charles H. O'Shei and remodeled in 1941. Bee, a later owner who co-owned the Palmer-Bee Company, sold the factory behind his house to Oakland Community College in 1965. He later donated the rest of his estate to the college. The factory is now the George A. Bee Administration Center. The guest house is the Doris Mosher Foundation building. (Courtesy of Cranbrook Archives.)

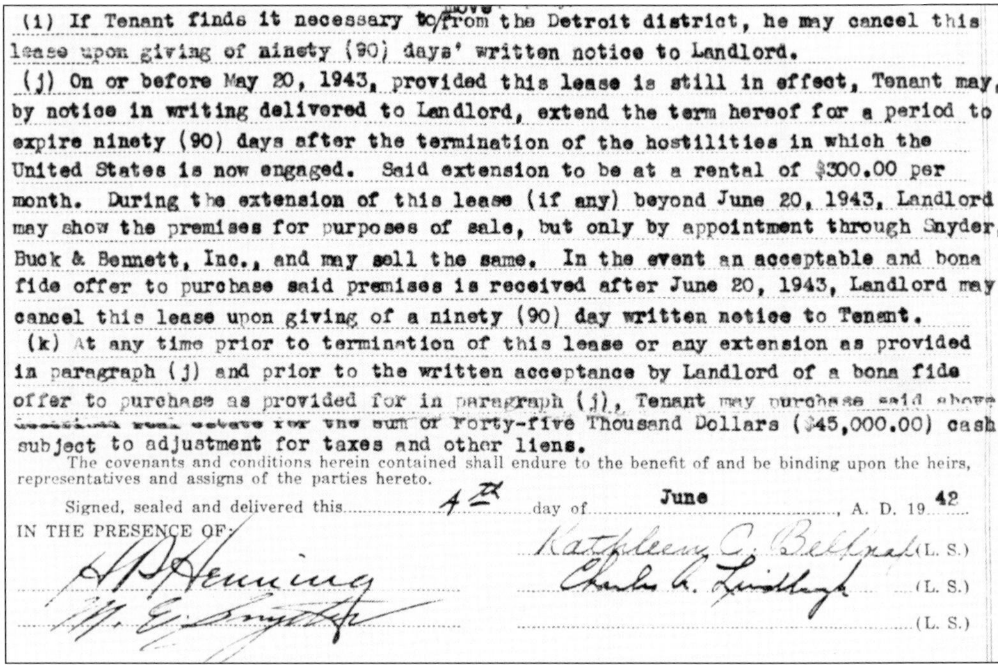
(i) If Tenant finds it necessary to move from the Detroit district, he may cancel this lease upon giving of ninety (90) days' written notice to Landlord.

(j) On or before May 20, 1943, provided this lease is still in effect, Tenant may, by notice in writing delivered to Landlord, extend the term hereof for a period to expire ninety (90) days after the termination of the hostilities in which the United States is now engaged. Said extension to be at a rental of $300.00 per month. During the extension of this lease (if any) beyond June 20, 1943, Landlord may show the premises for purposes of sale, but only by appointment through Snyder, Buck & Bennett, Inc., and may sell the same. In the event an acceptable and bona fide offer to purchase said premises is received after June 20, 1943, Landlord may cancel this lease upon giving of a ninety (90) day written notice to Tenant.

(k) At any time prior to termination of this lease or any extension as provided in paragraph (j) and prior to the written acceptance by Landlord of a bona fide offer to purchase as provided for in paragraph (j), Tenant may purchase said above [illegible] for the sum of Forty-five Thousand Dollars ($45,000.00) cash subject to adjustment for taxes and other liens.

The covenants and conditions herein contained shall endure to the benefit of and be binding upon the heirs, representatives and assigns of the parties hereto.

Signed, sealed and delivered this 4th day of June, A. D. 1942

IN THE PRESENCE OF: H. P. Henning, M. E. Snyder Jr.

Kathleen C. Belknap (L. S.)

Charles A. Lindbergh (L. S.)

(L. S.)

While Charles Lindbergh worked at Willow Run during World War II, he leased two different houses in Bloomfield Hills. This photograph shows his signature to lease the William J. Belknap property on Cranbrook Road, which was known as Belwood. The lease period was for one year beginning in June 1942. The rent was $300 per month. Designed by Albert Kahn, the house was built for Ralph Stone and was formerly called Stonelea. (Courtesy of Harry C. Walsh.)

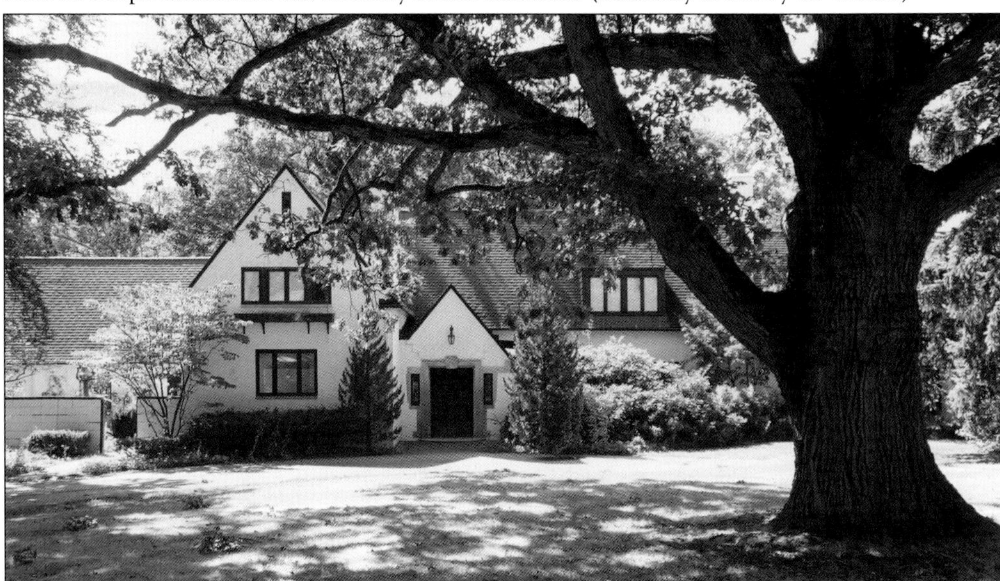

This is the house on North Cranbrook Road that Charles Lindbergh rented for his family while he worked at Willow Run. His wife, writer Anne Morrow Lindbergh, lived here with their children. She studied art at Cranbrook Academy of Art while residing here and wrote *The Steep Descent* in a trailer that was set back in the woods. (Photograph by and courtesy of Richard Orton.)

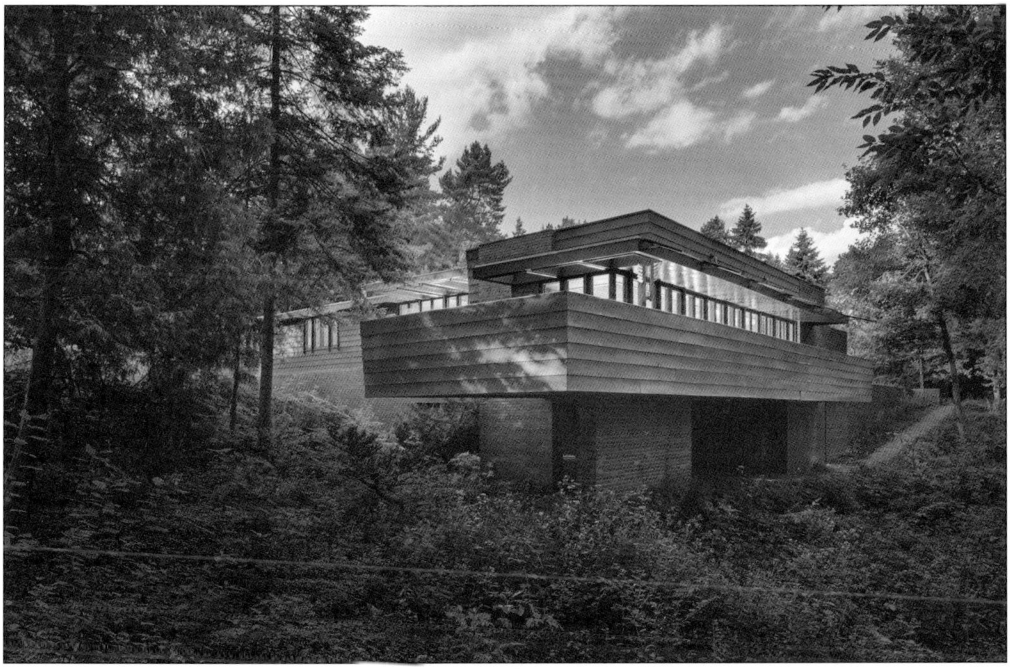

The Affleck House on Woodward Avenue was the first Frank Lloyd Wright–designed house in the Detroit area and the only one constructed within the city limits of Bloomfield Hills. Built in 1941 for Gregor S. and Elizabeth B. Affleck, the house cantilevers over a steep wooded hill and pond. The house is considered one of Wright's finest examples of Usonian architecture. (Courtesy of Lawrence Technological University.)

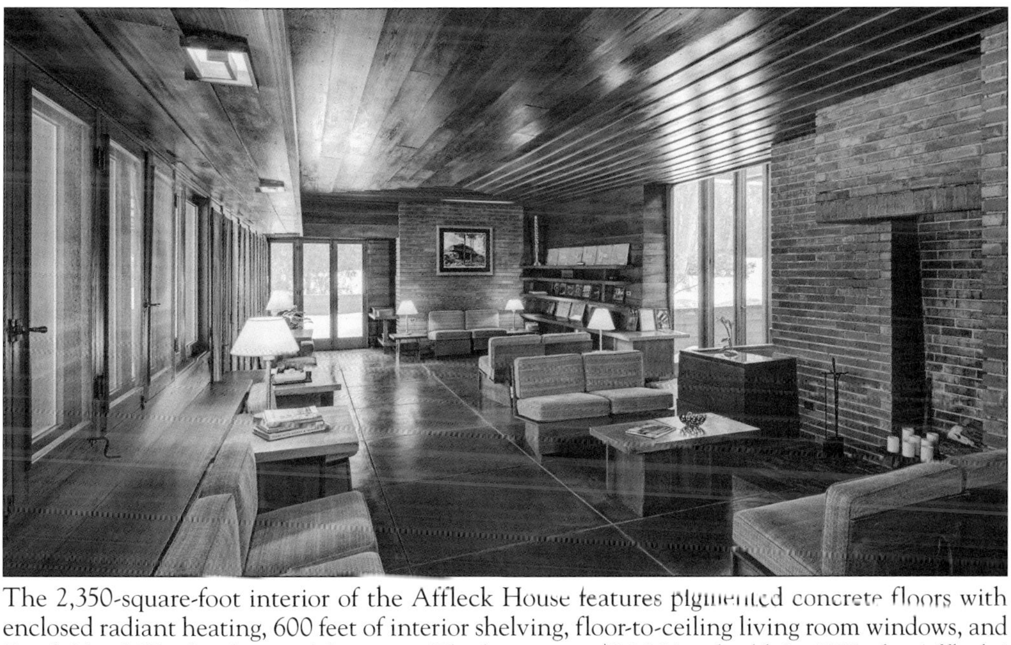

The 2,350-square-foot interior of the Affleck House features pigmented concrete floors with enclosed radiant heating, 600 feet of interior shelving, floor-to-ceiling living room windows, and Frank Lloyd Wright–designed furniture. The house cost $26,000 to build. In 1978, the Afflecks' children donated the house to Lawrence Technological University for use as a teaching resource. (Courtesy of Lawrence Technological University.)

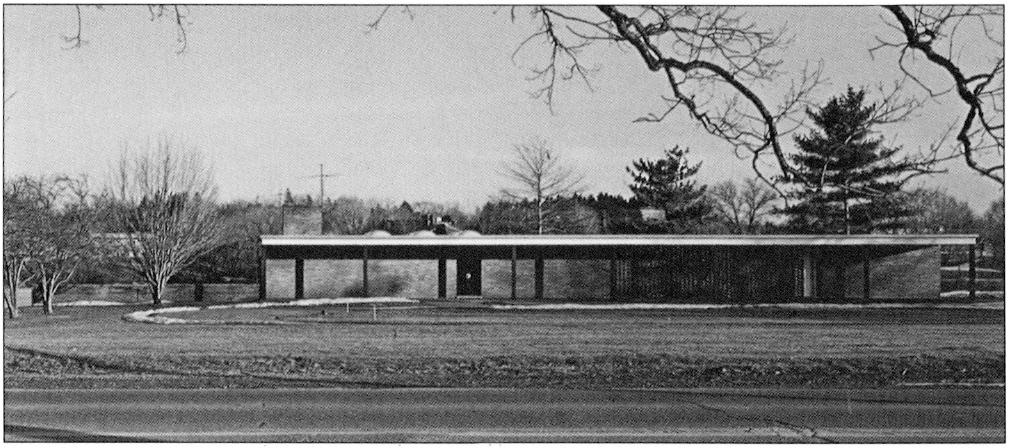

In 1953, architect Edward Durrell Stone designed this modern home overlooking Vhay Lake. Designed for Carney Matheson, this low, sleek house with no windows on the north side opens up dramatically on the south side facing the lake. A staircase descends from the street level to the large lakeside living room. (Author's collection.)

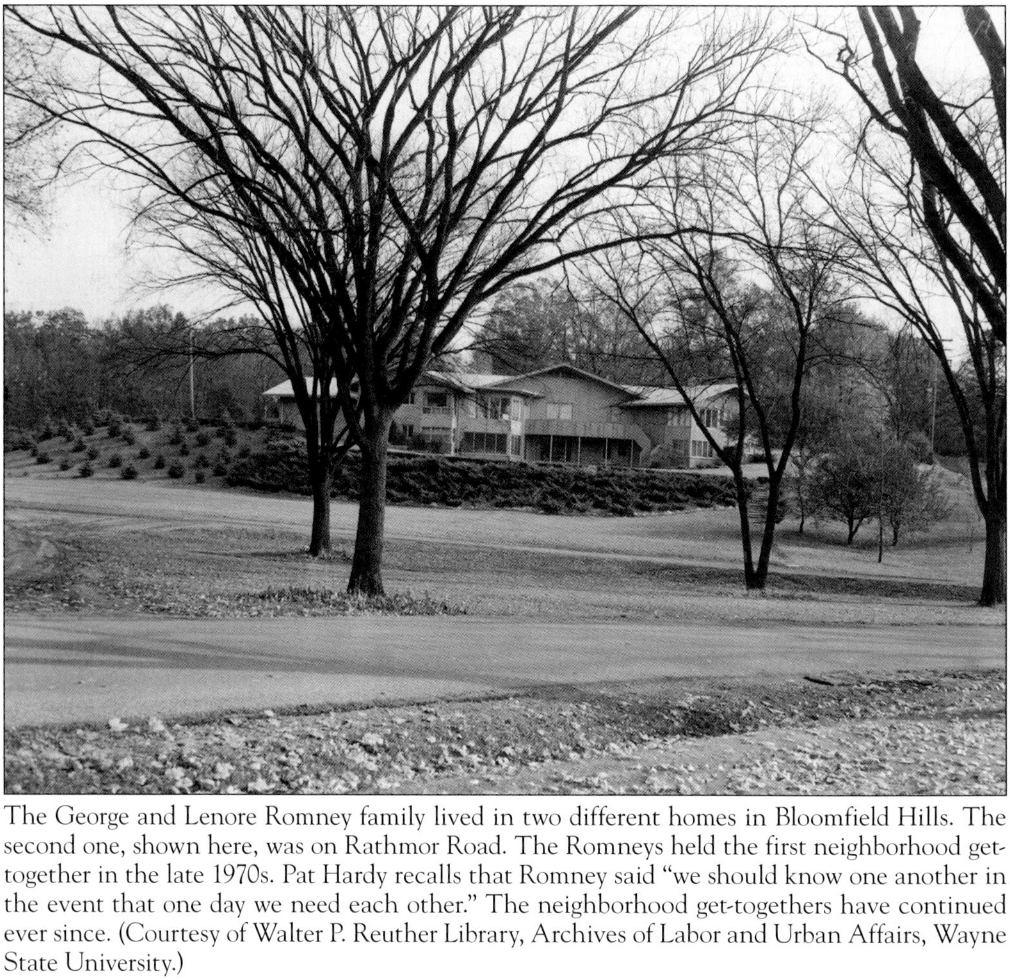

The George and Lenore Romney family lived in two different homes in Bloomfield Hills. The second one, shown here, was on Rathmor Road. The Romneys held the first neighborhood get-together in the late 1970s. Pat Hardy recalls that Romney said "we should know one another in the event that one day we need each other." The neighborhood get-togethers have continued ever since. (Courtesy of Walter P. Reuther Library, Archives of Labor and Urban Affairs, Wayne State University.)

Three

The Cranbrook Vision

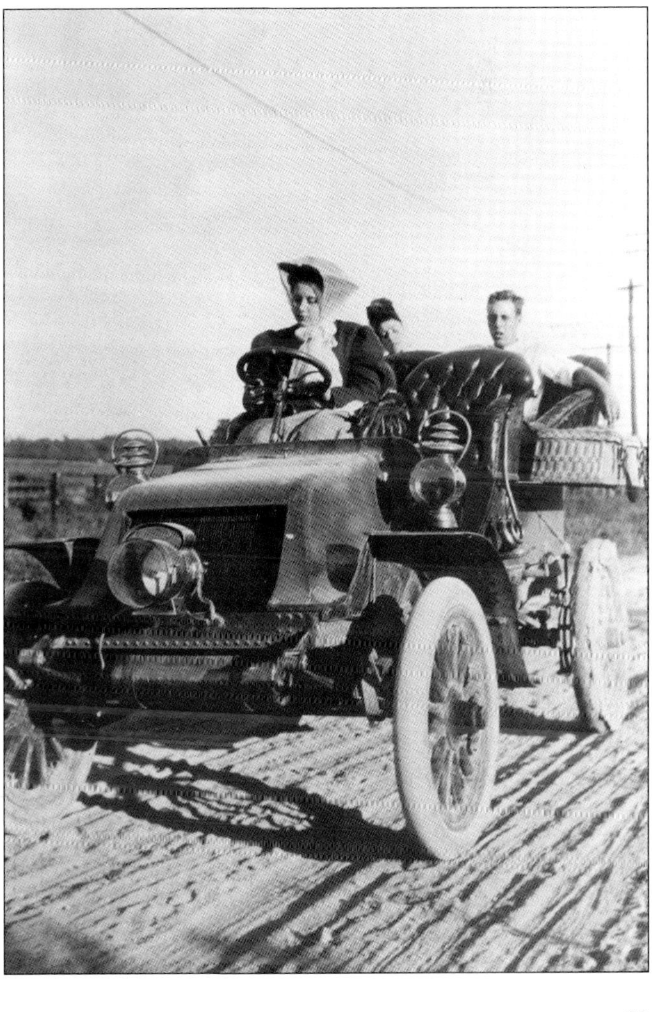

This 1904 photograph of the George Booth family's first car, a Winton, motoring along a dirt road, is representative of the great change that was about to take place in Bloomfield Hills, up until then a farming community. Many wealthy Detroiters who went touring northward in their new horseless carriages discovered the area's rolling hills and country atmosphere and began building weekend and summer homes there. (Courtesy of Cranbrook Archives.)

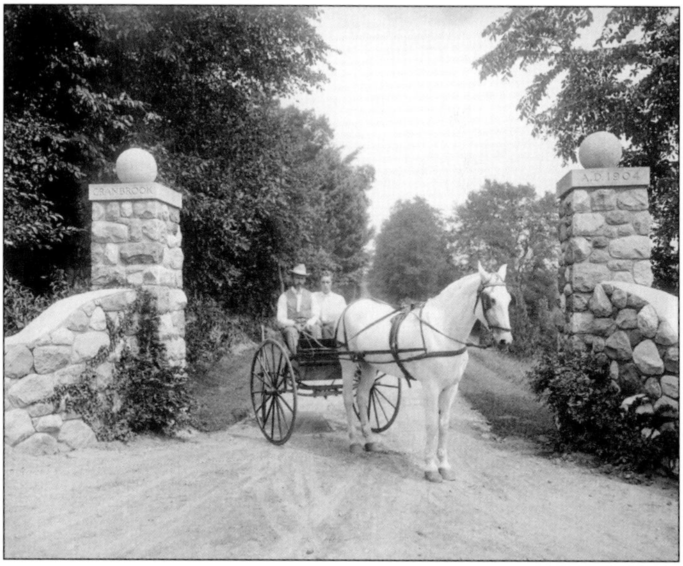

George Gough Booth bought Samuel Alexander's run-down farm in Oakland County's Bloomfield Township and named it Cranbrook after his father's former home in England. In this 1906 photograph, George Booth (left) and his son James Scripps Booth are in a carriage at the south end of the mall that would later become Cranbrook Road. (Courtesy of Cranbrook Archives.)

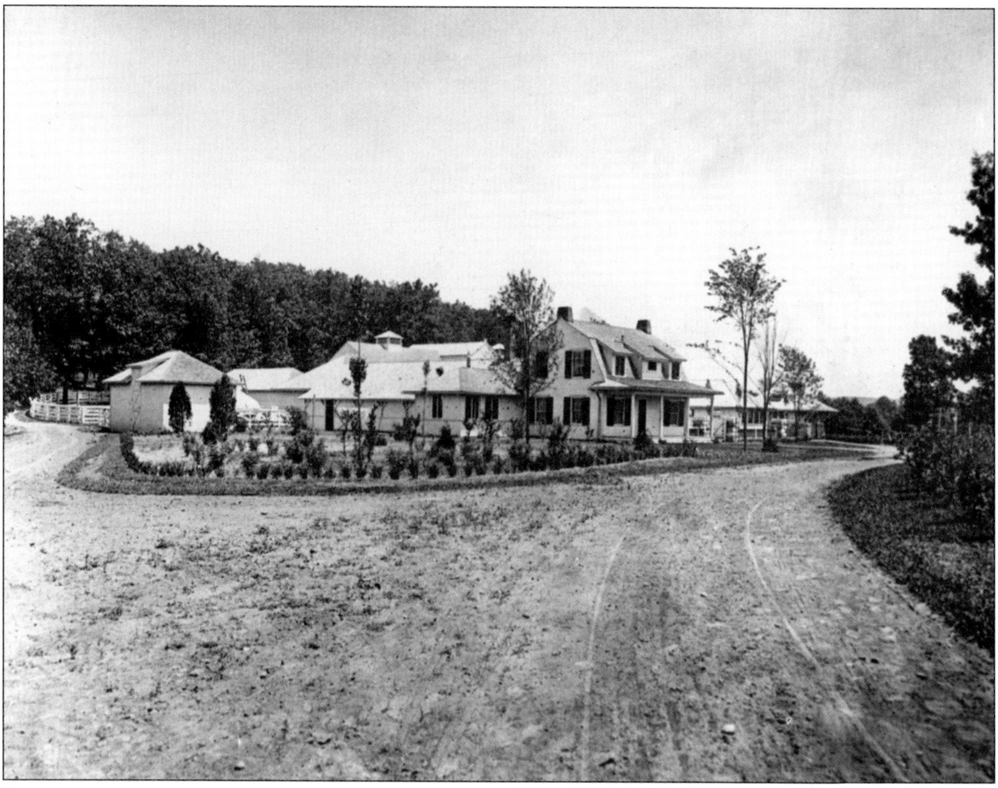

This c. 1905 photograph shows Farm Group No. 1, which Booth built on the property that would eventually become Kingswood School. The hill can be seen on the left, and the lake, not yet fully developed, would soon be on the right. The farm superintendent lived in the farmhouse. Booth created a sustainable working farm but, over time, developed other visions for the property. (Courtesy of Cranbrook Archives.)

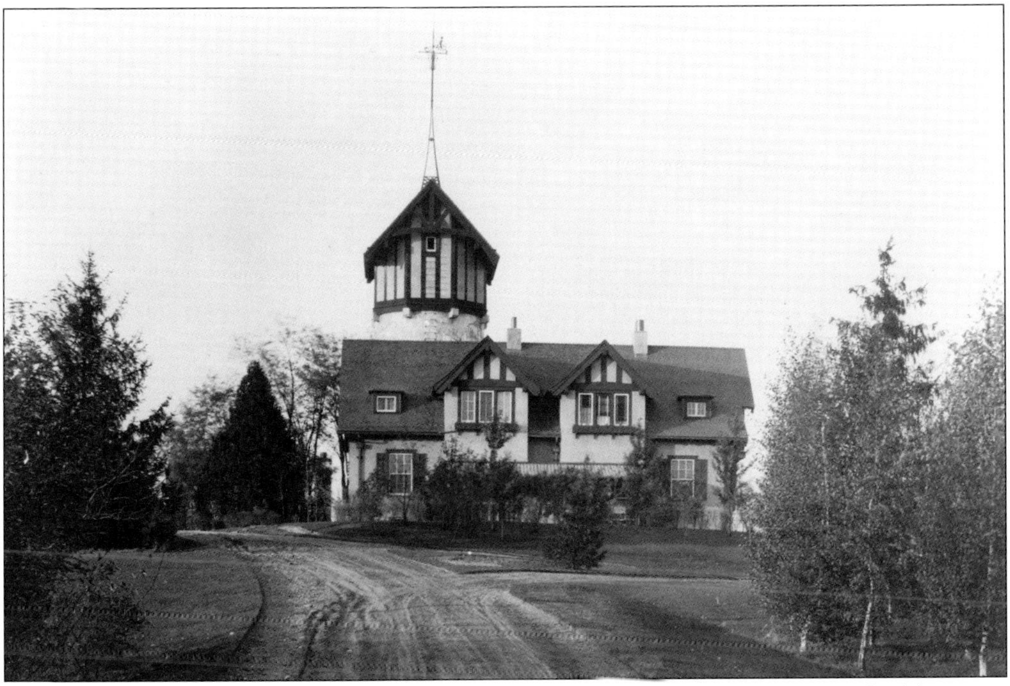

Tower Cottage, pictured here in 1908, was designed by Albert Kahn. It is one building in a complex of service buildings that Booth added to the southeast portion of the Cranbrook property. During the summer of 1913, James Scripps Booth, his wife, and their new baby lived in Tower Cottage. The tall structure behind the cottage is the original water tower. (Courtesy of Cranbrook Archives.)

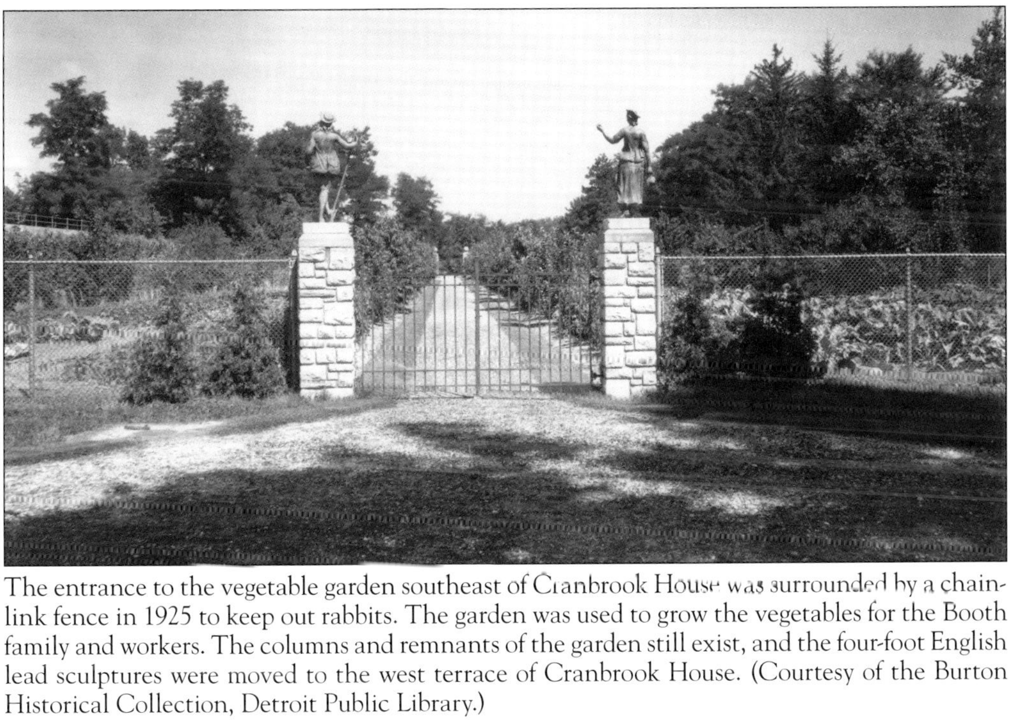

The entrance to the vegetable garden southeast of Cranbrook House was surrounded by a chain-link fence in 1925 to keep out rabbits. The garden was used to grow the vegetables for the Booth family and workers. The columns and remnants of the garden still exist, and the four-foot English lead sculptures were moved to the west terrace of Cranbrook House. (Courtesy of the Burton Historical Collection, Detroit Public Library.)

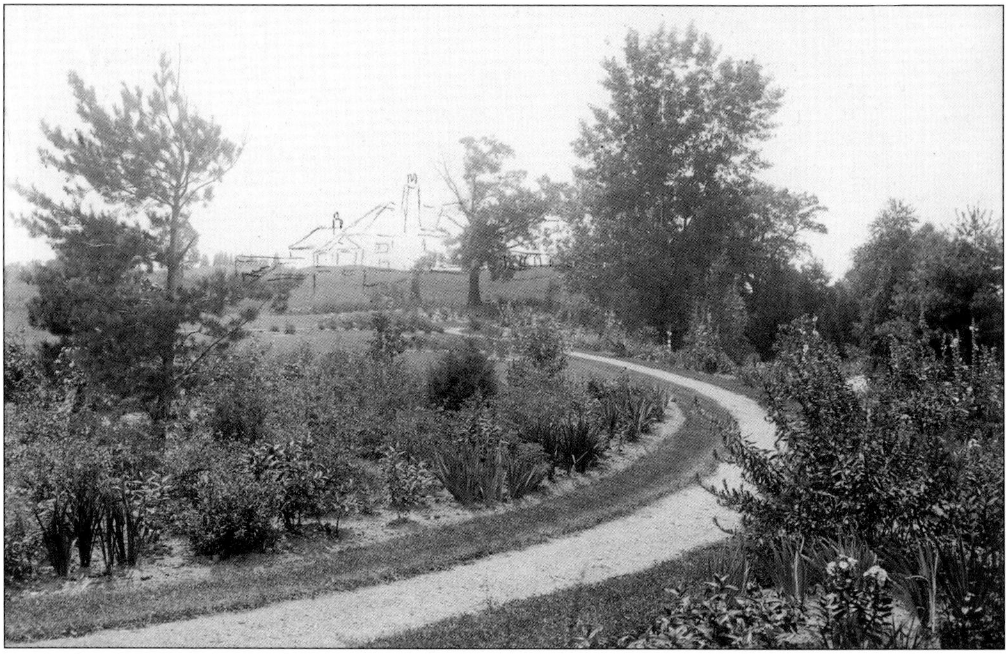

Look closely to see the rendering of Cranbrook House in this c. 1906 photograph. George Booth envisioned Cranbrook House and its placement on the property before Albert Kahn designed and built it. Although not formally trained as an architect, Booth understood perspective and sketched many of his ideas for Cranbrook before he shared them with his architects. (Courtesy of Cranbrook Archives.)

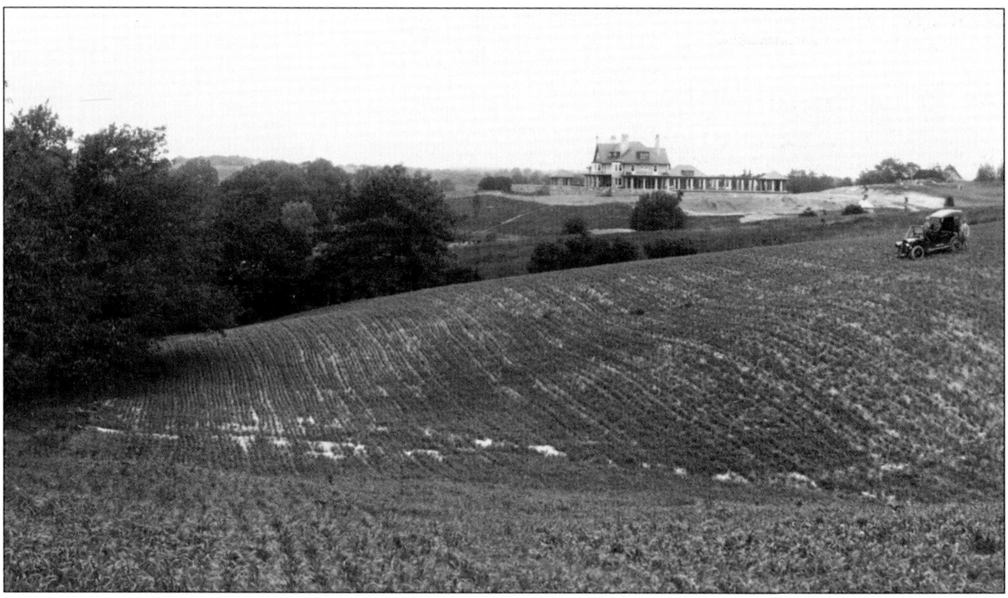

The property that George Booth purchased from Samuel Alexander was clearly a palette for Booth's visions of what could be. This distant view from around 1910, showing Cranbrook House before additions were made, gives a good idea of the property's characteristics at that time. The farmland would soon give way to the building of the educational community. (Courtesy of Cranbrook Archives.)

In 1915, George Gough and Ellen Scripps Booth pause at the steps of the garden of Cranbrook House, perhaps taking a moment to enjoy the fruits of their labor up to that point. The couple would reside at Cranbrook the rest of their lives and raise five children there, and both lived to be 84 years old. (Courtesy of Cranbrook Archives.)

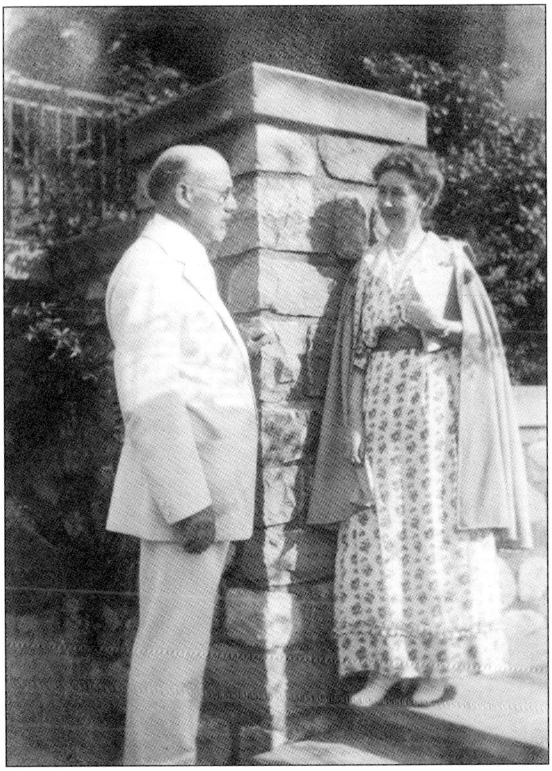

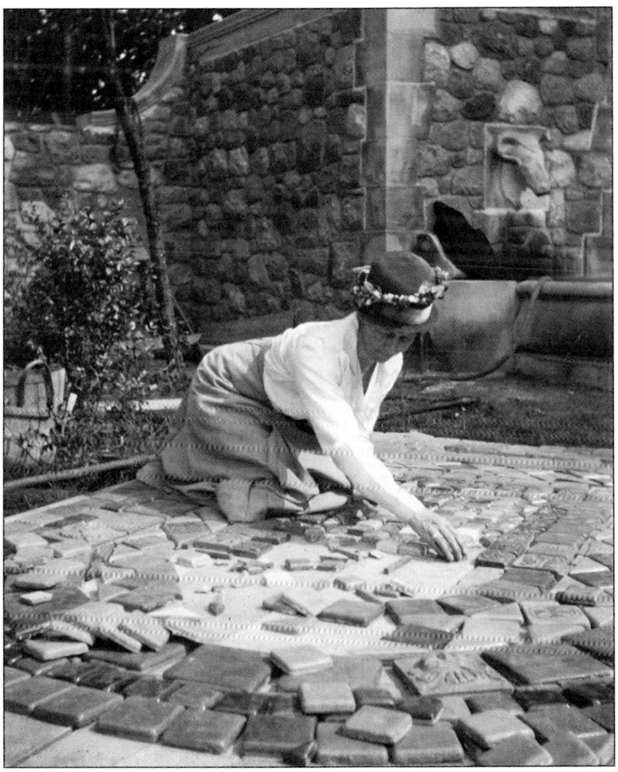

Mary Chase Perry Stratton, who founded Pewabic Pottery in Detroit, was involved with Cranbrook in several ways. In this 1916 photograph, she is laying out blue and green Pewabic tiles for the Rainbow Fountain backsplash. Since the fountain was fed by an artesian well, some of the tiles would turn shades of orange. (Courtesy of Cranbrook Archives.)

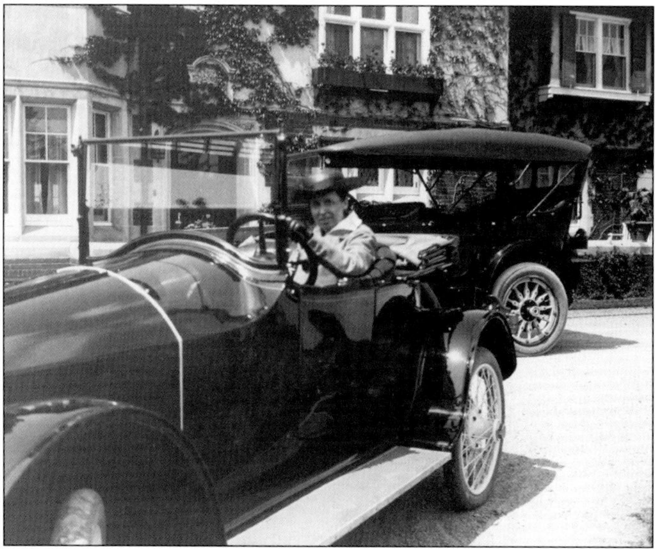

In 1916, Alexandrine McEwen visited Cranbrook House in her Scripps-Booth car, which was designed by James Scripps Booth. Alexandrine, her sister Katherine McEwen, and George Booth were cofounders in 1906 of the Detroit Society of Arts and Crafts, which was inspired by the British Arts and Crafts movement that emphasized beauty and craftsmanship. The society evolved over time to become the College for Creative Studies. (Courtesy of Cranbrook Archives.)

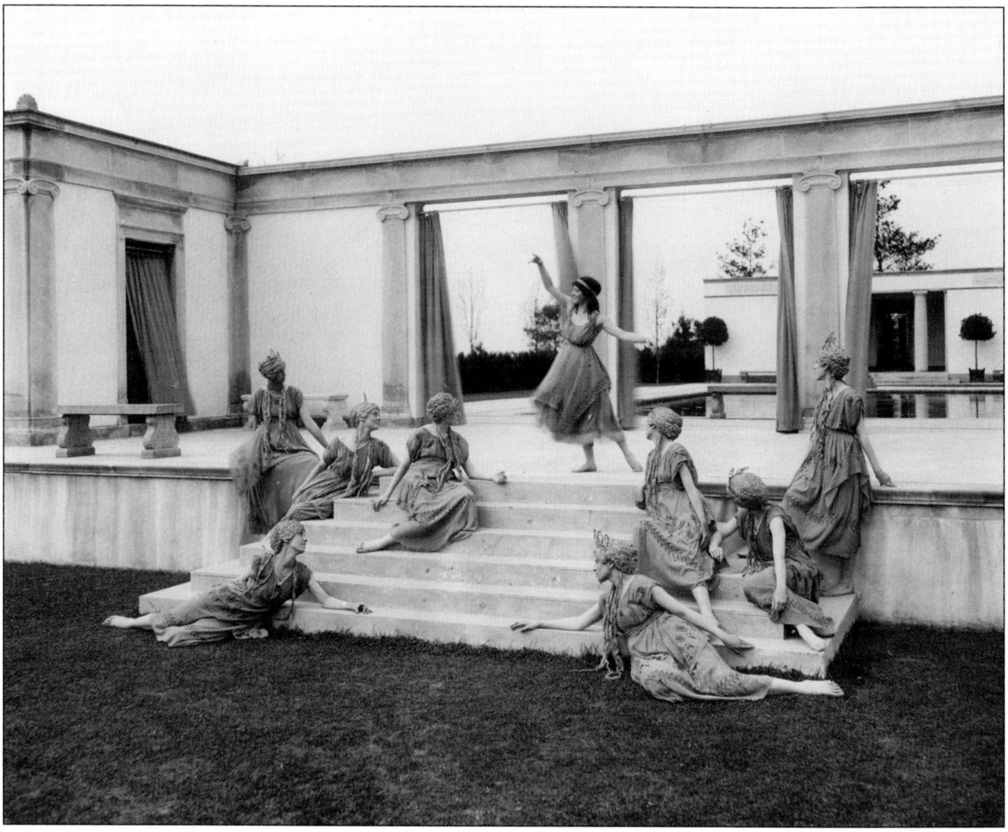

The Greek Theatre was designed by Marcus Burrowes and built in 1916. The first play produced there was *Cranbrook Masque* by Sidney Coe Howard, which had a 132-member cast. Unfortunately, a storm came up during the opening performance and scattered the audience. As a result, George Booth decided to build a covered open pavilion on Lone Pine Road to give shelter when needed. (Courtesy of Cranbrook Archives.)

This 1917 photograph shows the buildings in Farm Group No. 2, which were designed by Marcus Burrowes for efficient, scientific farming. After more than a few years of farming, however, Booth decided that the profession was problematic and began making other plans. In 1925, Eliel Saarinen designed Cranbrook School for Boys on the footprint of Farm Group No. 2. (Courtesy of Cranbrook Archives.)

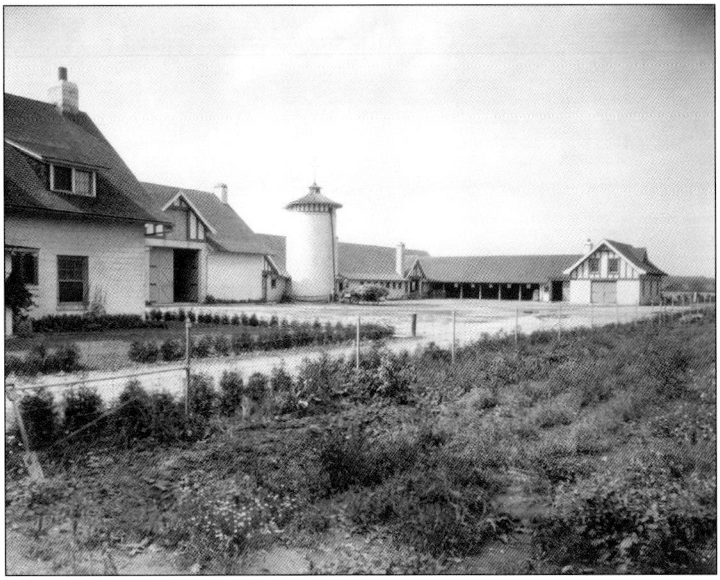

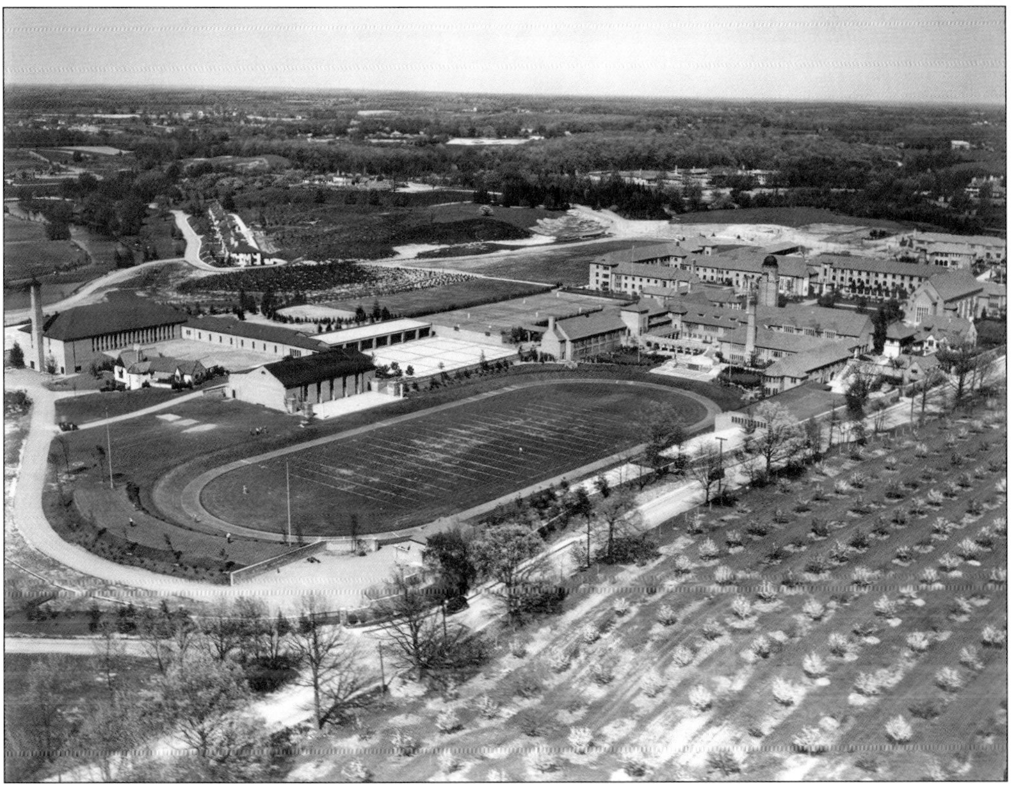

This 1931 aerial view looking to the southwest of the Cranbrook School campus shows the football oval as well as the conversion of the former Farm Group No. 2 buildings. On the south side of Lone Pine Road are apple orchards, which would later be cleared to build one of the city's largest subdivisions. (Courtesy of Cranbrook Archives.)

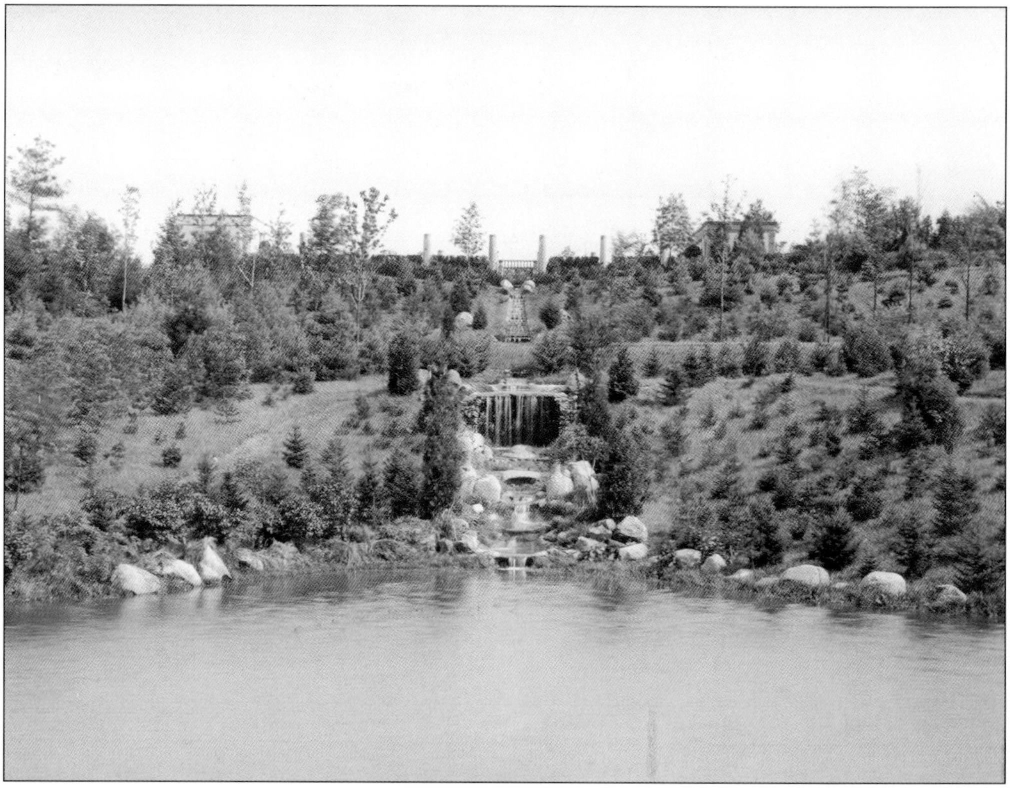

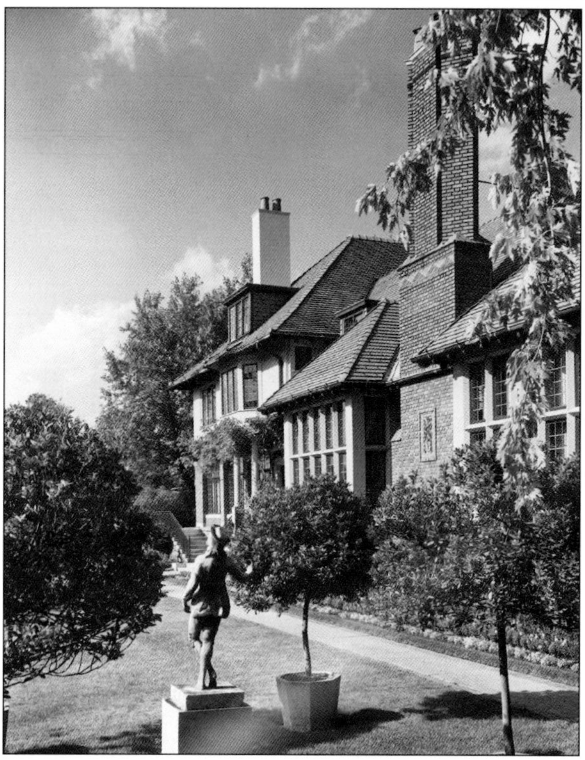

In 1914, when Henry Wood Booth was 77 years old, he planned a grotto with a series of cascades running into and forming a lake at the bottom. This grotto is now called Pineway Cascades. Aided by one helper, Booth made decorative use of the overflow from the swimming pool at the Greek Theatre. The stepped cascade, which broadens gradually, is now shaded by towering pines. Over the course of building Cranbrook, the Booths planted more than 150,000 trees. (Courtesy of Cranbrook Archives.)

This 1985 photograph shows a view of Cranbrook House long after it was finished. The lead sculpture of the shepherd that stood at the entrance to the vegetable garden so many decades before now faces his shepherdess, surrounded by lush landscaping and tall trees, just as the Booths had planned. (Courtesy of Cranbrook Archives.)

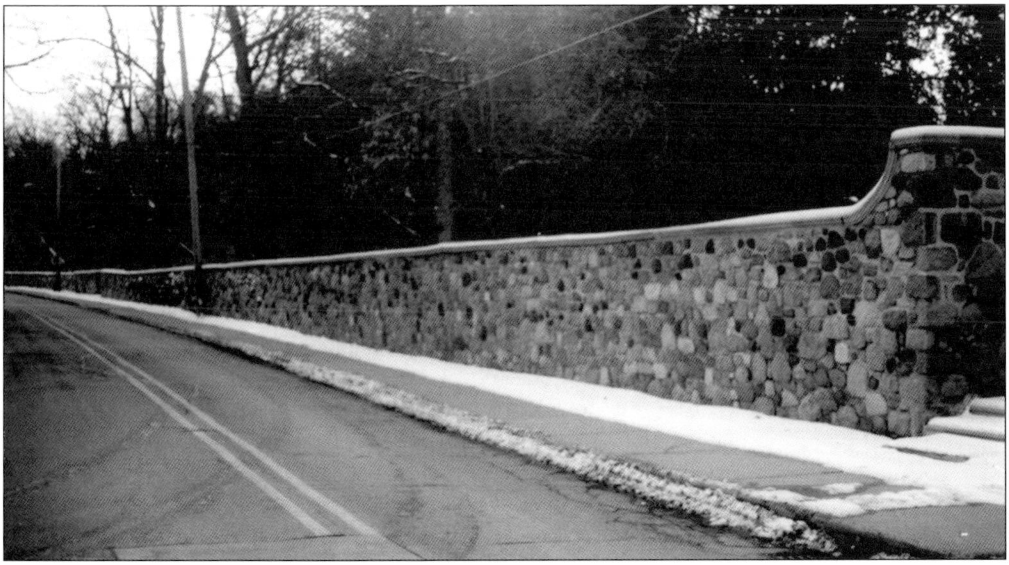

Stone walls reminiscent of those found in England are ubiquitous in Bloomfield Hills. Ten thousand years ago, the glaciers retreated from this area and left behind huge stones and boulders that they had dragged down from Canada. Field stones are so plentiful that travelers along this city's major roads will see walls that go on for more than a quarter-mile. (Courtesy of Harry C. Walsh.)

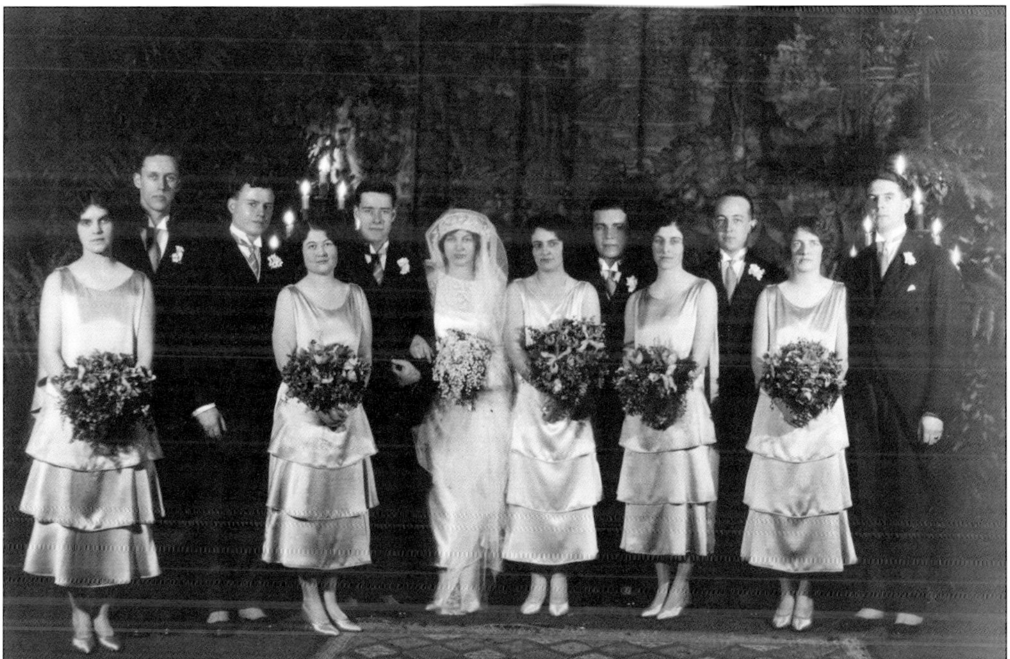

In February 1925, Florence Booth, daughter of George and Ellen Booth, married James Beresford in the Cranbrook House library. As a wedding gift, the couple received a home built for them on Lone Pine and Goodhue Roads. Shown from left to right are Carolyn Farr, Henry Booth, Edwin Beresford, Jean Thompson, James Beresford, Florence Beresford, Betsy Austin, unidentified, Katherine Shiell, Jenness Newcomb, Frances Shaw, and Raymond Smith. (Courtesy of Cranbrook Archives.)

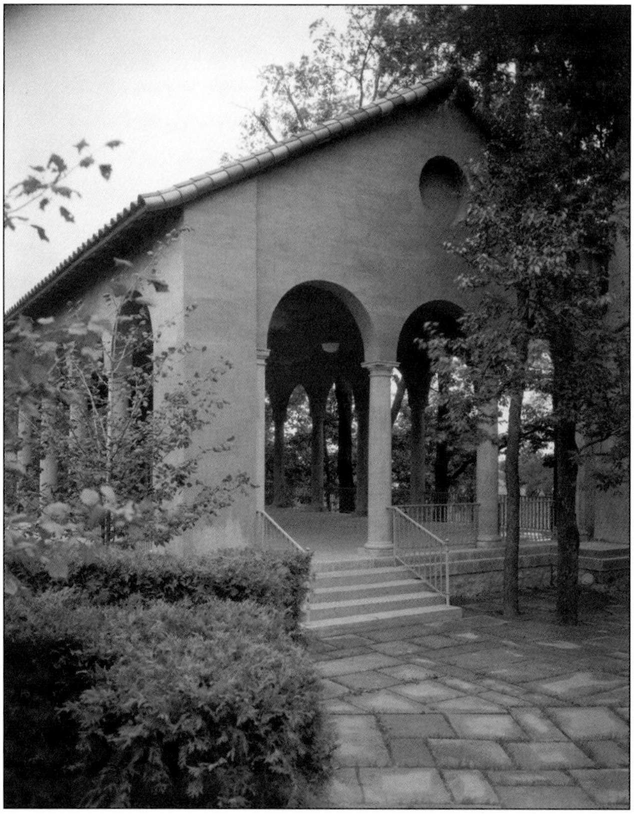

This c. 1924 photograph shows a view of what was originally designed by Albert Kahn as an open-air "garden house." In 1930, glass was installed between the arches to protect the interior from the weather. (Courtesy of Cranbrook Archives.)

Tremendous work went into building Cranbrook. In this c. 1926 photograph, Lone Pine Road is being lowered. To the right is the fieldstone wall that is familiar to passersby today. To the right of the wall is Farm Group No. 2, also known as the Cranbrook Farm, which produced dairy products that were sold to Bloomfield-area residents. Portions of this farm were remodeled or rebuilt to become the Cranbrook School for Boys. (Courtesy of Cranbrook Archives.)

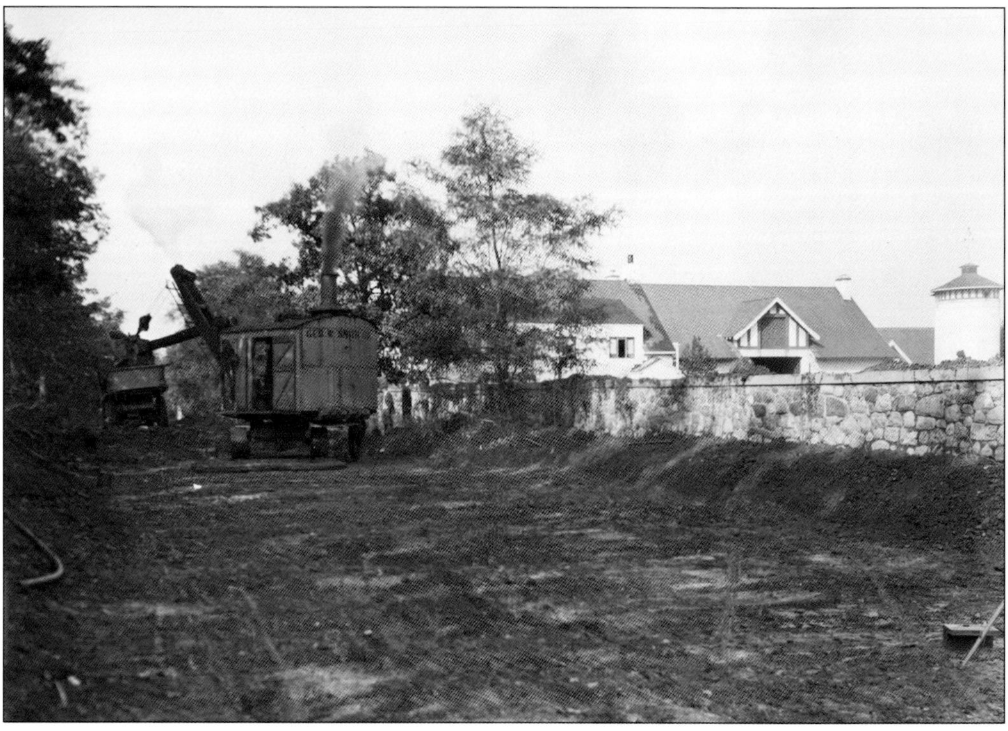

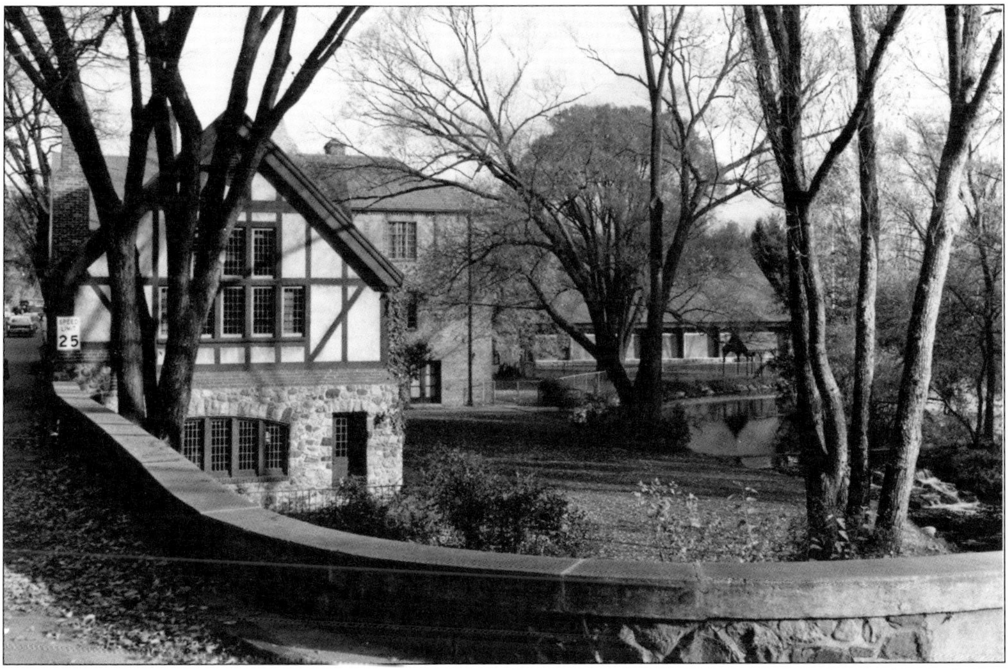

Brookside School Cranbrook was a day school for children in kindergarten through grade six and was designed by George Gough Booth. Booth's son Henry was the architect. Shown here is the south side of the school, which originally served as a community meetinghouse built in 1918. This 1959 view looks north from Lone Pine Road and shows a play area with the river running near it. (Courtesy of Cranbrook Archives.)

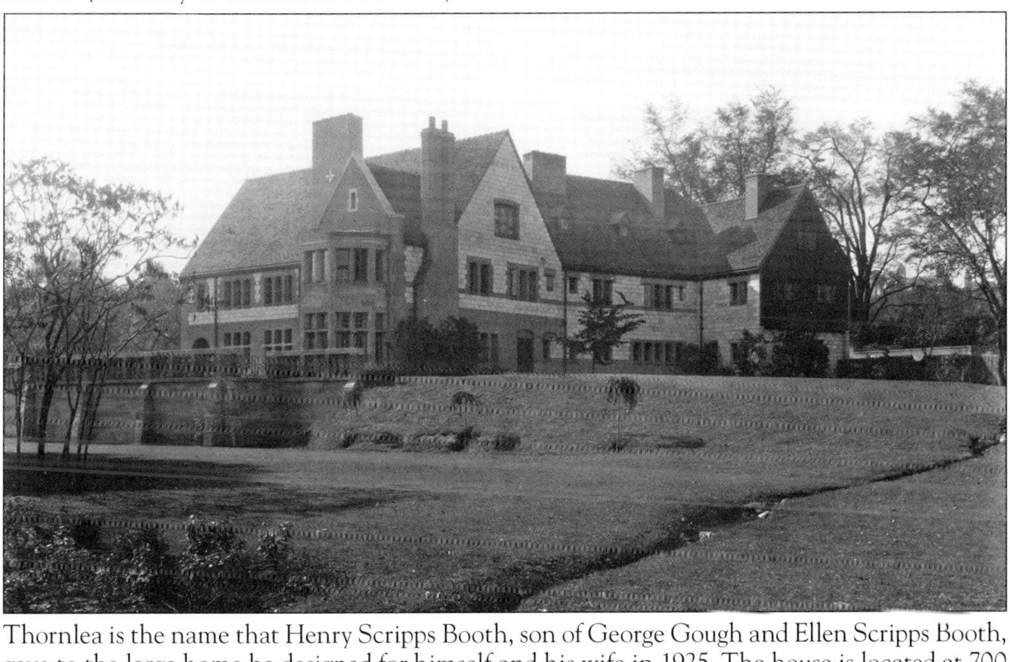

Thornlea is the name that Henry Scripps Booth, son of George Gough and Ellen Scripps Booth, gave to the large home he designed for himself and his wife in 1925. The house is located at 700 Cranbrook Road and looks out over a branch of the Rouge River. The Booths later bequeathed Thornlea to Cranbrook for use as an intellectual center. (Courtesy of Cranbrook Archives.)

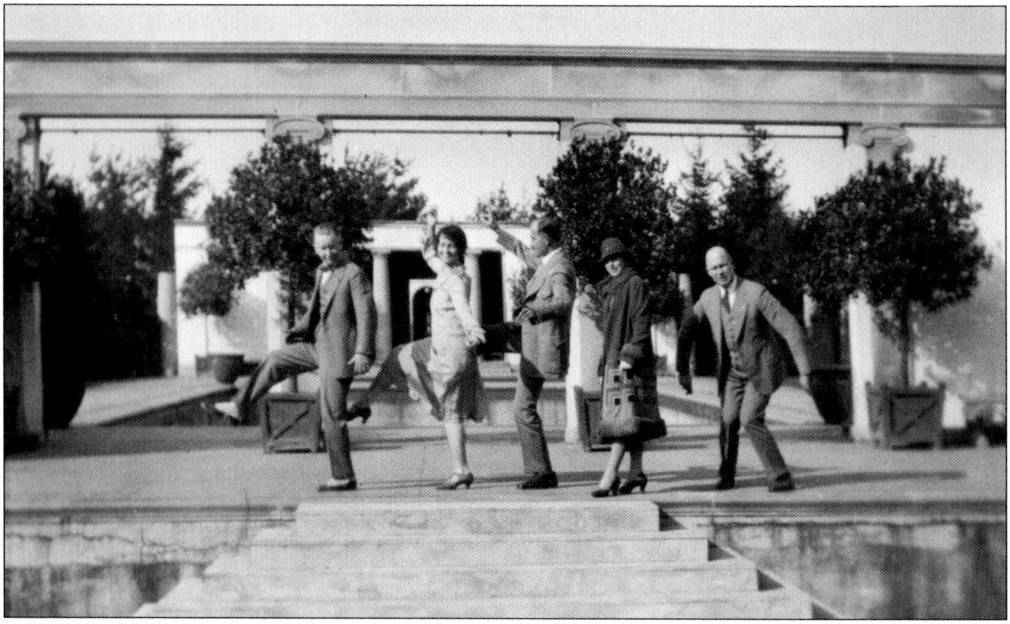

The Saarinens and a few of their friends enjoy a lighthearted moment on the Greek Theatre stage around 1928. From left to right are Eliel Saarinen, Leopoldine Maroti, Geza Maroti, Loja Saarinen, and an unidentified person. Geza Maroti created several sculptural adornments for Cranbrook School for Boys as well as sculpture and mosaics for the Fisher Building in Detroit. (Courtesy of Cranbrook Archives.)

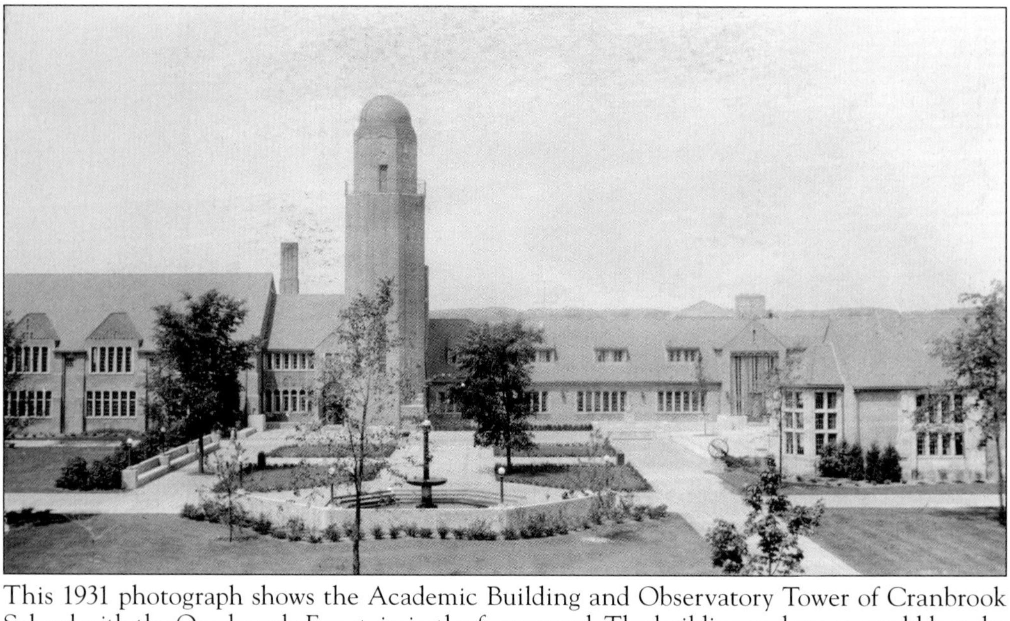

This 1931 photograph shows the Academic Building and Observatory Tower of Cranbrook School with the Quadrangle Fountain in the foreground. The building and tower would later be renamed Hoey Hall and Hoey Tower in honor of Harry D. Hoey, the headmaster of Cranbrook School from 1950 to 1964. The Quadrangle Fountain was erected in 1927 and is a replica of the Monreale Cathedral Fountain in Palermo, Italy. (Courtesy of Cranbrook Archives.)

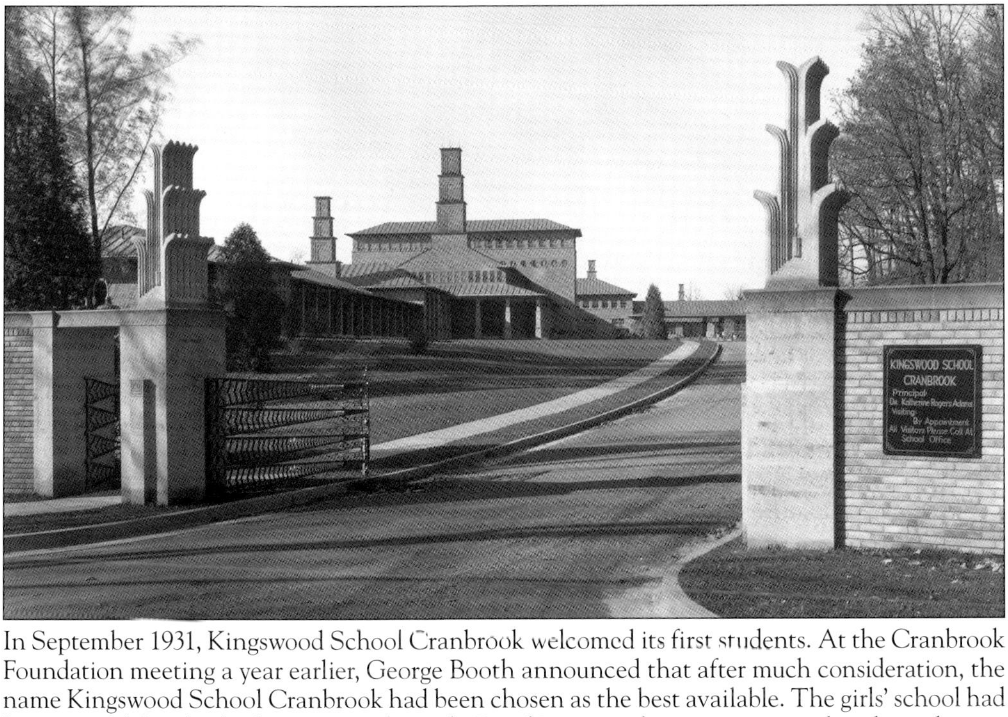

In September 1931, Kingswood School Cranbrook welcomed its first students. At the Cranbrook Foundation meeting a year earlier, George Booth announced that after much consideration, the name Kingswood School Cranbrook had been chosen as the best available. The girls' school had been named for Elizabeth Kingswood Booth, Booth's paternal great-great-grandmother, who was born in Cranbrook, Kent, England, on August 23, 1749. (Courtesy of Cranbrook Archives.)

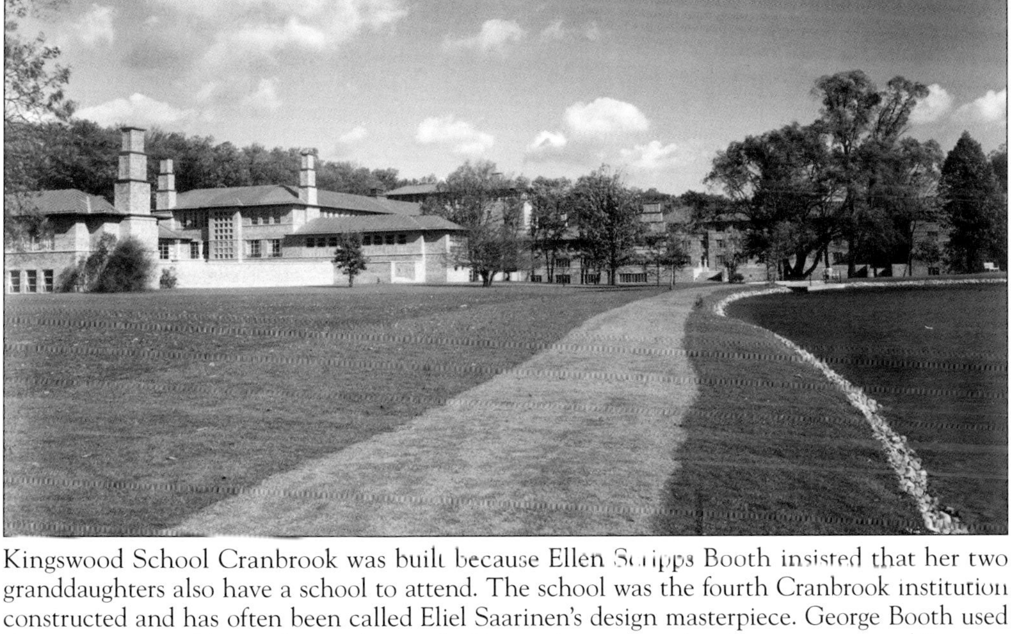

Kingswood School Cranbrook was built because Ellen Scripps Booth insisted that her two granddaughters also have a school to attend. The school was the fourth Cranbrook institution constructed and has often been called Eliel Saarinen's design masterpiece. George Booth used the opportunity of lowered costs during the Depression to complete its construction. (Courtesy of Cranbrook Archives.)

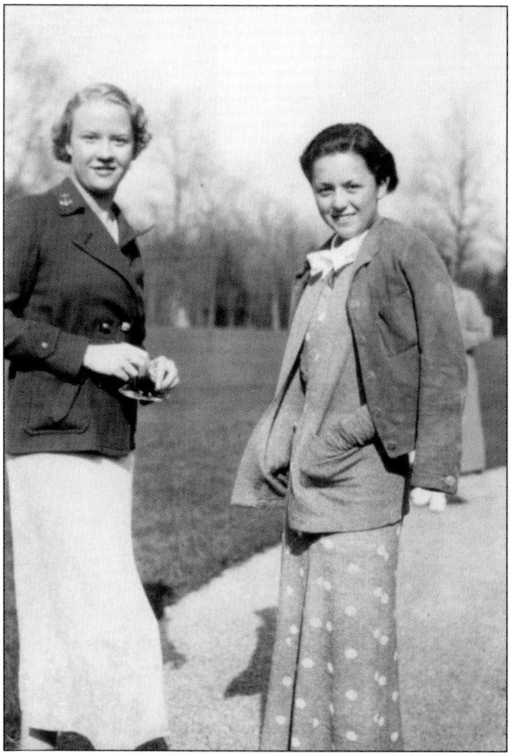

Florence Schust (Knoll) and Betty VanSlambrouck, left, stop to pose for this photograph around 1933 at Kingswood School. Schust went on to study architecture with Eliel Saarinen at Cranbrook Academy of Art as well as with Walter Gropius and Mies van der Rohe. After marrying Hans Knoll, she and her husband worked together to expand Knoll Associates, which became world famous for design. (Courtesy of Cranbrook Archives).

In 1933, this formal dance was held at Kingswood. Dances and dance classes were an important aspect of social training for students at Kingswood and Cranbrook Schools. According to author Elizabeth C. Clark, even the younger boys at Cranbrook were taught "the amenities of ballroom behavior, how to bow to a lady, shake hands properly, say the right thing, and move with a partner to the sedate rhythms of the fox trot." (Courtesy of Cranbrook Archives.)

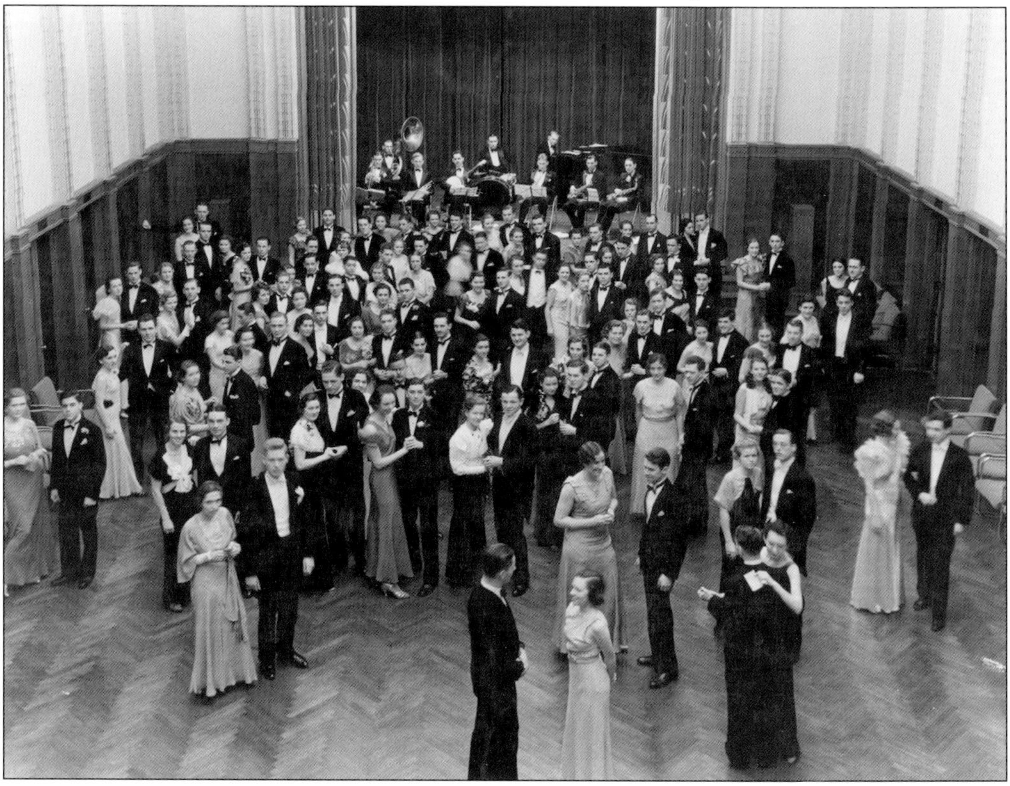

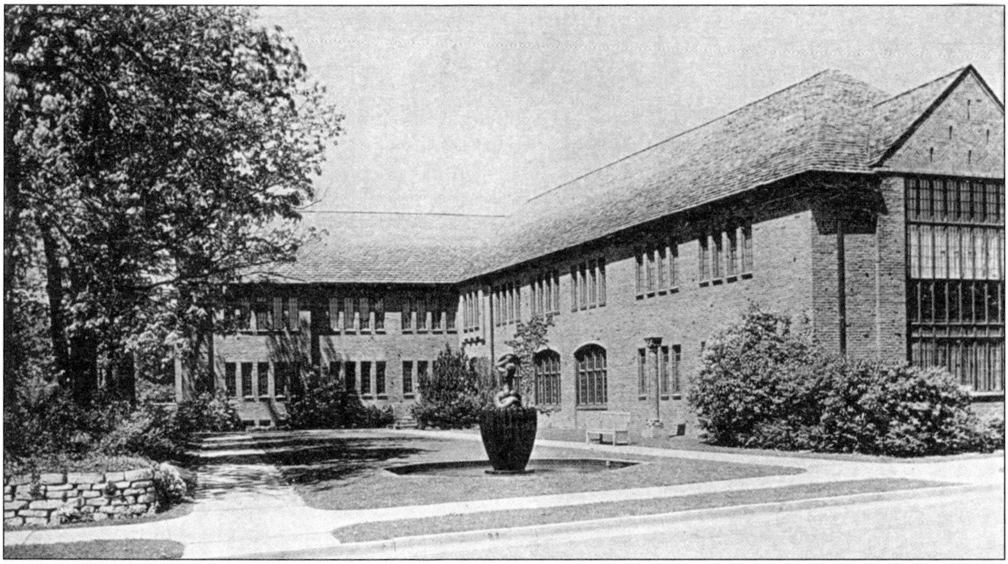

The postcard shows the Cranbrook Academy of Art Administration Building on Academy Way. In 1932, this building housed the library, museum, and painting and etching classes and was called the Art Academy Building. The eight-foot-tall bronze fountain in front is *Triton with Shell* and was designed in 1916 by Carl Milles in Sweden. Milles donated the fountain to Cranbrook in 1929. (Courtesy of Postcard Collection, Bentley Historical Library, University of Michigan.)

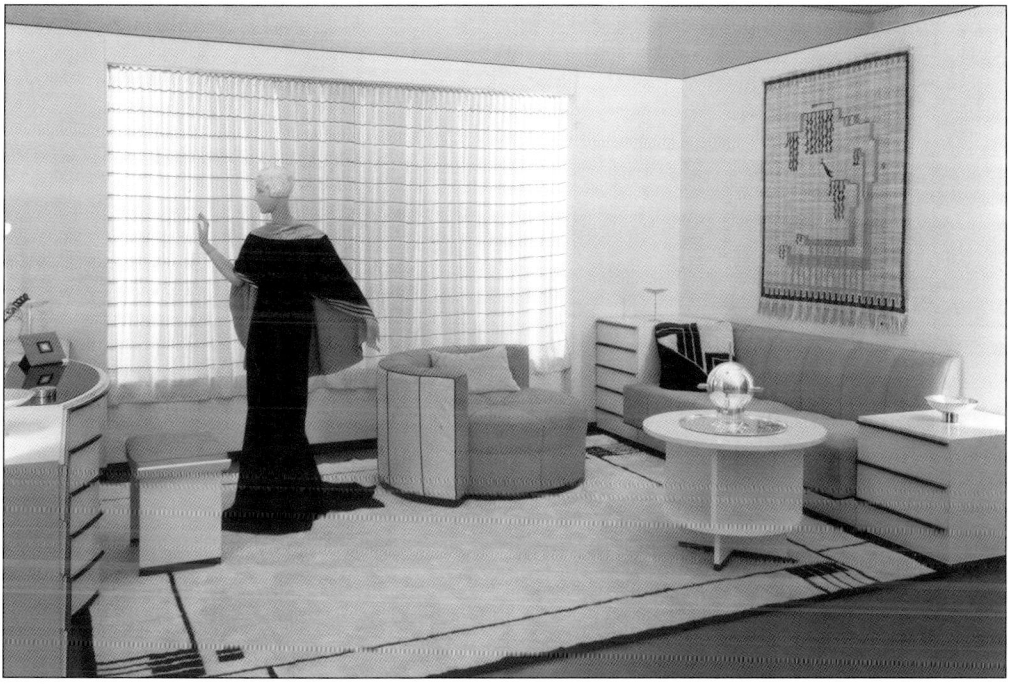

In 1935, *Room for a Lady* was part of an exhibition called Contemporary American Industrial Design held at the Metropolitan Museum of Art. Loja Saarinen created the lady's and bedroom's textiles, while Eliel Saarinen designed everything else, including the furniture and silver pieces. These types of exhibitions showcased the creativity of the artists and promoted the enormous talent residing at Cranbrook. (Courtesy of Cranbrook Archives.)

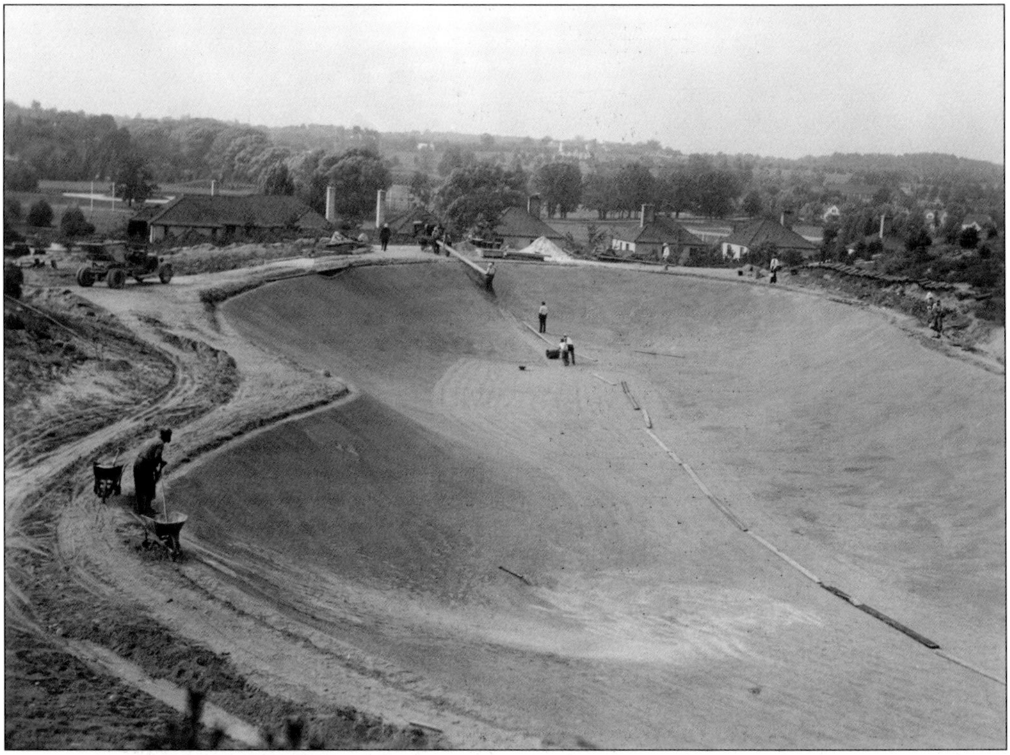

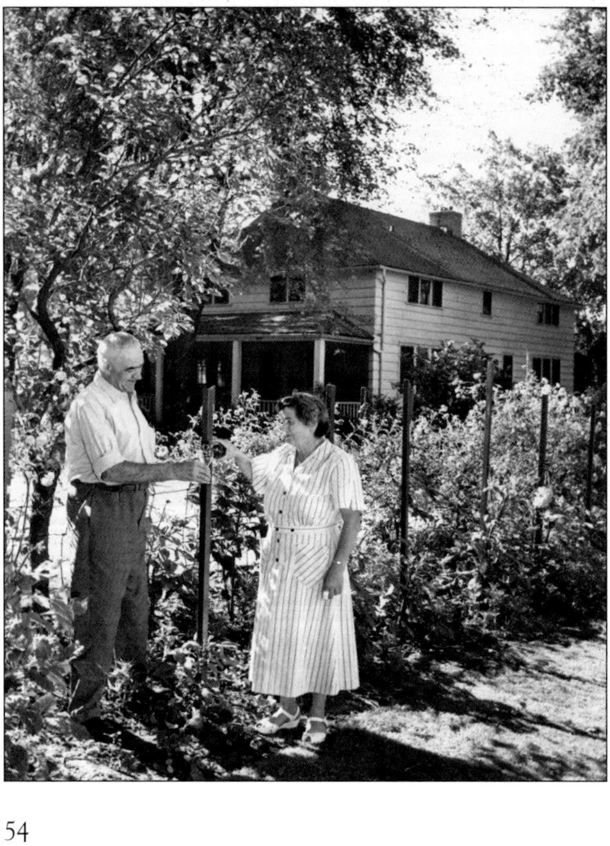

Workers are busy in 1934 building Lake Jonah, which was designed in the shape of a whale. Lake Jonah is 650 feet long, 75 feet wide, and 12 feet at its deepest point. For nearly 60 summers, students and faculty from the Cranbrook Schools as well as day camp students would swim in the lake or take swimming lessons there. (Courtesy of Cranbrook Archives.)

Around 1952, Michael and Michela Vettraino stand in the garden of their Valley Way home. Michael was superintendent of grounds at Cranbrook for 53 years. In 1955, Piazza Vettraino was dedicated in honor of 50 years of service. The Vettrainos' son, Dominick Vettraino, also worked at Cranbrook for more than 50 years, and also served as a Bloomfield Hills commissioner and as mayor in 1958. (Courtesy of Cranbrook Archives.)

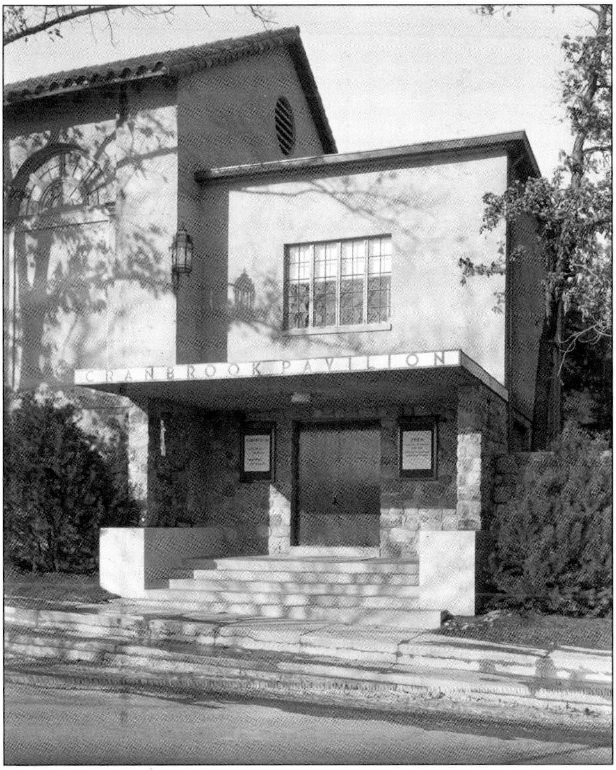

This 1935 view of the Cranbrook Pavilion entrance on Lone Pine Road is recognizable today as St. Dunstan's. Between 1930 and 1934, Eliel Saarinen supervised the enclosing of the arcades in concrete and stucco to create an indoor exhibition space for the Cranbrook Academy of Art. In 1932, St. Dunstan's Theatre Guild of Cranbrook was granted permanent use of this structure. The guild is named for the patron saint of the arts. (Courtesy of Cranbrook Archives.)

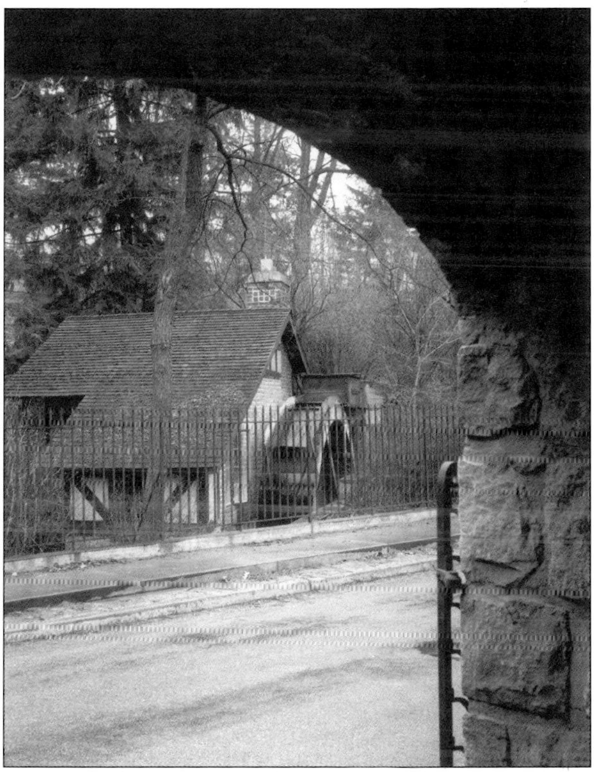

This current Morris Mill and waterwheel were built by the Booths on the site of the historic Stiff's Flouring Mill. Viewed in 1948 from Brookside School, the mill was rebuilt in 1917 as a pumping station. However, its new design better reflected the English style Booth was using for Cranbrook. The mill pumps water uphill to the Greek Theatre pool. That water cascades down to Grotto Lake, eventually discharging into Kingswood Lake, which replenishes the millrace. (Courtesy of Cranbrook Archives.)

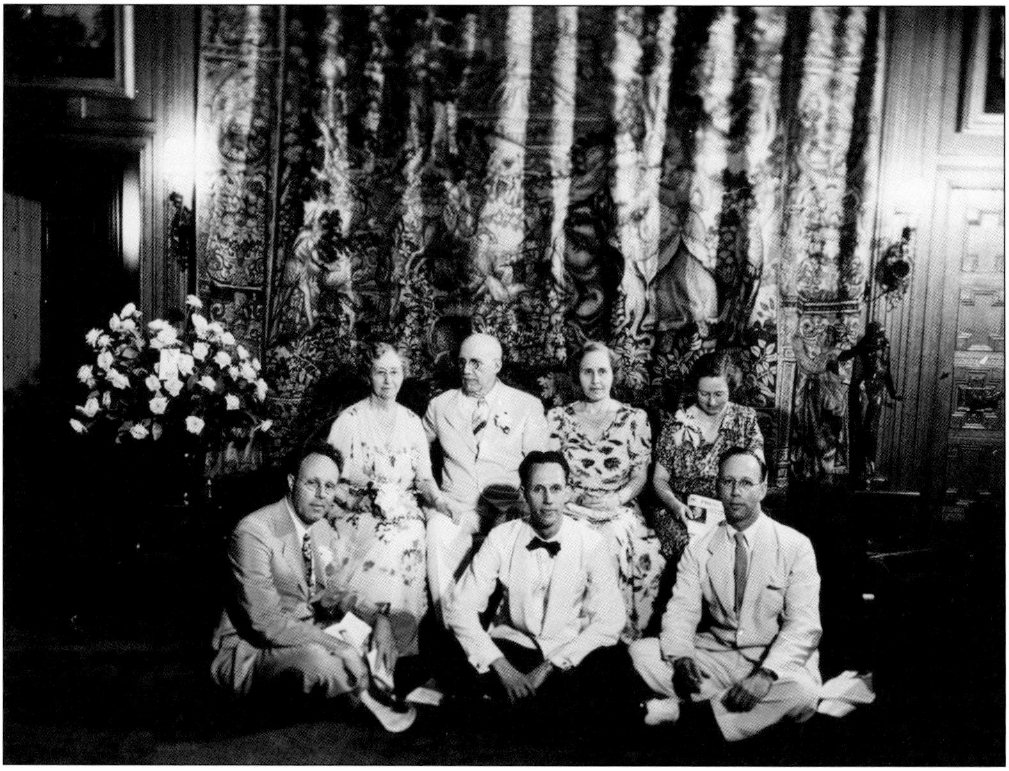

In 1937, George Gough Booth and Ellen Scripps Booth gathered with their children for this 50th wedding anniversary photograph. Pictured are, from left to right, (front row) the Booths' sons —James, Henry, and Warren; (back row) Ellen Scripps and George Gough Booth and their daughters, Grace and Florence. (Courtesy of Cranbrook Archives.)

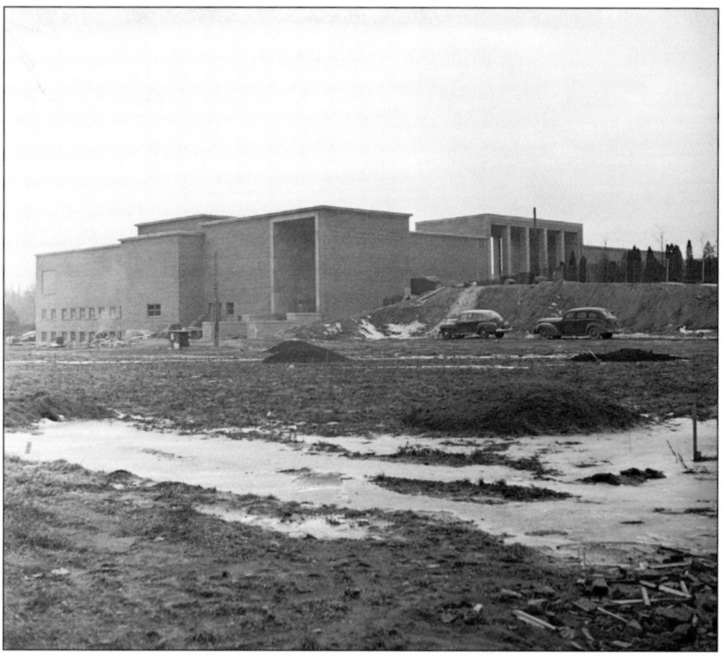

In February 1941, the Cranbrook Art Museum and Library were still under construction. By 1942, Cranbrook Academy of Art would incorporate as a Michigan institution of higher learning. Designed by Eliel Saarinen and based on George Booth's ideas, the museum and library, along with the arts and crafts studios and living quarters along Academy Way, would constitute a community where instructors and students lived and worked together. (Courtesy of Cranbrook Archives.)

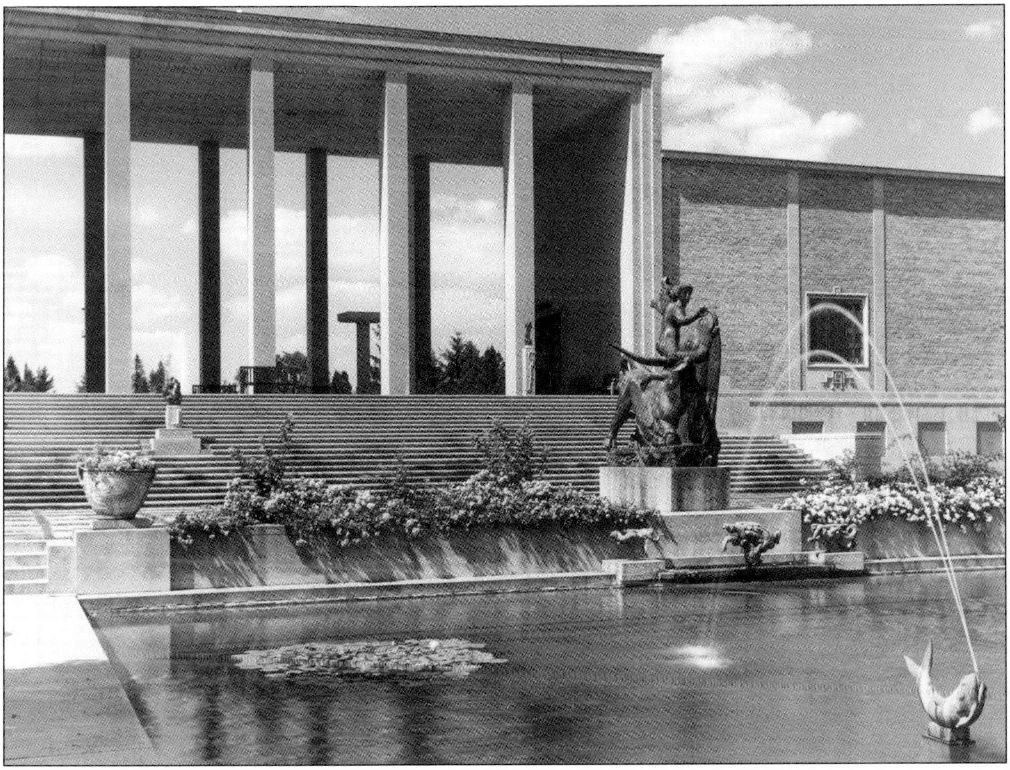

In this 1946 view of the Cranbrook art galleries' peristyle, Carl Milles's bronze sculpture *Europa and the Bull* graces the foreground. The continent of Europe is named for Europa, a princess from Greek mythology. Milles's bronze version of Europa was completed in 1926 and shows her climbing onto the bull's back just before she is kidnapped and carried away to the island of Crete. (Courtesy of Cranbrook Archives.)

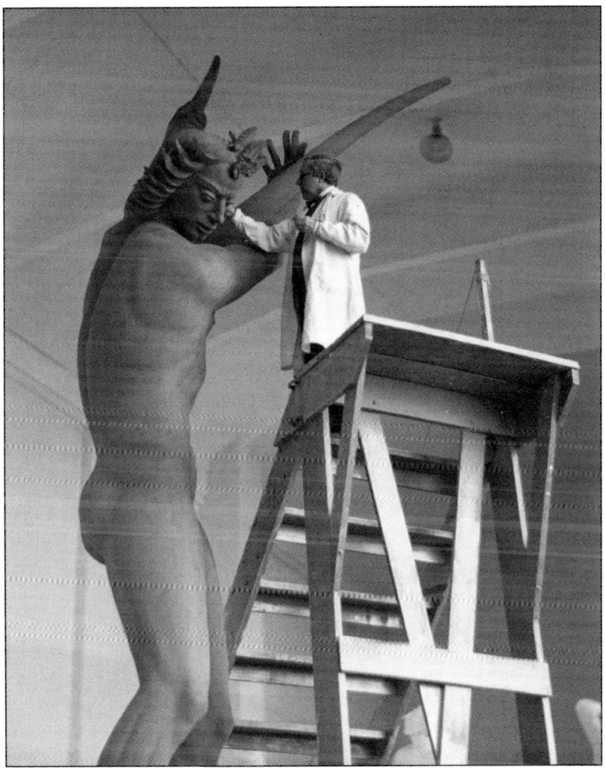

Carl Milles (1875–1955) sculpts the figure of Orpheus in his studio at Cranbrook Academy of Art in 1934, the same year he became head of the Sculpture Department. The finished sculpture was placed in front of the concert hall in Stockholm, Sweden. Milles was the resident sculptor at Cranbrook Academy of Art until 1950. (Courtesy of Cranbrook Archives.)

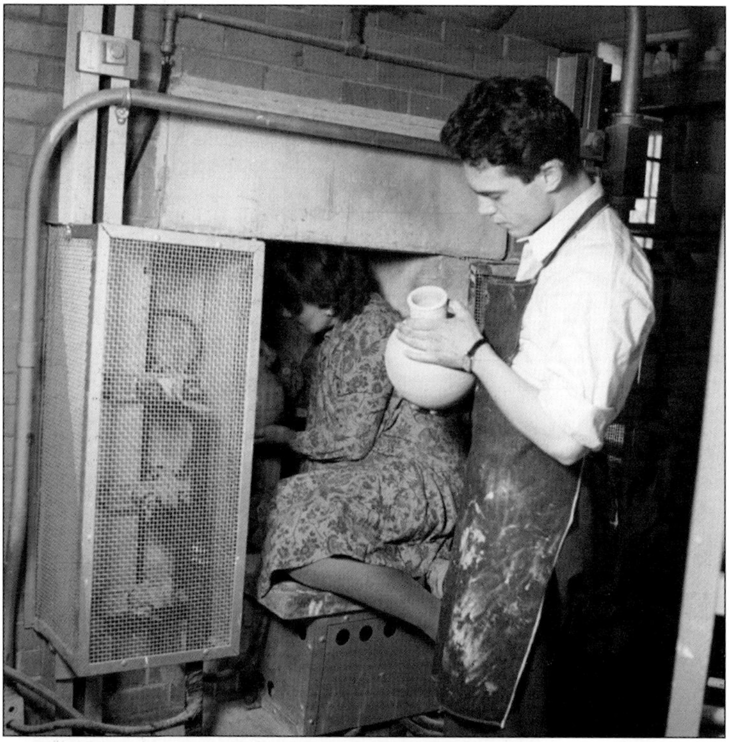

Ceramist Maija Grotell loads the ceramics studio kiln in 1939 while Cranbrook Academy of Art student Harry Weese (front) examines some pottery. Grotell was head of the Cranbrook Academy of Art's Ceramic Department from 1938 to 1966. Weese studied city planning and textiles as well as pottery while at Cranbrook. He went on to become a prominent architect who designed the Washington Metro. (Courtesy of Cranbrook Archives.)

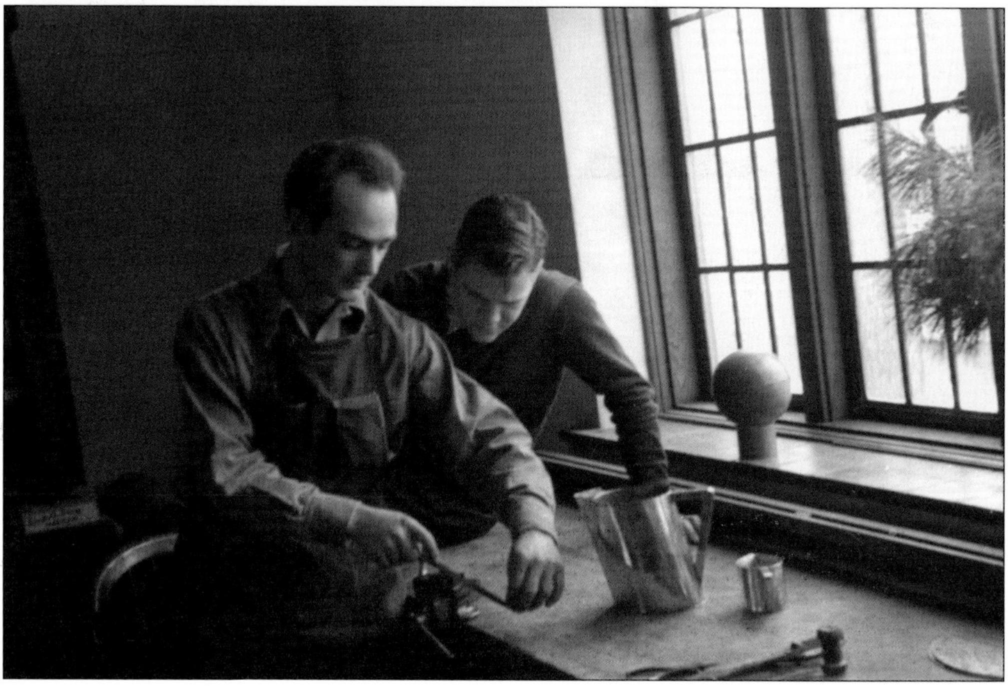

Harry Bertoia works at Cranbrook Academy of Art as an instructor of metalcraft with an unidentified student in 1939. Like all of the other instructors, he was also a working artist. Through his innovative furniture design and sculpture, he would become a major contributor to American modern design. (Courtesy of Cranbrook Archives.)

Charles Eames (left) and Eero Saarinen share a moment with Warren Booth (right) at the opening of the Cranbrook Academy of Art Faculty Exhibition in 1939. Eames eventually led the academy's Design Department and became renowned for his furniture design. Saarinen, the son of Eliel Saarinen, went on to design the St. Louis Arch, the GM Tech Center, and other world-famous structures. (Courtesy of Cranbrook Archives.)

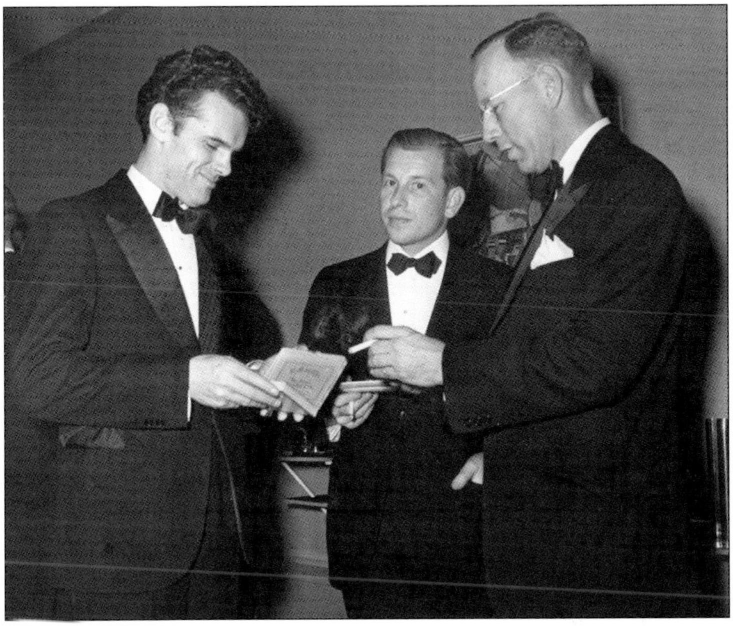

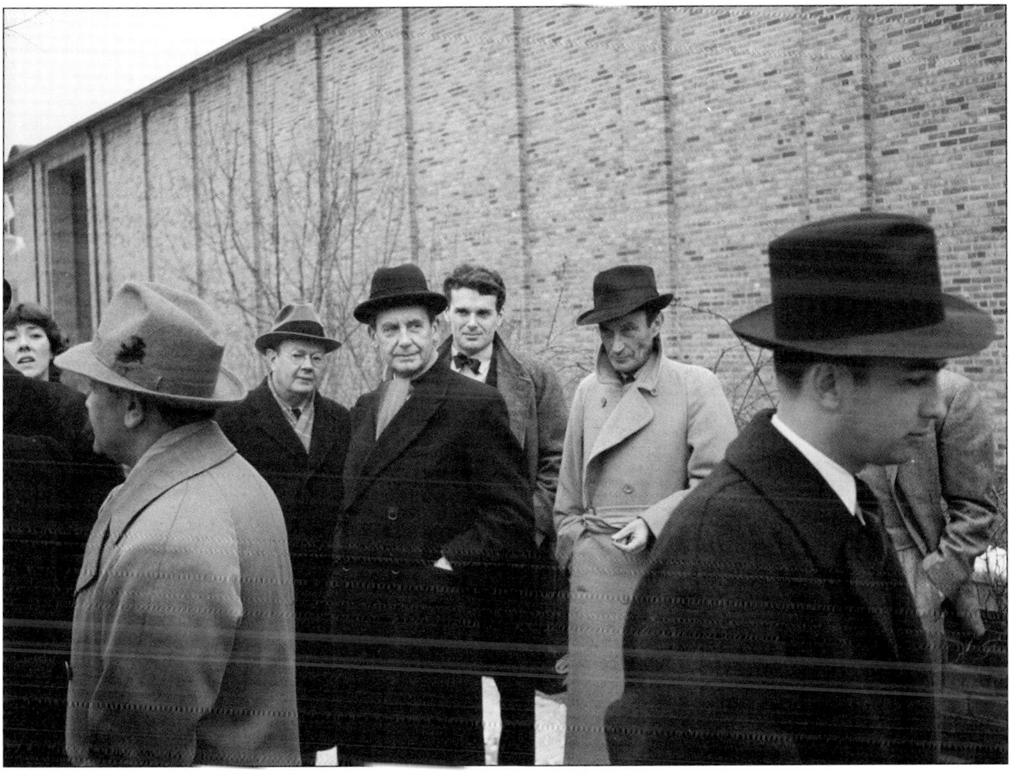

Several pioneering architects visited Cranbrook over the years. In the midst of these architects attending a convention in 1940 is Walter Gropius, founder of the Bauhaus. From left to right are Lily Swann Saarinen, Richard Hudnut, Gropius, Charles Eames, and three unidentified men. Also in attendance but not shown here were Eliel and Eero Saarinen. (Courtesy of Cranbrook Archives.)

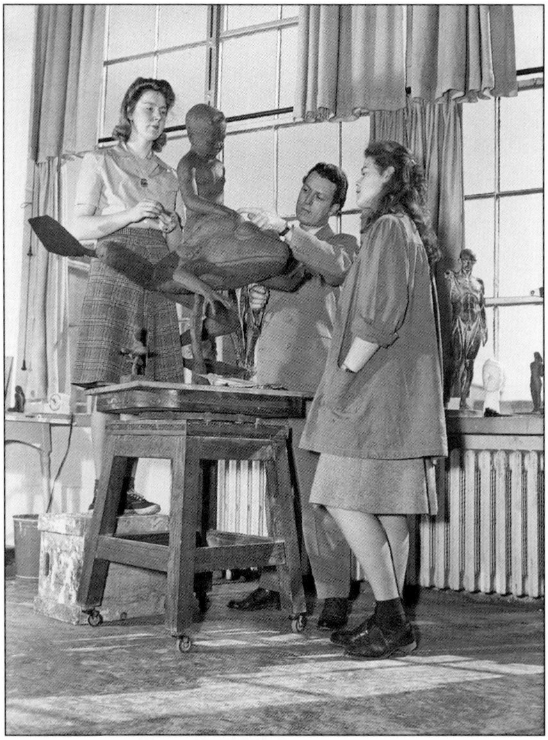

In 1942, Marshall Fredericks confers with students in his sculpture workshop at Cranbrook Academy of Art. In 1932, he was invited by his own former instructor, Carl Milles, to teach at the academy, which he did until 1942. Fredericks completed many commissions and has several sculptures on the Cranbrook campus. He is perhaps best known locally for his monumental sculpture *The Spirit of Detroit*. (Courtesy of Cranbrook Archives.)

Ruth Adler Schnee (left) is shown in this 1946 design class at Cranbrook Academy of Art. Born in Germany, she and her family fled Germany after Kristallnacht. Schnee would later become a prominent designer of textiles and interiors. To her right are students Frederick Lauritzen, unidentified, Gordon Lawson, and Martha Middleton Lauritzen. (Courtesy of Cranbrook Archives.)

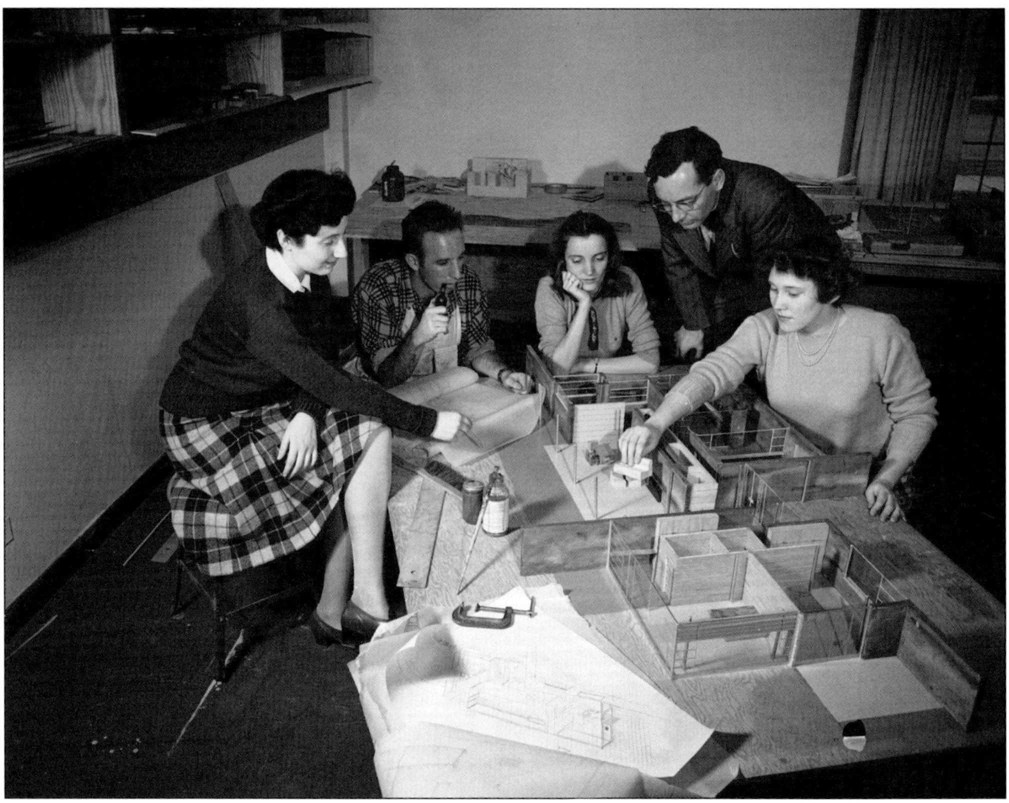

In 1945, architect Frank Lloyd Wright (right) lectured at Cranbrook and toured the campus with Eliel Saarinen. This was only one of several visits, as these two renowned architects were also good friends. (Courtesy of Cranbrook Archives.)

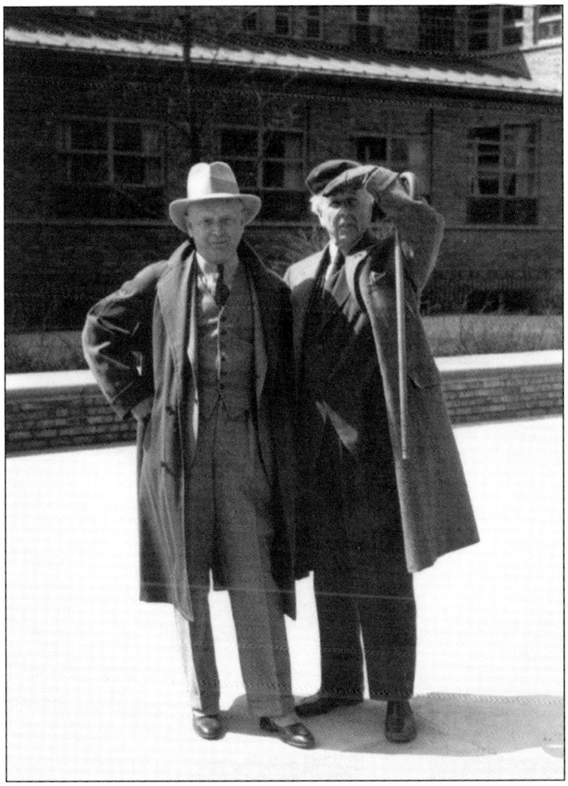

In 1942, Cranbrook Academy of Art student Oliver LaGrone displays several of his maquettes. LaGrone, who studied sculpture with Carl Milles, created more than 500 sculptures during his lifetime. He was also a poet whose writing was included in *New Negro Poets: USA*, edited by Langston Hughes. A scholarship established by his church in his name helped many other students pursue a postsecondary education. (Courtesy of Cranbrook Archives.)

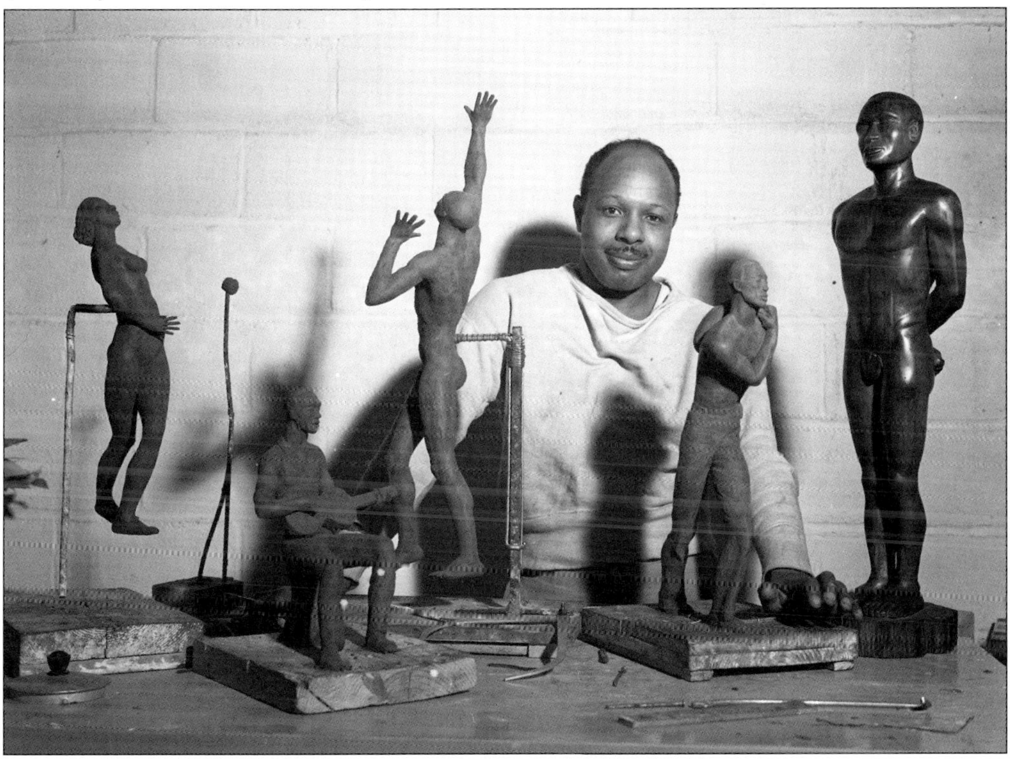

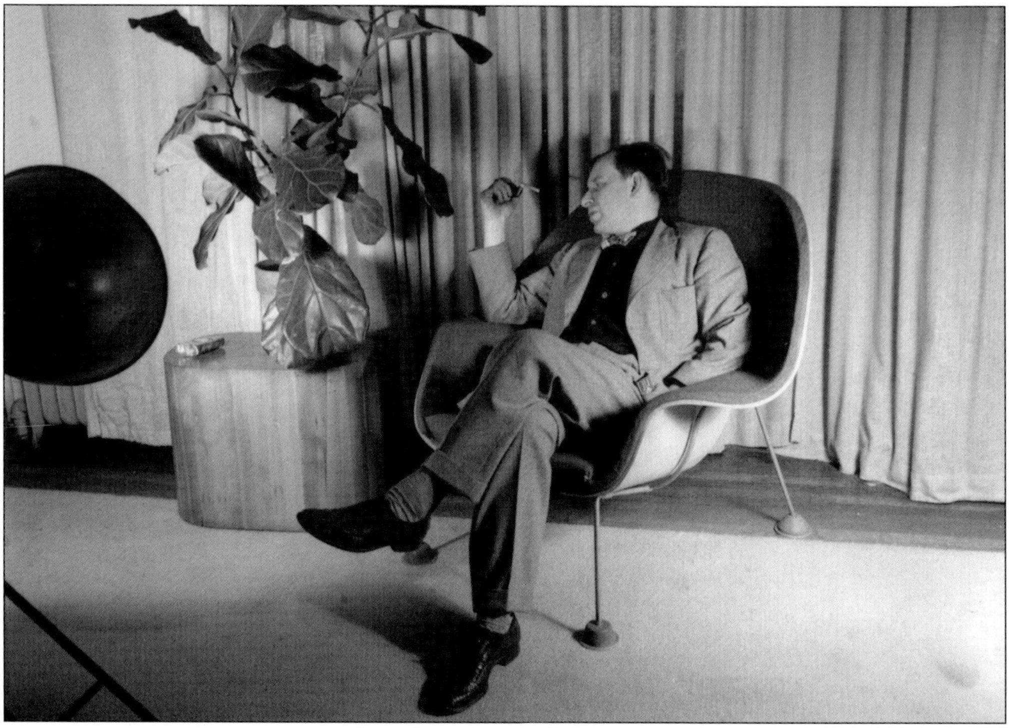

In 1947, Eero Saarinen takes a well-deserved rest in a prototype of the Womb Chair he designed. Saarinen had been designing furnishings for Cranbrook since his teens, and after teaming up with Charles Eames in 1940 and winning a prestigious award for molded furniture design, he continued exploring materials and designing innovative furniture. The Womb Chair is still manufactured by Knoll, Inc., today. (Courtesy of Cranbrook Archives.)

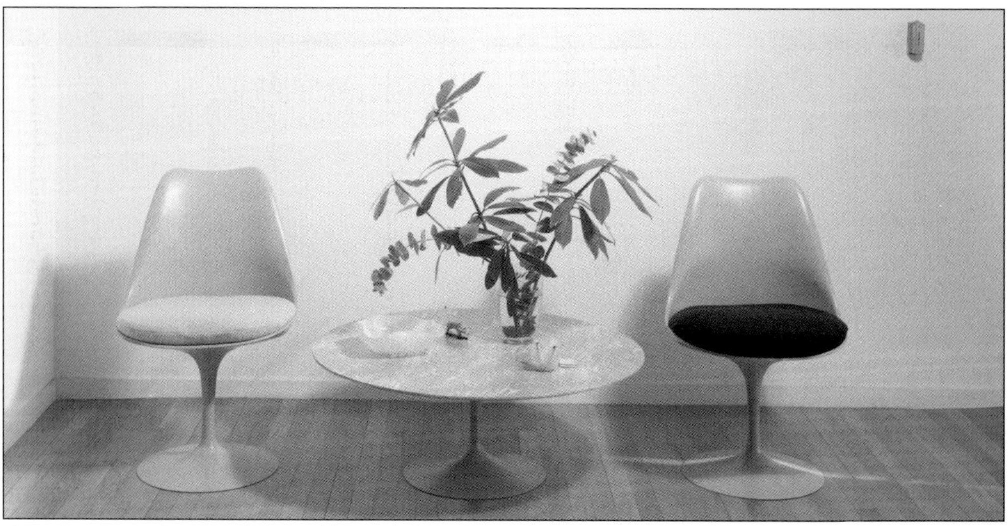

Eero Saarinen designed this table and chairs between 1954 and 1957; they became known as his Pedestal series. Each furniture piece had a single cast-metal base with a molded fiberglass chair or tabletop. To make each chair appear to be one single form, he had the metal bases and fiberglass seats manufactured in the same color. Seat pads and various tabletop materials were available. (Courtesy of Cranbrook Archives.)

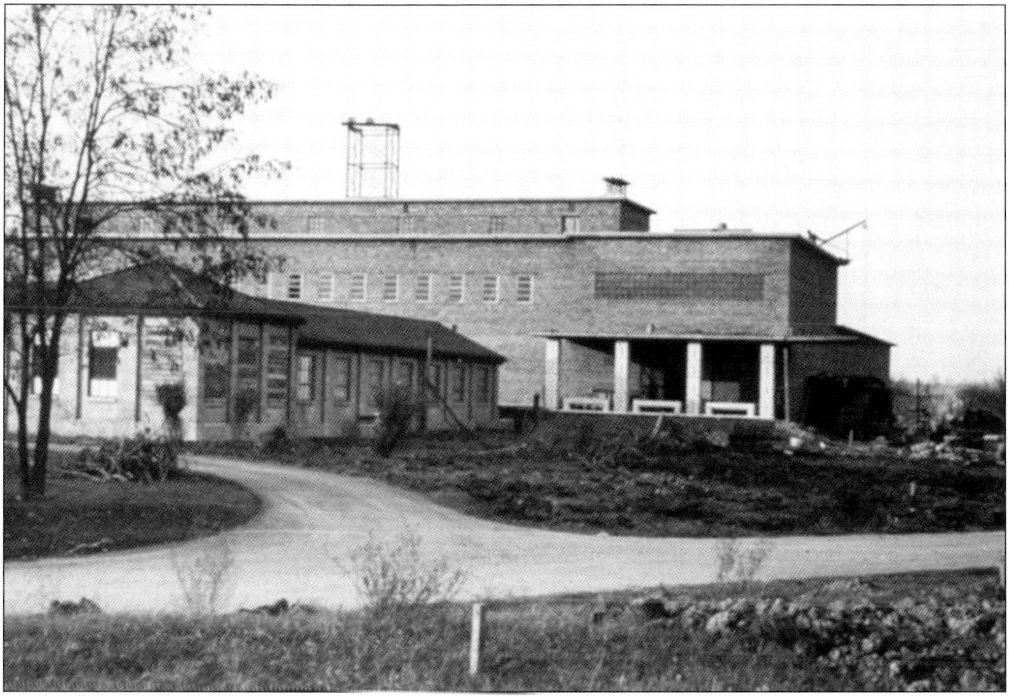

This photograph shows the Cranbrook Institute of Science under construction. The building was designed by Eliel Saarinen based on sketches provided by George Booth (who had designed the original building in 1930), and it opened in 1936. The museum included a domed planetarium, large displays of fossils and minerals, and educational dioramas that showed how life on Earth changed over time and how people adapted to those changes. (Courtesy of Cranbrook Archives.)

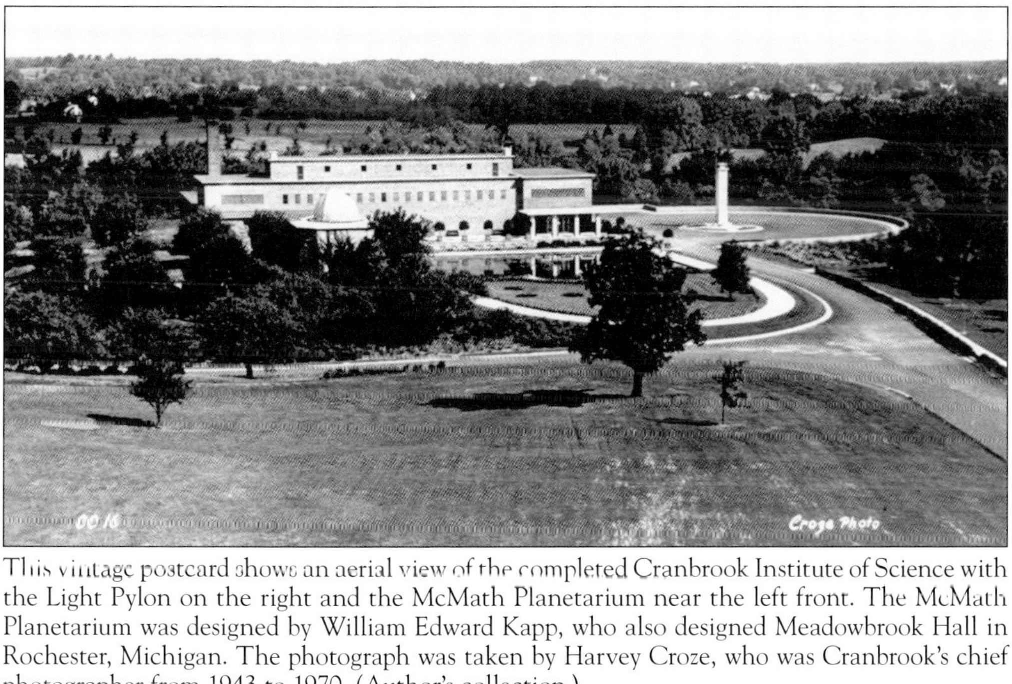

This vintage postcard shows an aerial view of the completed Cranbrook Institute of Science with the Light Pylon on the right and the McMath Planetarium near the left front. The McMath Planetarium was designed by William Edward Kapp, who also designed Meadowbrook Hall in Rochester, Michigan. The photograph was taken by Harvey Croze, who was Cranbrook's chief photographer from 1943 to 1970. (Author's collection.)

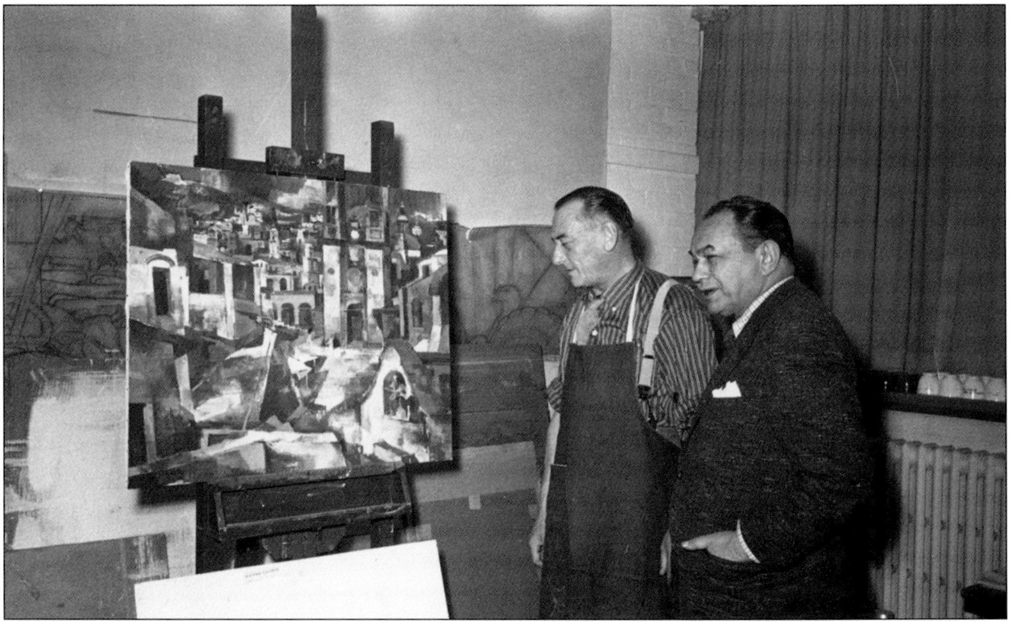

Zoltan Sepeshy (1898–1974) was director of the Department of Painting at Cranbrook Academy of Art for many years until he became president of Cranbrook in 1957 after Eliel Saarinen's death. In this December 1957 photograph, he is visited by actor and collector Edward G. Robinson (right). Sepeshy exhibited regularly and received the Samuel F.B. Morse gold medal from the National Academy of Design. (Courtesy of Cranbrook Archives.)

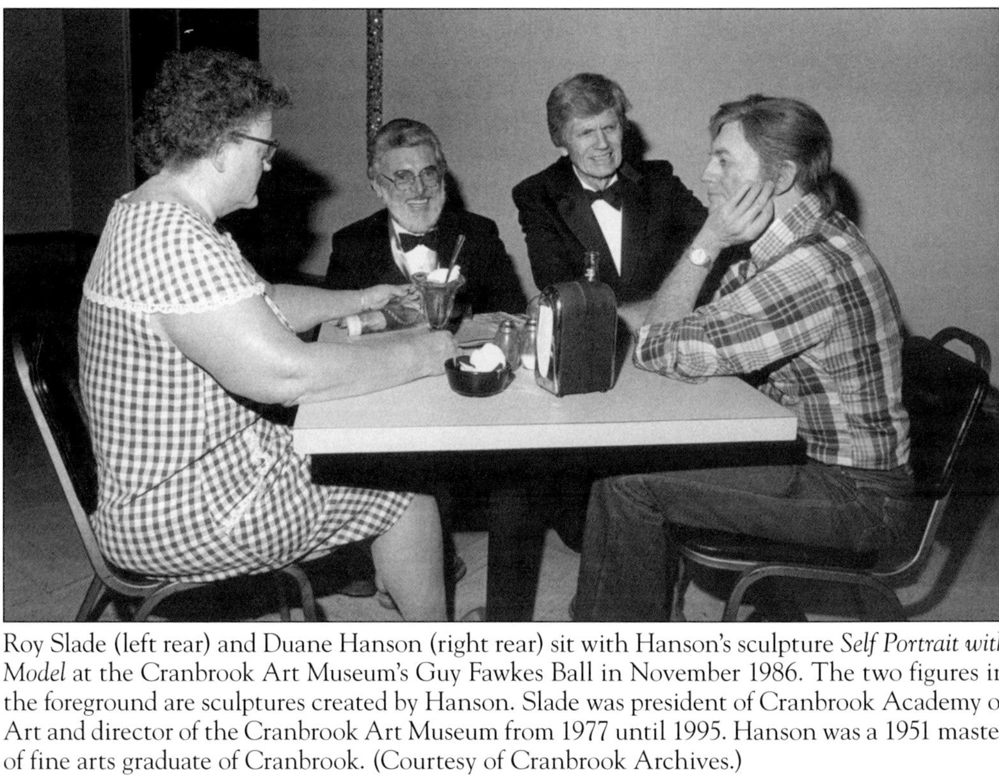

Roy Slade (left rear) and Duane Hanson (right rear) sit with Hanson's sculpture *Self Portrait with Model* at the Cranbrook Art Museum's Guy Fawkes Ball in November 1986. The two figures in the foreground are sculptures created by Hanson. Slade was president of Cranbrook Academy of Art and director of the Cranbrook Art Museum from 1977 until 1995. Hanson was a 1951 master of fine arts graduate of Cranbrook. (Courtesy of Cranbrook Archives.)

Four

Nooks and Crannies

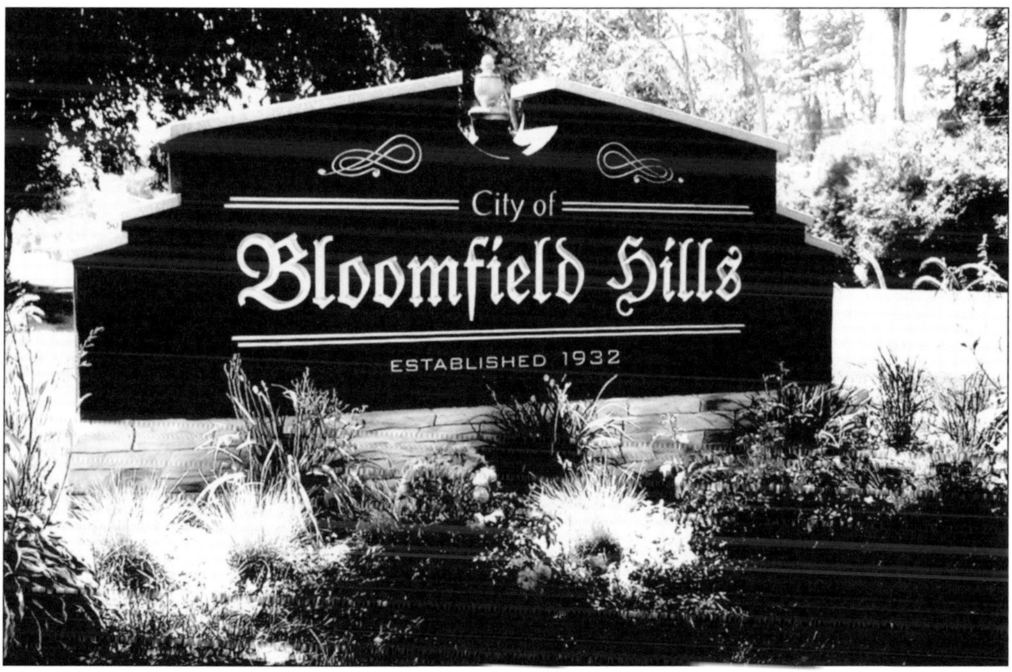

Majestic welcome signs on Woodward Avenue greet drivers as they cross the northern and southern city limits. They are printed in gold letters on a black background, the color requirement for all city signs. The signs were donated some years ago by resident Martin "Hoot" McInerney, legendary auto dealer and city benefactor. (Courtesy of Pat Hardy.)

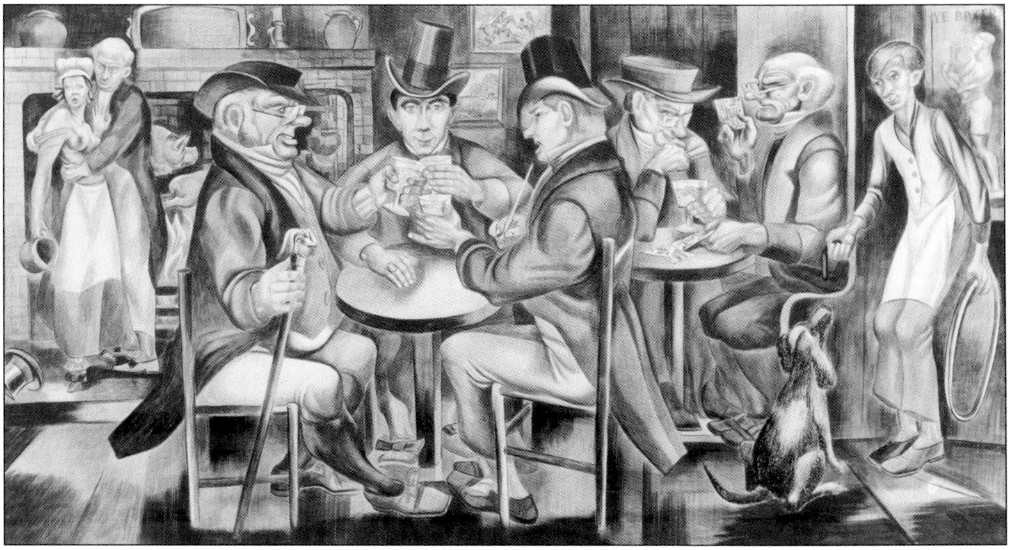

This 1944 photograph shows the Fox and Hounds mural created by Clifford B. West, a former student at Cranbrook Academy of Art and art teacher at Kingswood School. In the center of the painting, West has painted himself wearing a top hat and facing viewers. The Fox and Hounds was demolished in 2007. (Courtesy of Cranbrook Archives.)

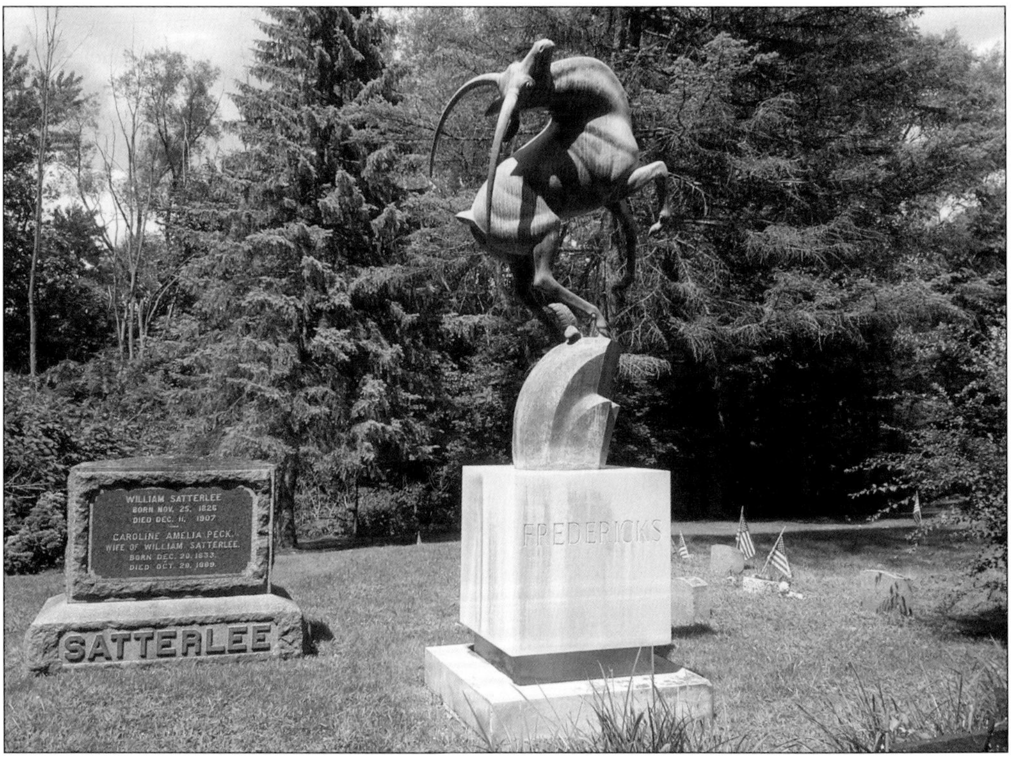

Many of Bloomfield Hills' pioneering families and other deceased residents are buried in Greenwood Cemetery in Birmingham. George and Ellen Booth and many of their family members are buried there. The surnames of some of Bloomfield's early settlers can also be found, including Satterlee and Trowbridge, as well as prominent artists' names, such as Fredericks. (Author's collection.)

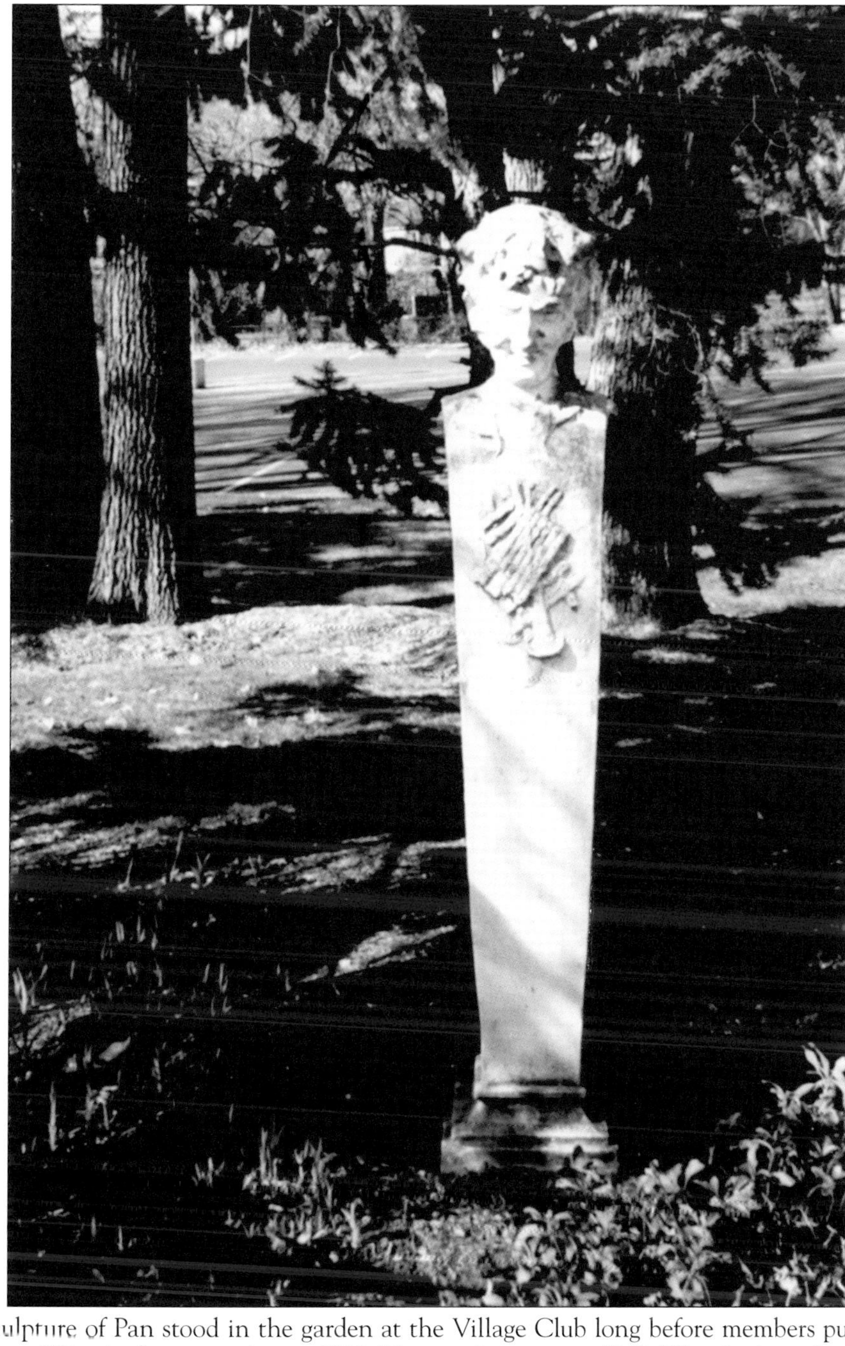

This sculpture of Pan stood in the garden at the Village Club long before members purchased the former Winningham mansion in 1961. The previous owner, C.C. Winningham, bought the property in 1919 and remodeled the former barn extensively during the 1920s. His daughter, Gail Winningham, used to play beneath the sculpture and remembers it with fondness. Gail had other play areas as well. For example, she used to hide in a small concealed space off of the entrance hall of the house and then jump out to surprise guests as they arrived for parties. (Courtesy of the Village Club.)

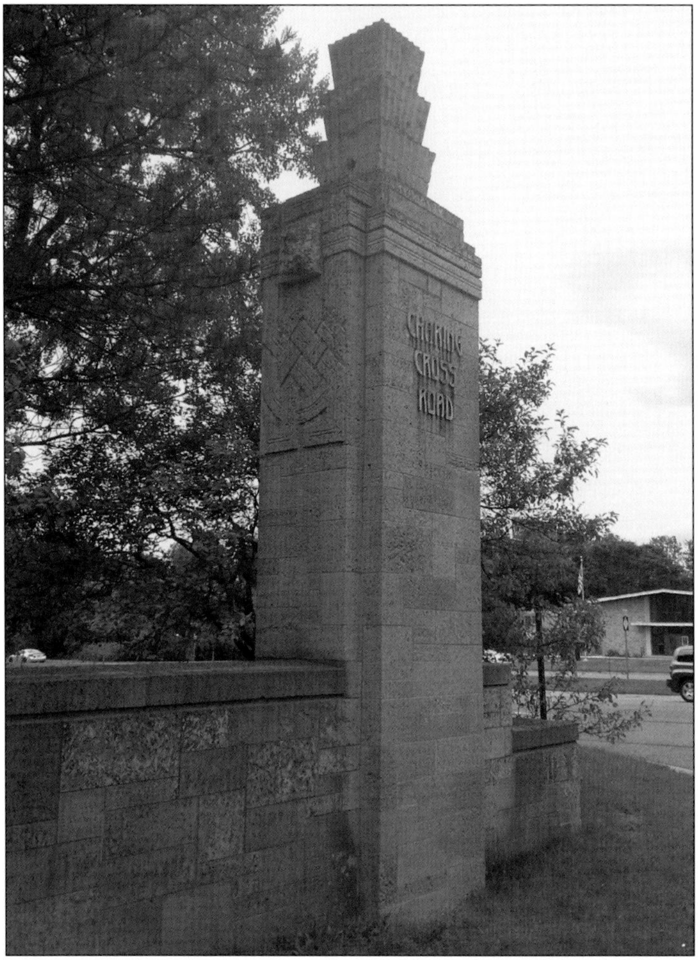

The entrance columns at Charing Cross Road and Woodward Avenue bear a striking resemblance to the many pillars and posts that Eliel Saarinen designed for Kingswood School Cranbrook. They have the same golden stone capped with a descending stack of flutes. However, these columns were designed between 1925 and 1930 as the entranceway to Bloomfield Estates, a Judson Bradway development. Their exact history remains a mystery, but they were not designed by Saarinen. (Author's collection.)

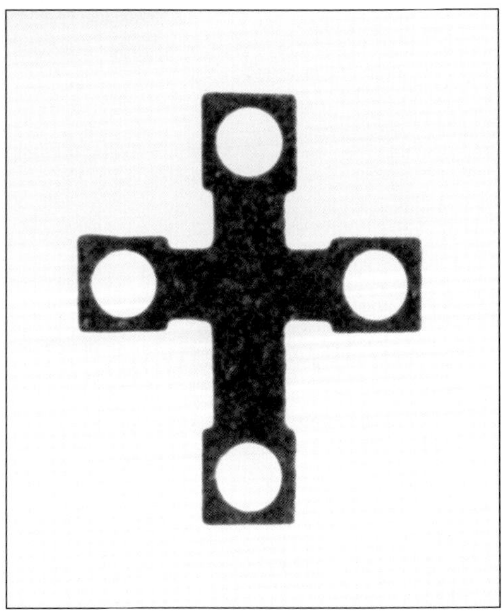

The distinctive cross that now serves as the logo for St. Hugo of the Hills was inspired by an event that occurred during the building of the original chapel. Mrs. Theodore (Alice) MacManus pointed out to the builder that she disliked the four stand-alone circular air vents on the chapel's exterior. The builder's solution was to connect the four circles to make a cross. (Courtesy of St. Hugo of the Hills.)

Eight figures strain to hear the music of Orpheus, the famous Greek singer and son of the muse Calliope and god Apollo in Greek mythology. The one figure who strains most, with his arms reaching toward the sky, is Beethoven, the only figure that sculptor Carl Milles identified as a real person when he completed this bronze sculpture fountain in 1936. This photograph was taken in 1948. (Courtesy of Cranbrook Archives.)

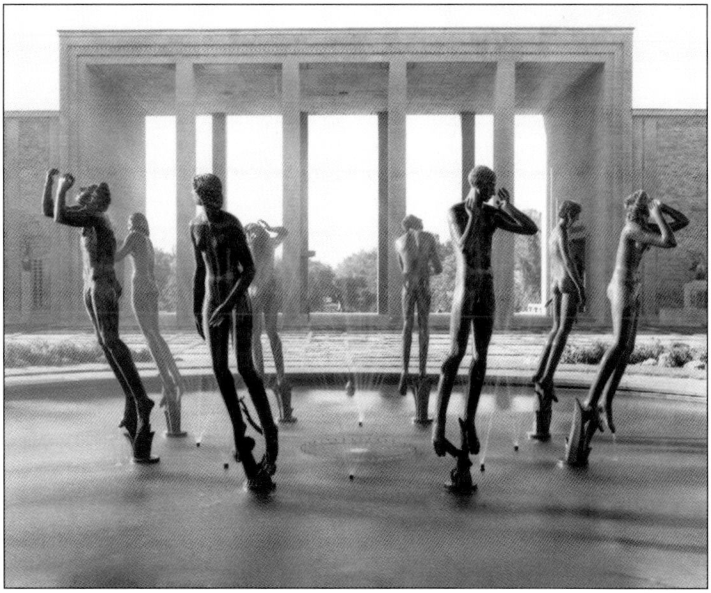

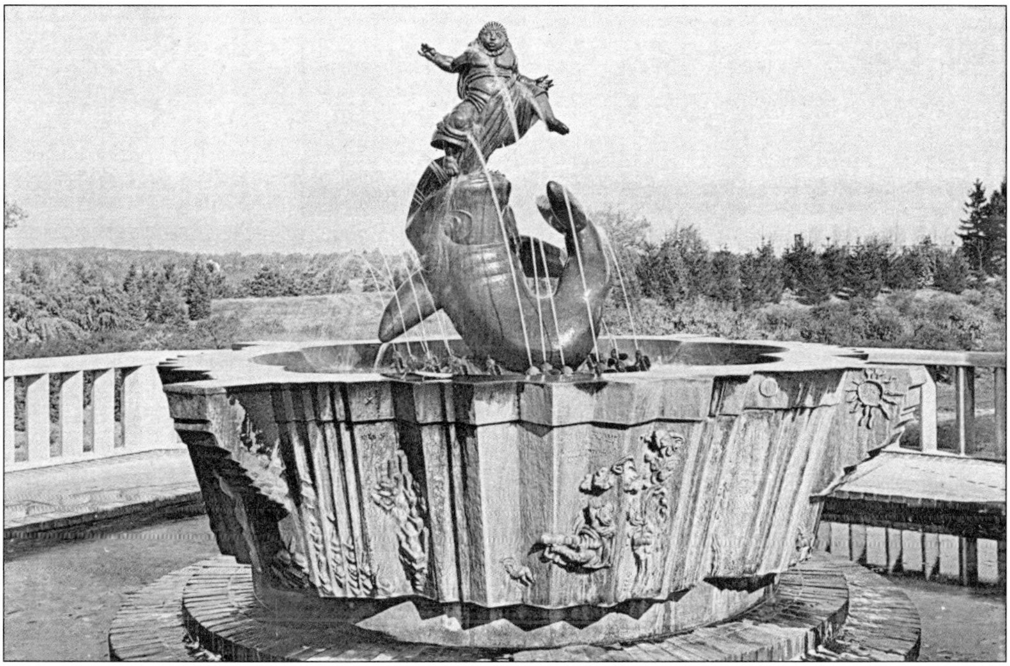

This postcard shows *Jonah and the Whale*, the first sculpture that Carl Milles made for Cranbrook in 1932. Scenes on the fountain's base illustrate the prophet preaching and sleeping before being disgorged. The bronze fountain was originally intended for Kingswood School. However, Milles's desire for an abundance of water required an overflow basin, so the fountain was placed overlooking Lake Jonah. (Courtesy of Postcard Collection, Bentley Historical Library, University of Michigan.)

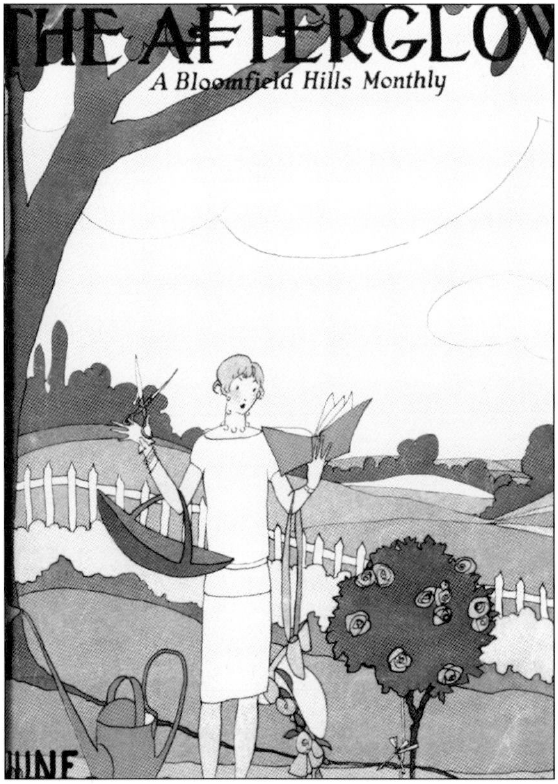

The *Afterglow* was a monthly magazine published between 1925 and 1927 that focused primarily on life in Bloomfield Hills. Each issue was 25¢ and contained photographs, advertisements, and articles on topics including Bloomfield's country homes and estates, local businesses, country club activities, and society news. Both the Birmingham Public Library and the Burton Historical Collection at the Detroit Public Library have issues. (Courtesy of Friends of Preservation Bloomfield.)

Cranbrook has the largest collection of Carl Milles's sculpture in the world outside of his home, Millesgården, in Lidingö, Sweden, now a national museum. In this photograph are Milles's bronze *Running Dogs* in the Quandrangle outside of the dining hall of Cranbrook School. Milles considered these dogs to be the hounds of Diana, goddess of the hunt. (Courtesy of Postcard Collection, Bentley Historical Library, University of Michigan.)

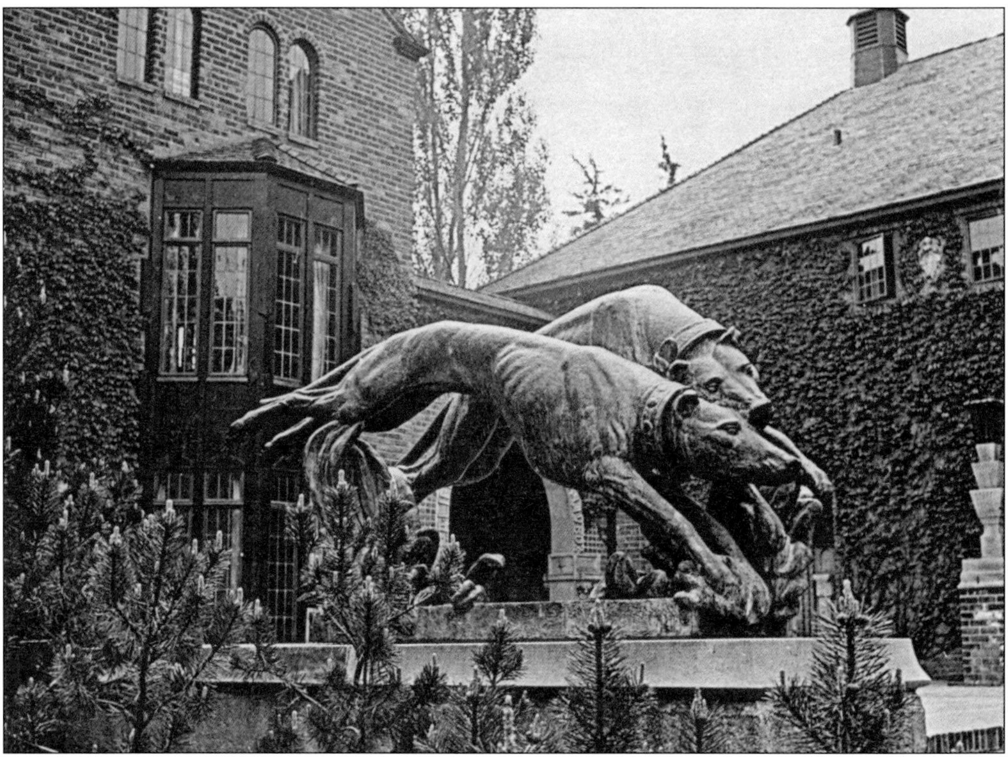

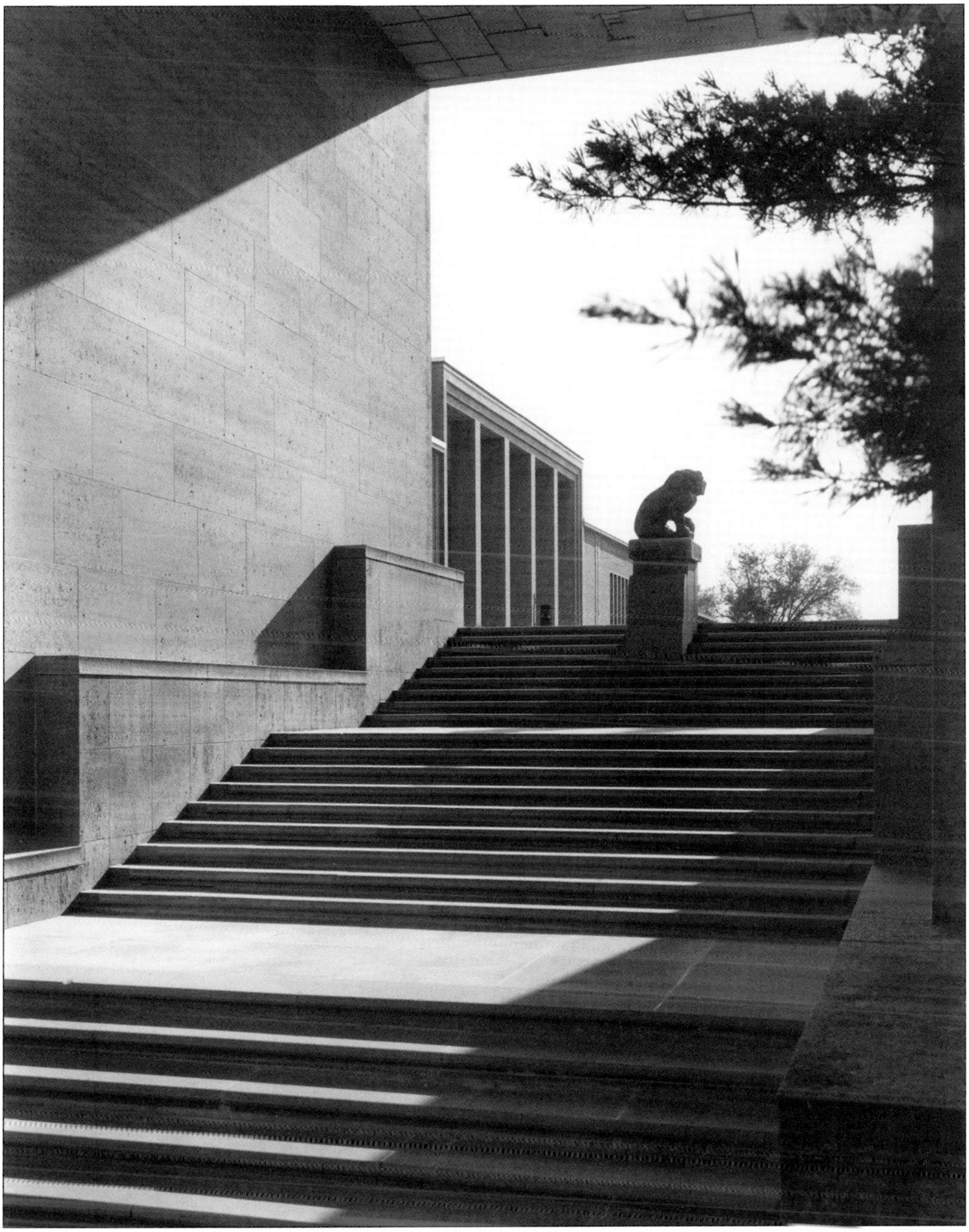

The stepped hill that leads down from the art museum to Cranbrook House is called the "Ramp of the Chinese Dog." The sixth-century sculpture is the *Chinese Dog* (actually a lion), which came from a temple in Chien Ting Fu Prefecture in Hebei. This photograph of the sculpture and ramp was taken in 1985. (Courtesy of Cranbrook Archives.)

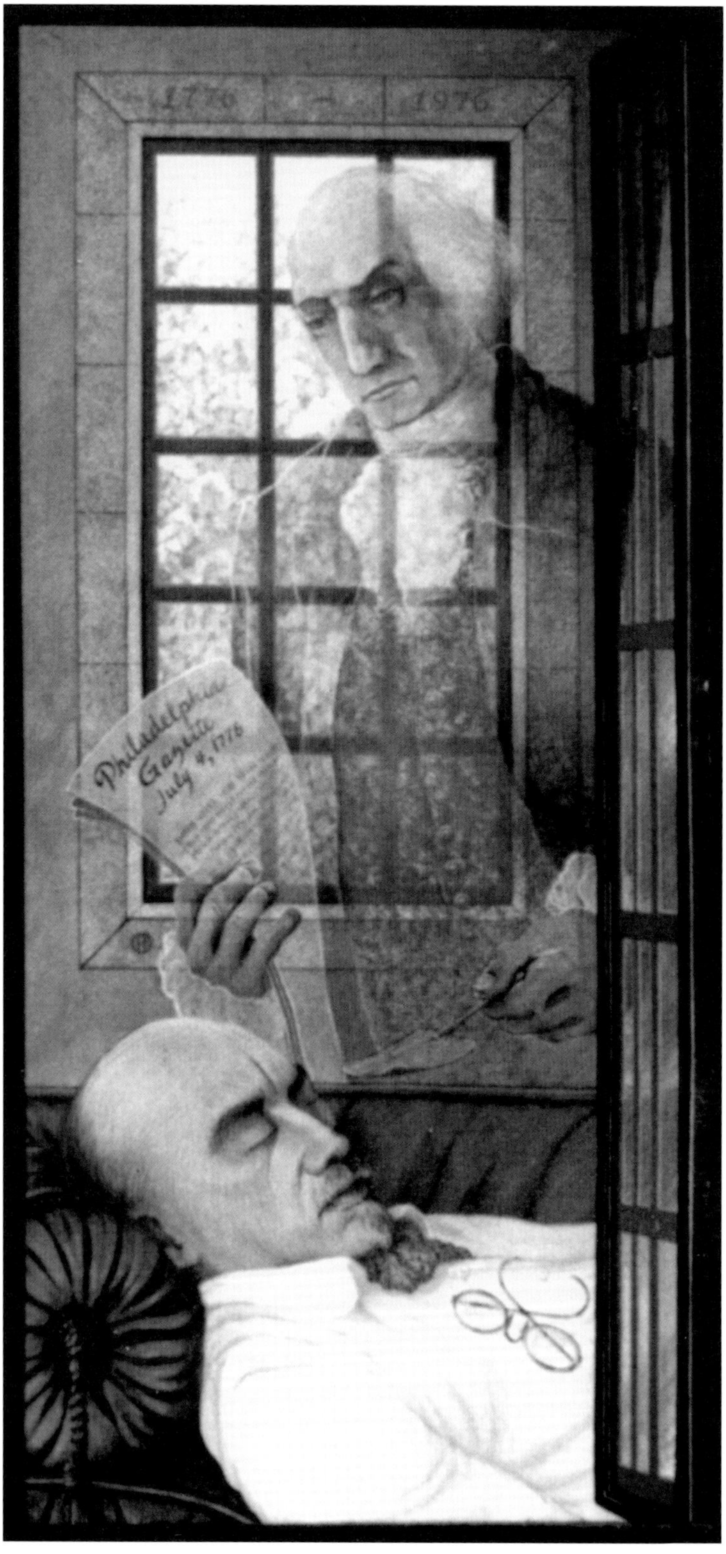

To commemorate the 200th anniversary of the United States, Henry S. Booth, son of George Booth, had a student from the Cranbrook Academy of Art paint this panel for a window in the Still Room of Cranbrook House. The painting shows George Washington using a feather to remove a fly from George Booth's nose. Intended to be humorous, the illustration nonetheless shows a serious Washington reminding Booth of his greater responsibility to the community. A still room was traditionally a place for making brew in England, but at Cranbrook House, the word *still* meant "quiet," and it was where George Booth rested. The couch and window are actual objects on the other side of the panel, and the ceiling within is richly decorated with illustrations by James S. Booth, artist and son of George Booth. (Author's collection.)

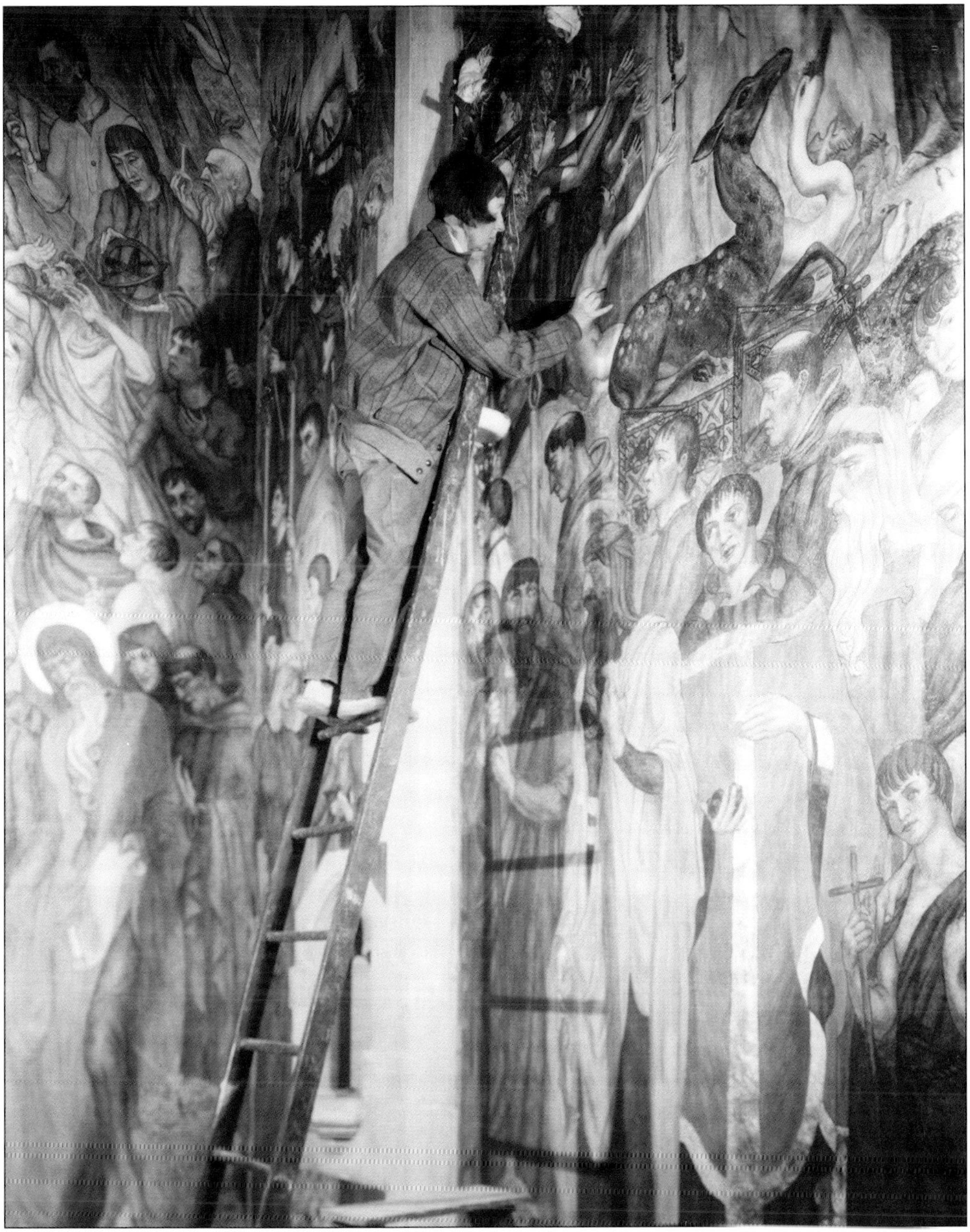

Katherine McEwen worked on the fresco surrounding the high altar of Christ Church Cranbrook from 1925 to 1928. According to an article about her in the September 1927 issue of the *Afterglow*, she was awarded the contract for painting the fresco in a sealed competition. However, her reputation was already well known because in years prior she had painted a decorative scene over the fireplace in the Cranbrook Meeting House. According to Henry Scripps Booth in the *Pilgrim's Guide to Christ Church Cranbrook*, the subject of the fresco is the aggressive Church on the left and the realm of ideas rather than action on the right. The design ascends from the earthly Church at the base to the celestial choirs above. (Courtesy of Walter P. Reuther Library, Archives of Labor and Urban Affairs, Wayne State University.)

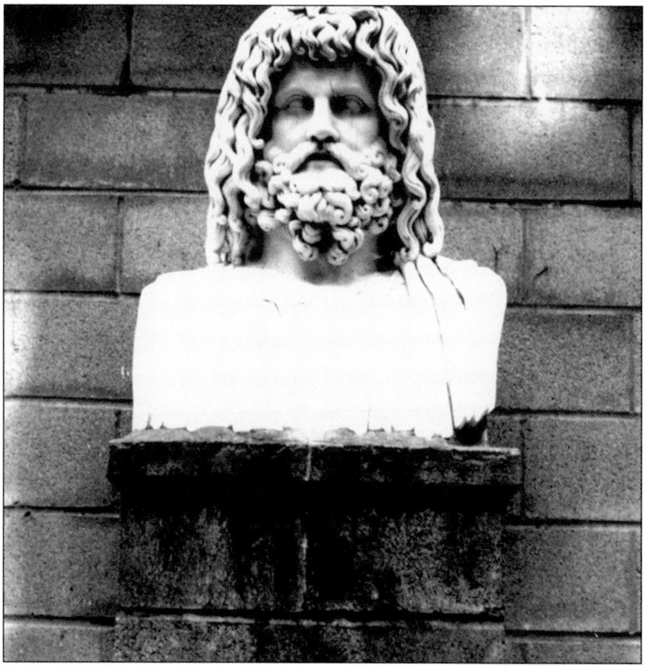

In 1961, Henry S. and Carolyn Farr Booth purchased this early 19th-century Carrara marble statue of Zeus in England and donated it to Cranbrook. Prior to this time, the sculpture had decorated Mansion House in Scotland for more than 100 years. Visitors to Cranbrook can make Zeus weep by stepping lightly on one of the panels to the right of the pedestal, hence its name *Weeping Zeus*. (Author's collection.)

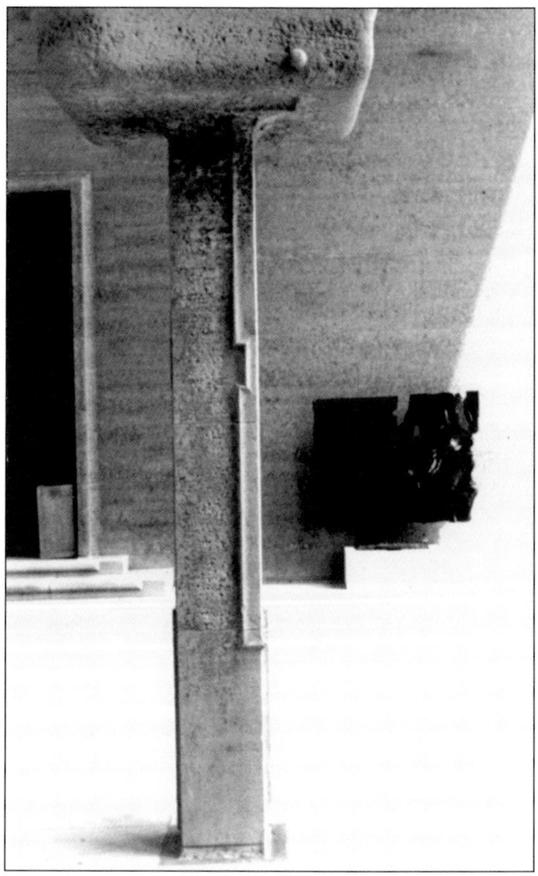

In 1962, Cranbrook Academy of Art metals instructor Harry Bertoia created this cast bronze piece titled *Ossabaw Echoes*, which was inspired by the natural environment of Ossabaw Island off the coast of Georgia. Mrs. Robert Daisley donated it to the academy in memory of her late husband. (Author's collection.)

Sven Hedin was a noted explorer in Asia and a longtime friend of sculptor Carl Milles. This three-foot-high sculpture outside the Cranbrook Institute of Science was created in 1932 and shows Hedin astride a "ship of the desert" using a navigator's sextant. Milles said that he had to study how to make a camel without copying the Chinese, whose sculpture he admired. (Author's collection.)

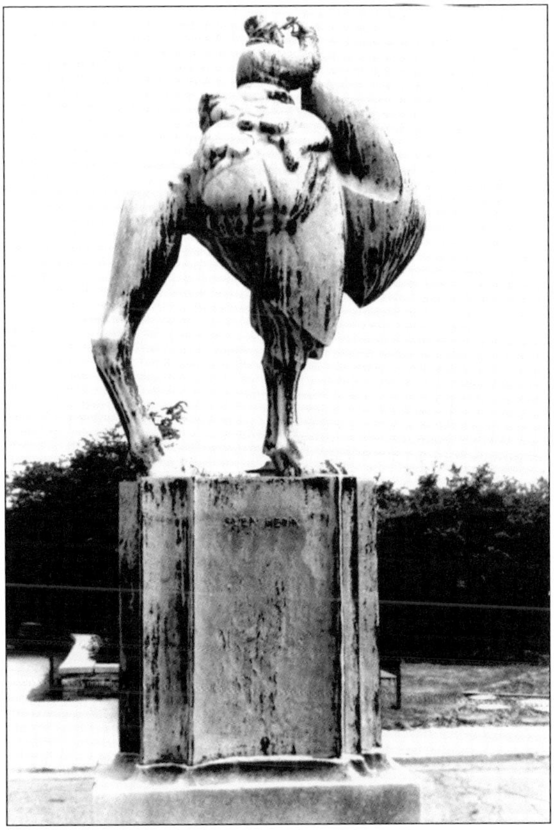

The bas-relief *Founder's Award* on the exterior of the Cranbrook Institute of Science was created by Marshall Fredericks in honor of the Booths. The design was later adapted for the Founder's Medal, which is awarded from time to time for distinguished service to Cranbrook. The bronze pair of running boars was designed by Carl Milles. The boars are reminiscent of the larger ones that flank Nichols Gate on Lone Pine Road. (Author's collection.)

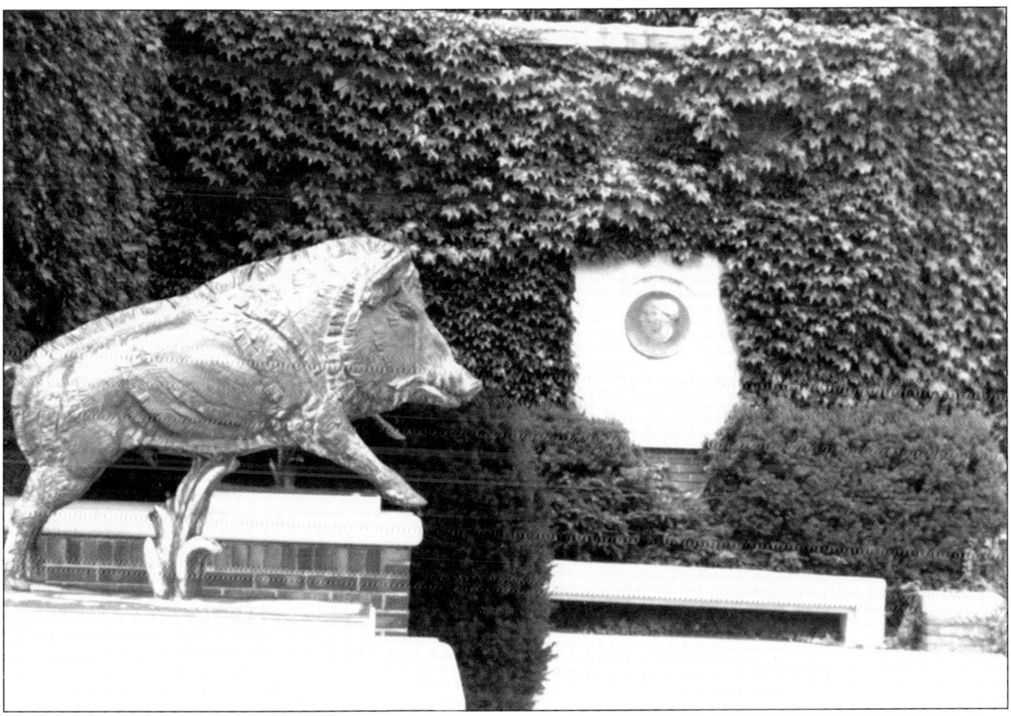

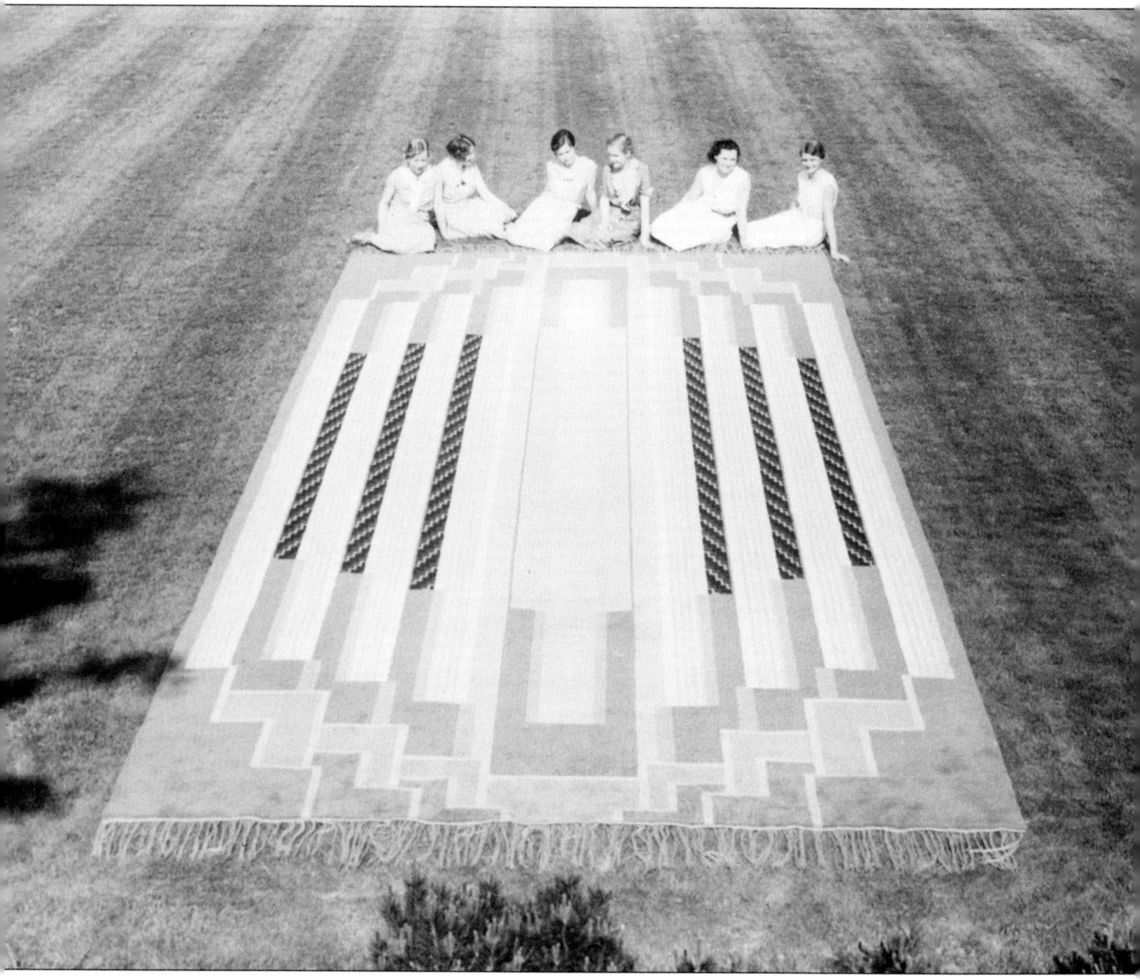

In 1931, Swedish weavers who worked for Studio Loja Saarinen have gathered on the lawn with a rug designed by Loja for Reception Hall I at Kingswood School. From left to right are an unidentified woman, Lillian Holm, three unidentified women, and Ruth Ingvarsson. Studio Loja Saarinen was founded in 1928 as a commercial weaving studio and produced a variety of textile products in addition to rugs for the Cranbrook campus and other clients. Additional products included curtains, tablecloths, and tapestries. During the 1920s and 1930s, the studio employed a staff made up mostly of Swedish women who had immigrated to the United States. Today, Kingswood has the largest school weaving studio in North America, with 60 looms. (Courtesy of Cranbrook Archives.)

Five

SCHOOLS

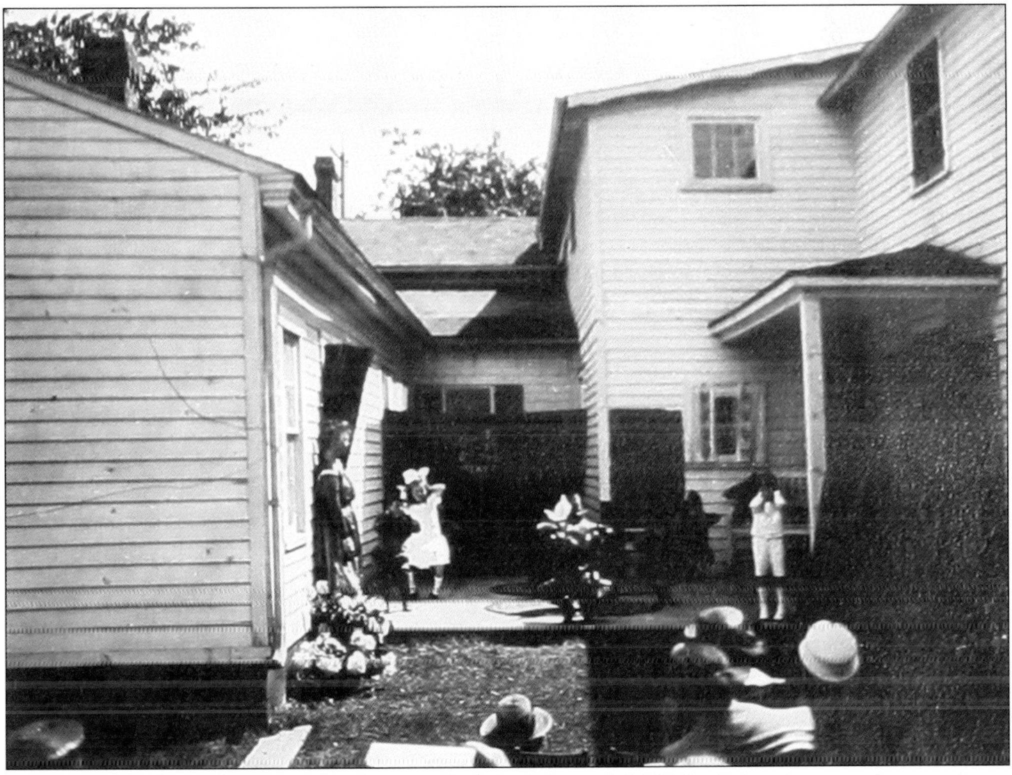

The Bloomfield Hills Seminary, later called the Bloomfield Hills School, opened as a private elementary school in 1912 in the former home of Ezra Parke at the corner of Lone Pine Road and Woodward Avenue. This photograph shows children acting in a play there. When World War I began, enrollment dropped, and the school closed in November 1918. (Courtesy of Cranbrook Archives.)

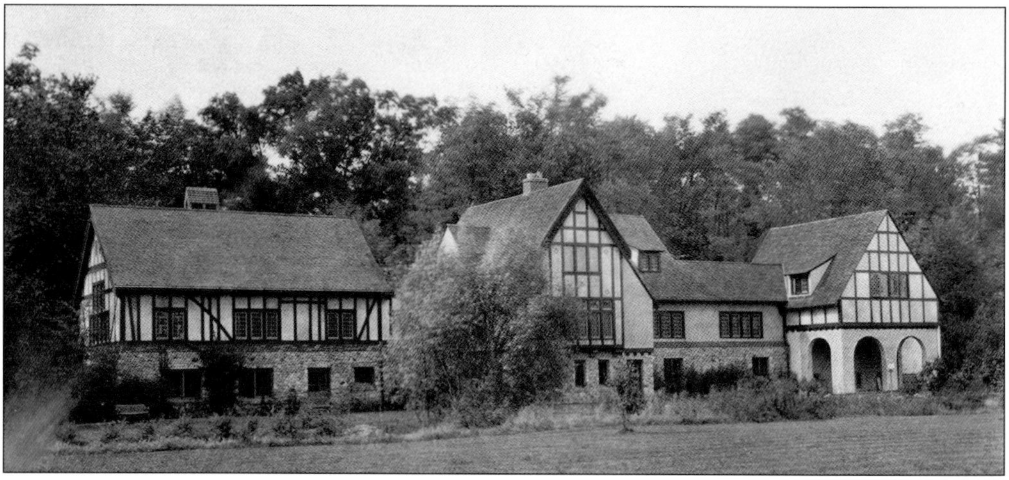

In 1922, local families met to organize another private Bloomfield Hills School for children. The Booths leased them the meetinghouse for this purpose for $1 a year. In 1925, the Booths created the Children's School Trust, providing income for the school. By 1930, the school's name was changed to Brookside School Cranbrook to avoid confusion with Bloomfield Hills public schools. (Courtesy of the Burton Historical Collection, Detroit Public Library.)

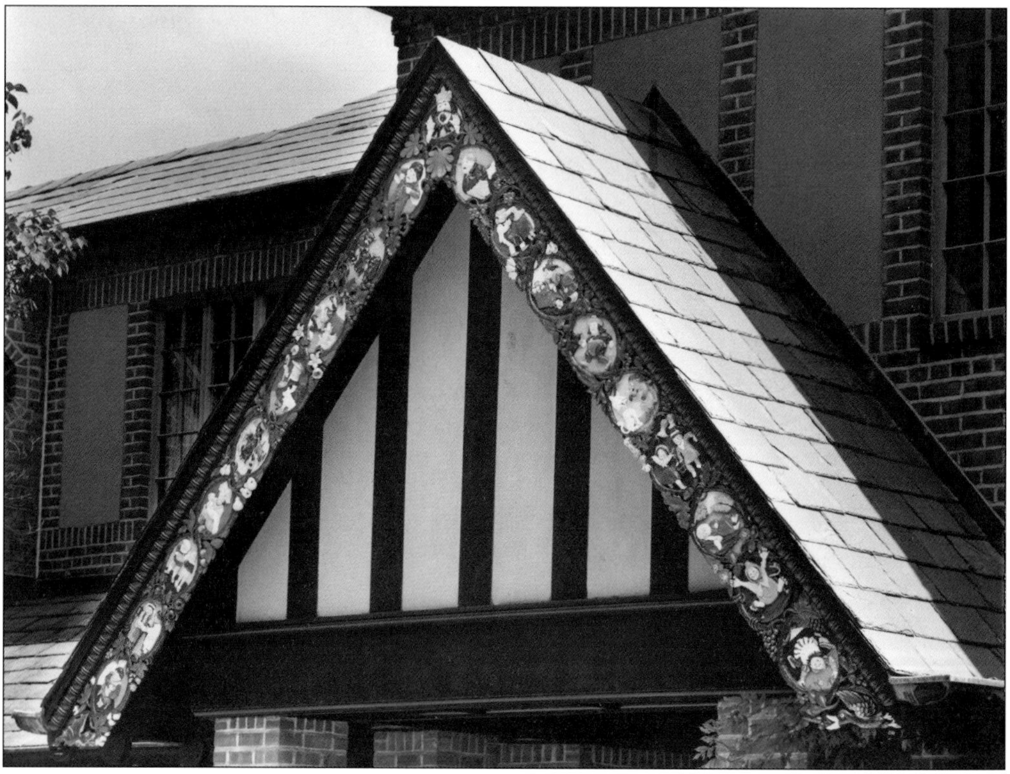

In 1923, Cranbrook founder George Booth made a sketch of Mother Goose nursery rhymes to decorate Brookside School. He then commissioned Detroit woodcarver Joachim Jungwirth to execute the designs that decorate one of the school's entrances and the oriel that faces Cranbrook Road. The carvings and the quaint cottage design of the buildings give the school a fairy-tale atmosphere suitable to childhood. (Courtesy of Cranbrook Archives.)

Children are shown leaving Brookside School Cranbrook on their first day of school in September 1945. More than a decade earlier, the school had reorganized on the country day plan, which emphasized an activity program, supervised play, and longer hours. The goals were to educate the whole child socially, scholastically, and physically. (Courtesy of Cranbrook Archives.)

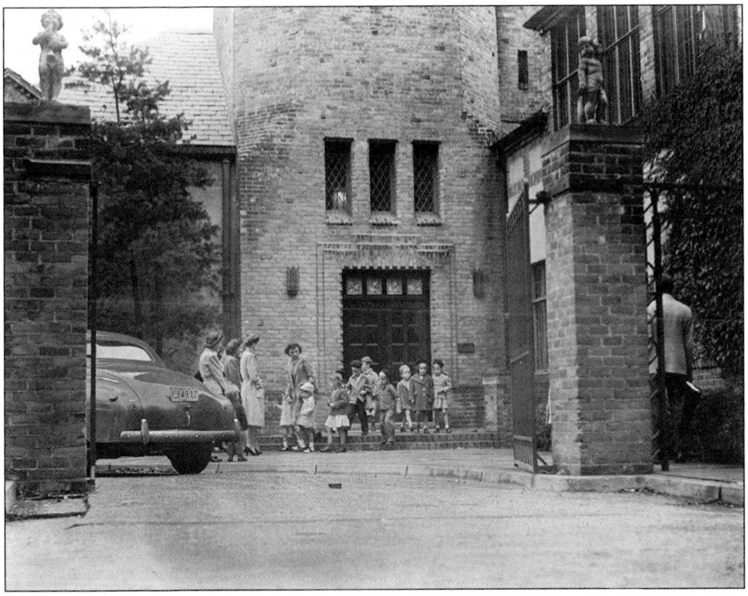

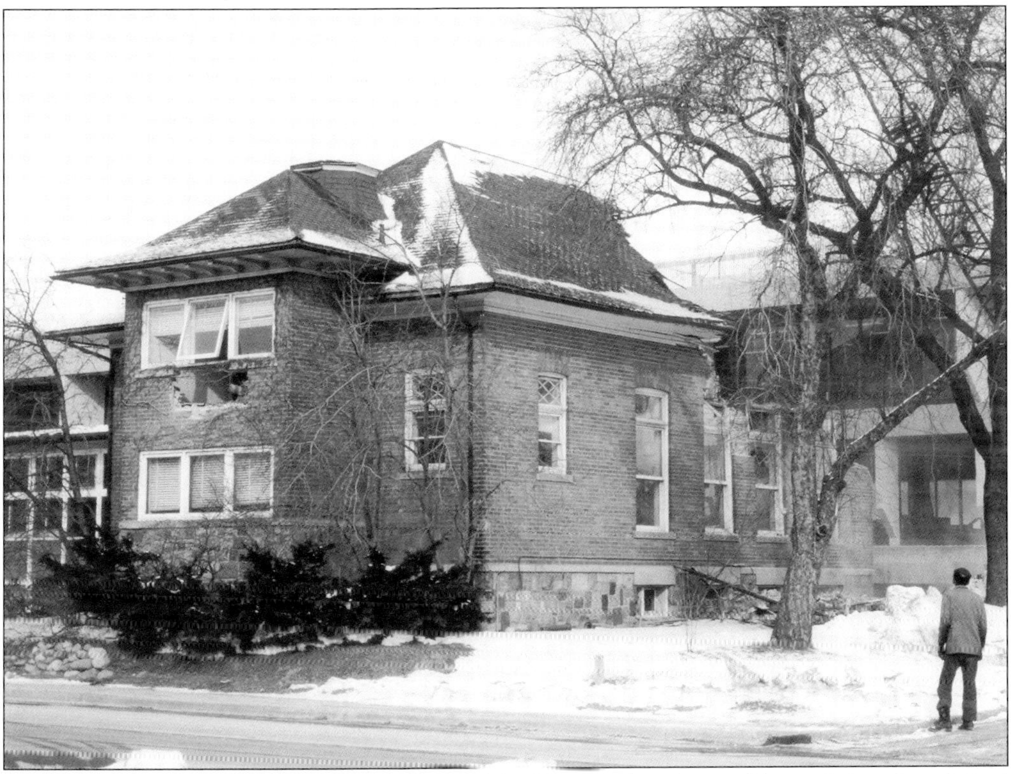

This photograph shows the old Circle School building and its later addition being demolished on Long Lake Road northwest of Woodward Avenue. The taller portion of the old school (right) was constructed in 1900 and was once a one-room frame school. The later addition to it was used for offices. The building was the office of Saarinen, Swanson & Saarinen. Then, when the firm split in 1947, it became Saarinen and Saarinen and, later, Swanson and Associates. (Courtesy of Paul DePorre.)

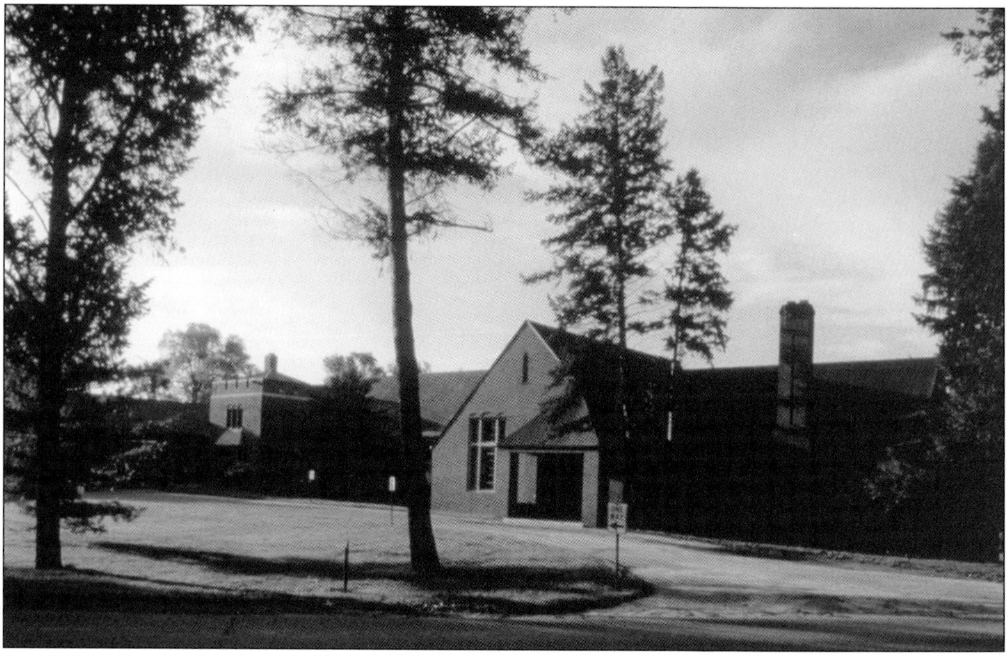

In 1925, Perry A. Vaughan sold his land to George Booth, who in turn donated the land to the school district. A school building designed by J. Robert F. Swanson was built on the land in 1932 and was called Bloomfield Hills School until 1955, when it was renamed Vaughan School in honor of Perry Vaughan. Today, the school is the Cranbrook Boys' Middle School. (Courtesy of Cranbrook Archives.)

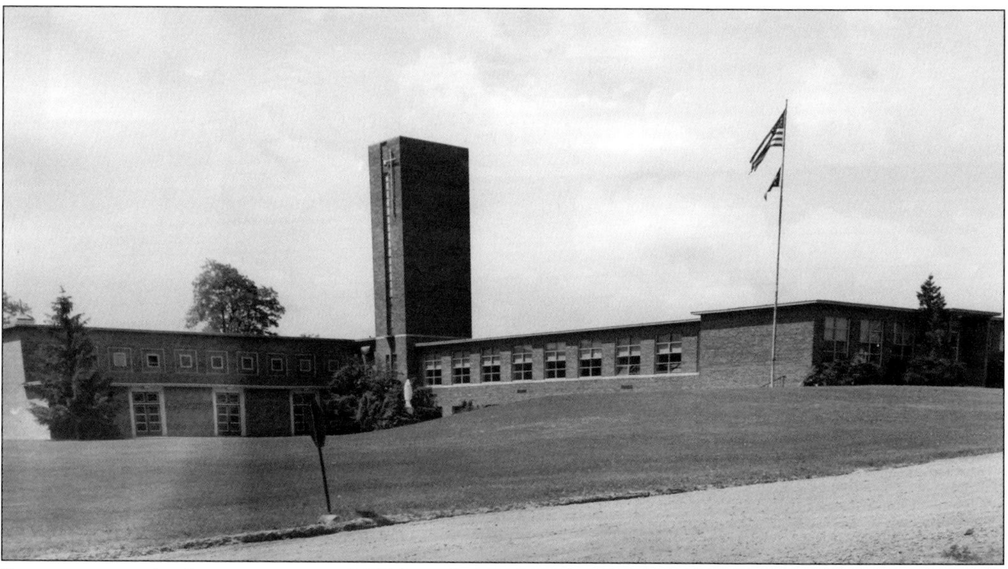

Beginning with the generosity of Walter O. Briggs, the first unit of the St. Hugo of the Hills School was completed in 1940. Fr. Francis T. Stack continued the school's expansion over the years. By 1968, additions to the school included a library and more classrooms, including those for art and science. The school was originally staffed by the Sisters, Servants of the Immaculate Heart of Mary. (Courtesy of St. Hugo of the Hills.)

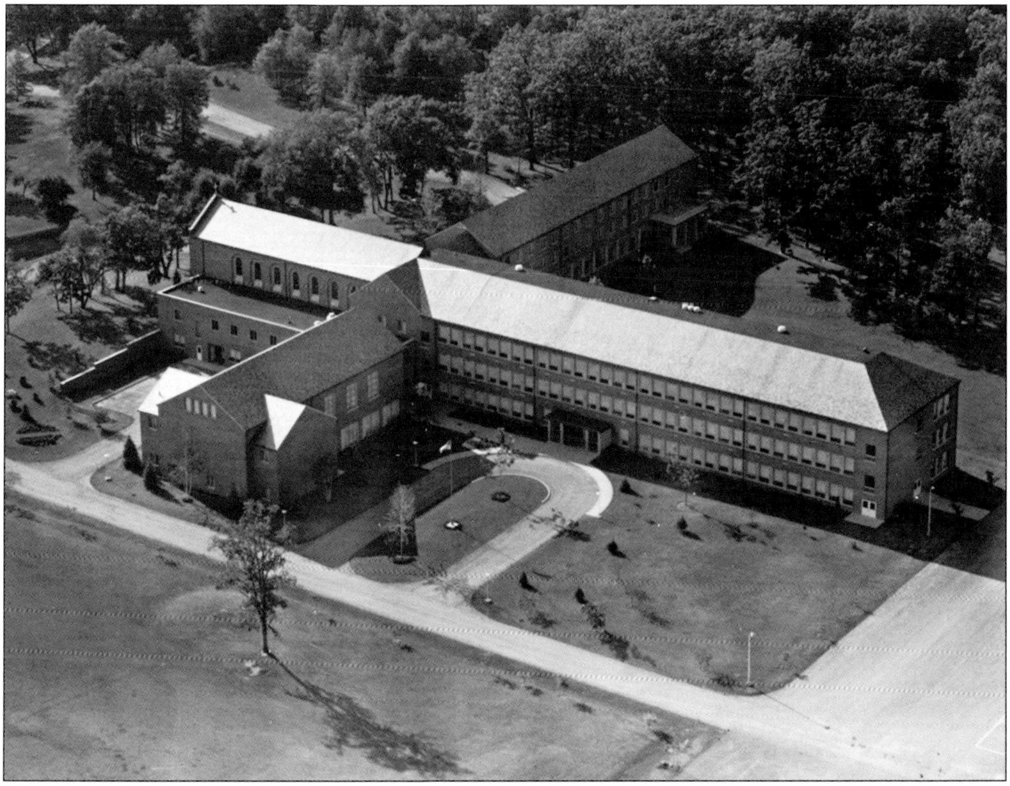

The Academy of the Sacred Heart moved from its Detroit location into its new building on Kensington Road in 1958. The academy, established in 1851, is Michigan's oldest independent school. Additional land for this Catholic college-preparatory school was purchased in 1964 from the Walter O. Briggs estate. The school is partially in Bloomfield Hills and partially in Bloomfield Township. (Courtesy of the Academy of the Sacred Heart.)

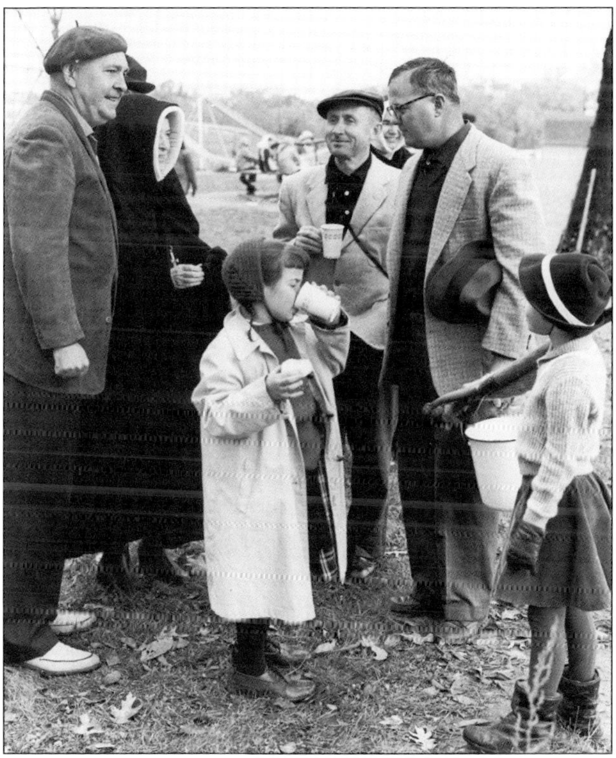

Children and adults gather in 1959 for tree planting on the new campus of the Academy of the Sacred Heart. Today, the former farmland on which the school is built is well wooded. (Courtesy of the Academy of the Sacred Heart.)

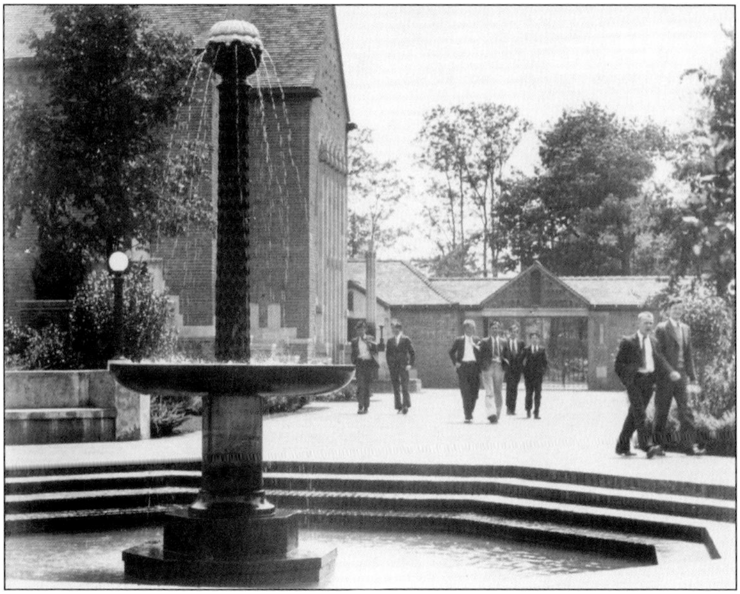

This 1934 view shows students walking in the Quadrangle of Cranbrook School for Boys. The "Quad," as it is also called, is in the heart of the campus and connects most of the main buildings, including the dining hall. The interior of the dining hall is cathedral-like and reminiscent of a hall typically found in British boarding schools. The campus was designed by Eliel Saarinen. (Courtesy of Cranbrook Archives.)

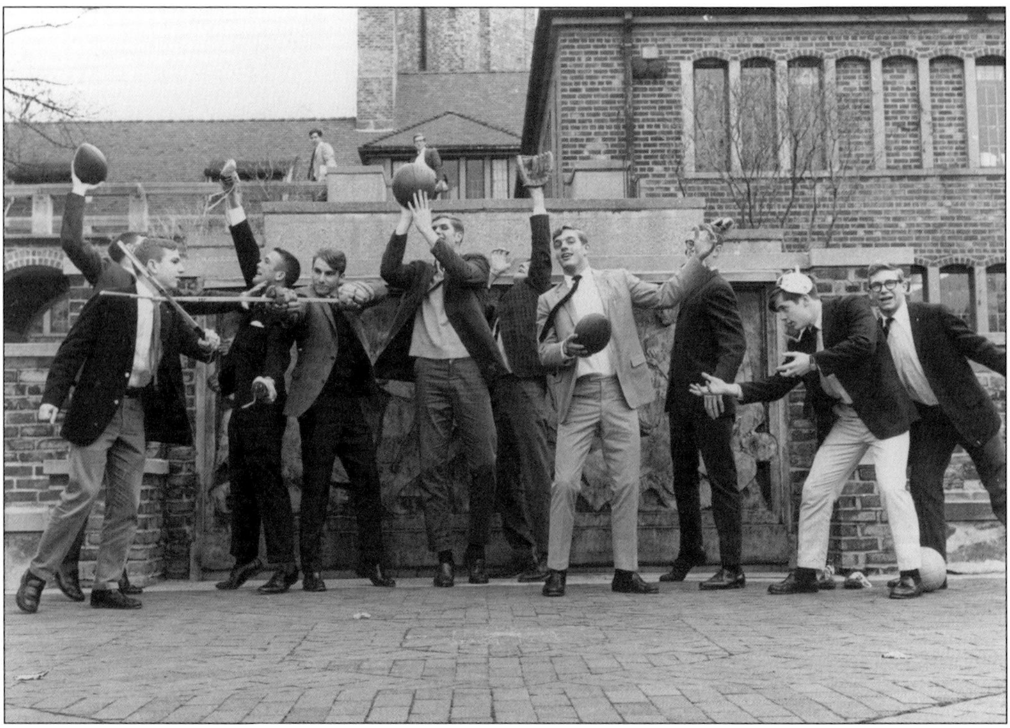

It's one for all and all for one in this November 1964 photograph showing the captains of the various Cranbrook School sports teams. The students at Cranbrook still regularly wore suits during this time, especially when they traveled by bus to away games. The turbulent 1960s would force change, however, and by 1968, this dress code was abandoned. (Courtesy of Cranbrook Archives.)

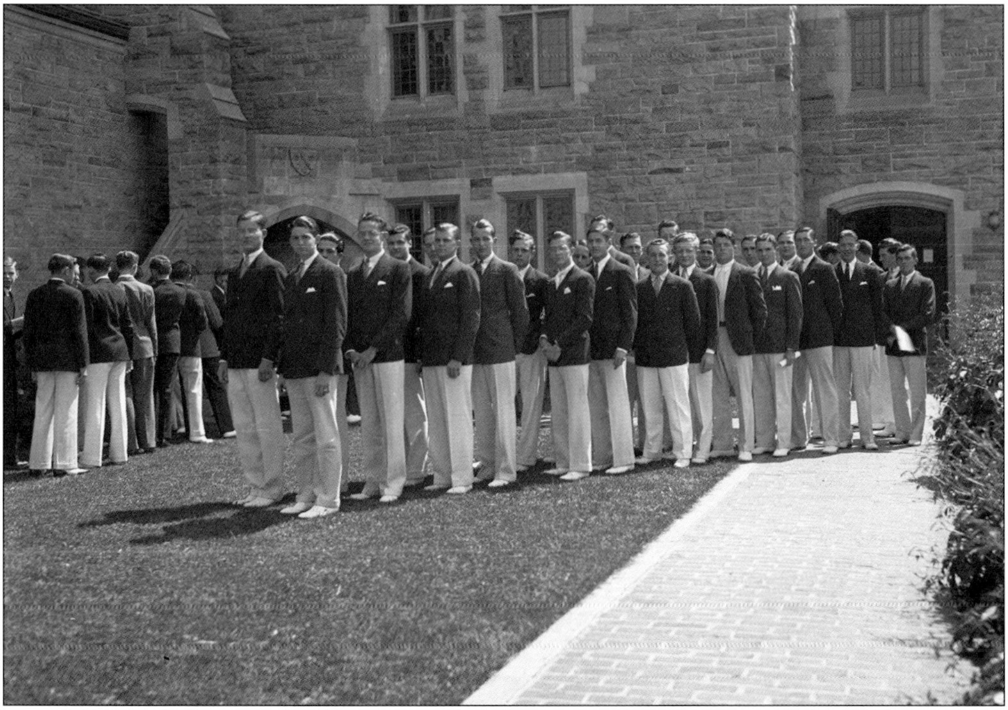

This dapper-looking group of gentlemen is the Cranbrook School graduating class of 1935. They are lined up outside of Christ Church Cranbrook, where their graduation ceremony is about to take place. The school, led at the time by Dr. William Stevens, set high goals for excellence in scholarship as well as conduct. (Courtesy of Cranbrook Archives.)

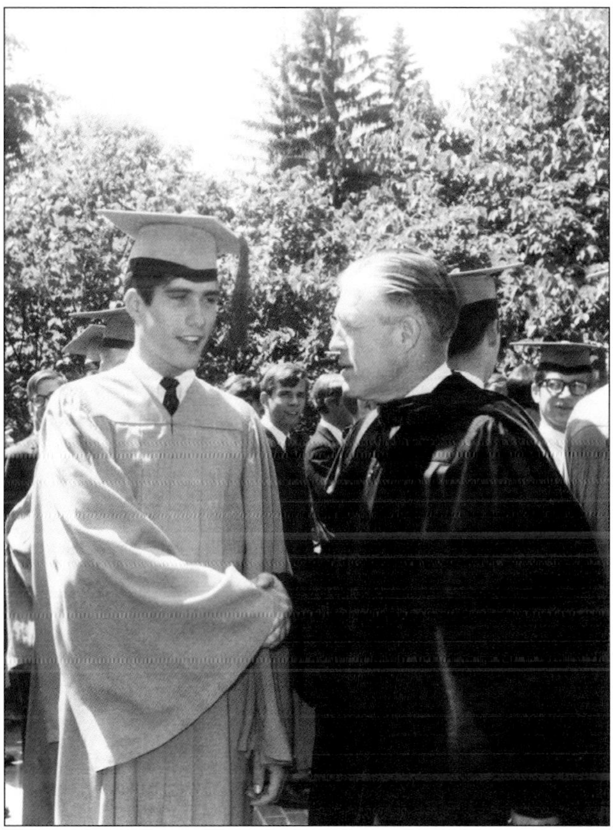

Cranbrook Schools have produced many illustrious graduates, and here is one of them. In this June 1965 photograph taken on Commencement Day for graduates of the Cranbrook School for Boys, Mitt Romney shakes hands with his father, George Romney, who at the time was governor of Michigan. Mitt later became governor of Massachusetts and also made two bids for the US presidency. (Courtesy of Cranbrook Archives.)

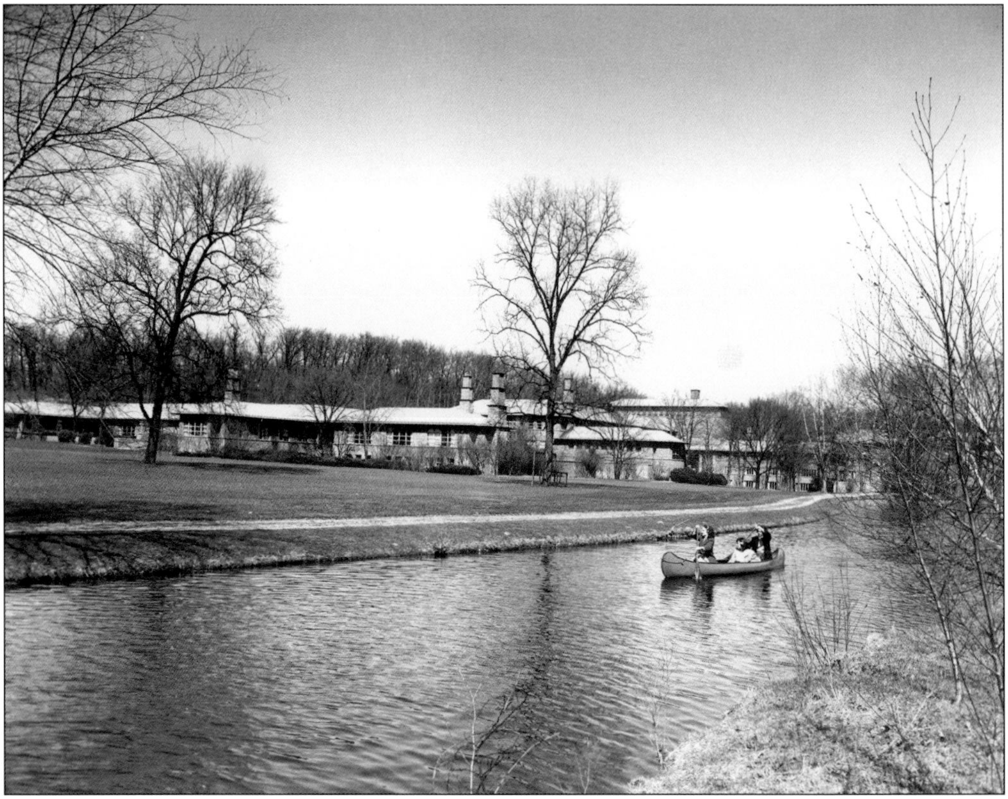

The view of Kingswood School for Girls from Kingswood Lake in 1947 may seem like an ideal one, but the building of the girls' school initially met with some resistance from George Booth. However, Ellen Scripps Booth, his wife, continued to push for its construction. Her initial gift of $200,000 in 1928 helped to jump-start the project. (Courtesy of Cranbrook Archives.)

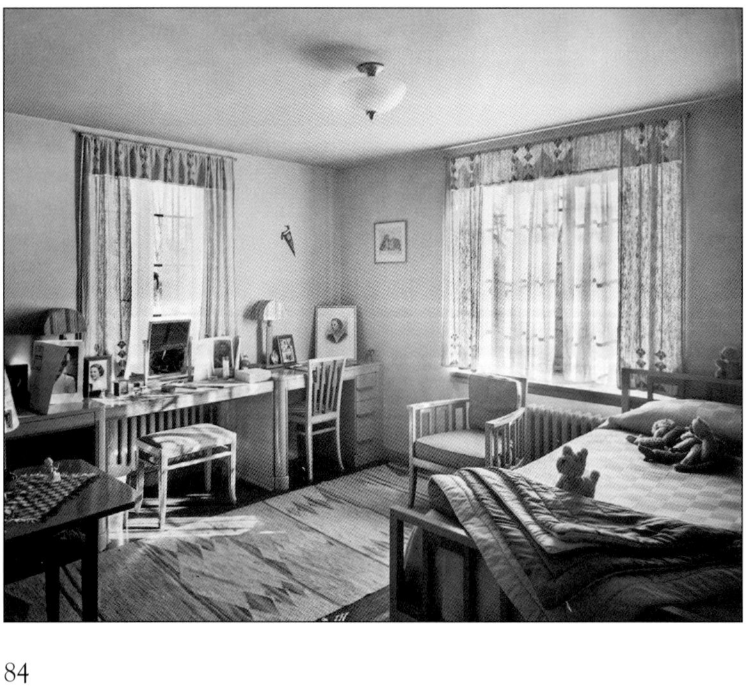

This 1937 photograph shows a typical girl's room at Kingswood School Cranbrook. The furniture, which was designed by Eero Saarinen, is still used in the rooms today. The main difference between then and now is not the overall change in decorating style but the single-room double bed. Most rooms this size now have bunk beds. (Courtesy of Cranbrook Archives.)

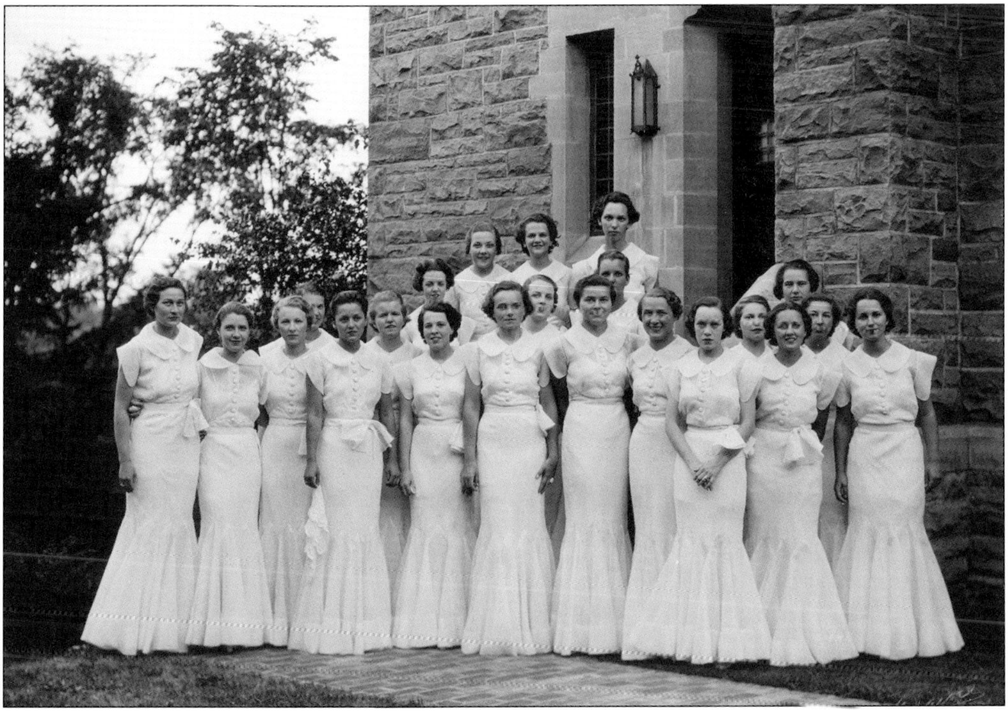

The Kingswood class of 1934 poses for a photograph in front of Christ Church Cranbrook, where all graduation ceremonies took place. The new graduates are wearing the customary white dresses. Fourth from the left in the front row is Florence Schust (Knoll). By 1940, the dress custom had changed, and graduating seniors also wore white caps and gowns. (Courtesy of Cranbrook Archives.)

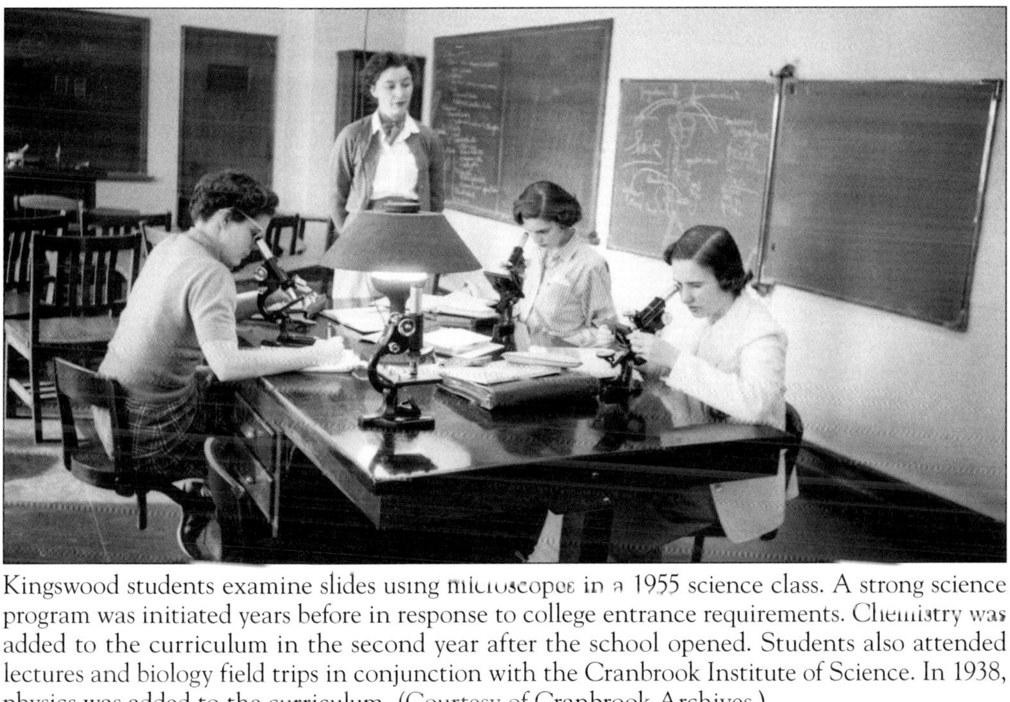

Kingswood students examine slides using microscopes in a 1955 science class. A strong science program was initiated years before in response to college entrance requirements. Chemistry was added to the curriculum in the second year after the school opened. Students also attended lectures and biology field trips in conjunction with the Cranbrook Institute of Science. In 1938, physics was added to the curriculum. (Courtesy of Cranbrook Archives.)

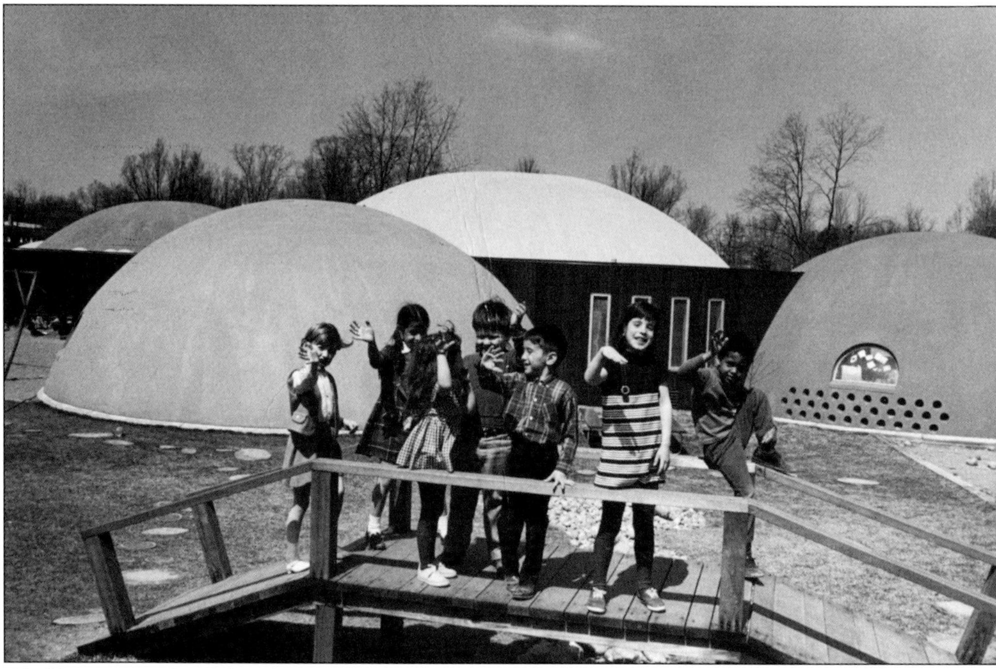

Children attending the Roeper School play in front of the dome-shaped buildings that were erected on the campus in 1969. Smaller domes contained classrooms, while larger ones housed a multi-purpose assembly and play area as well as an academic center with the library and science, social studies, art, and music facilities. (Courtesy of the Roeper School Archive, Roeper City and Country School, Inc.)

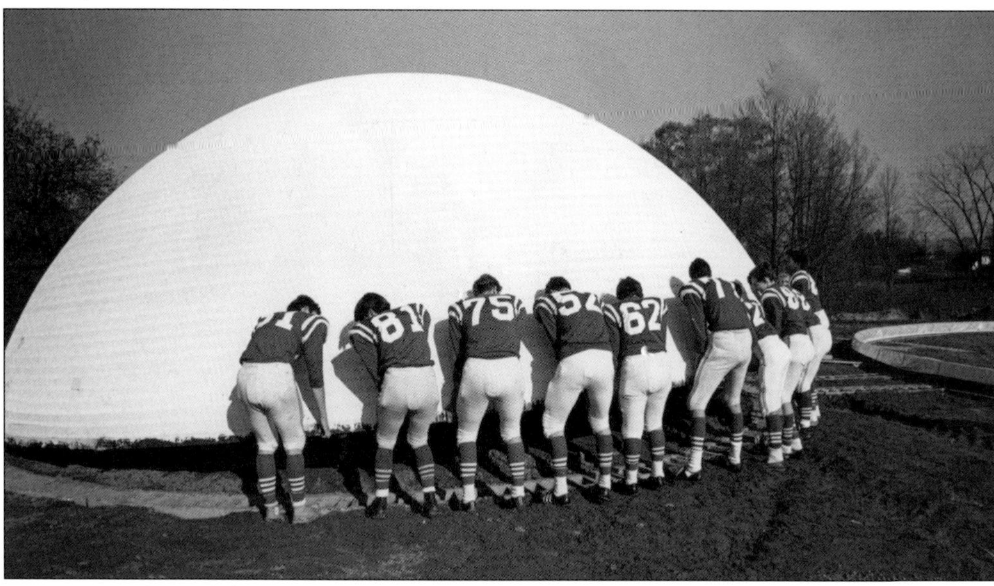

In 1967, members of the junior varsity football team at Roeper lift a "Spiral Generation" dome to show how light it was before it was anchored to its foundation. The Lower School Complex of domes was designed by Glen Paulsen and Associates Architects. The project was a creative experiment of the Dow Chemical Company using Styrofoam as a structural material. (Courtesy of the Roeper School Archive, Roeper City and Country School, Inc.)

Six

Clubs

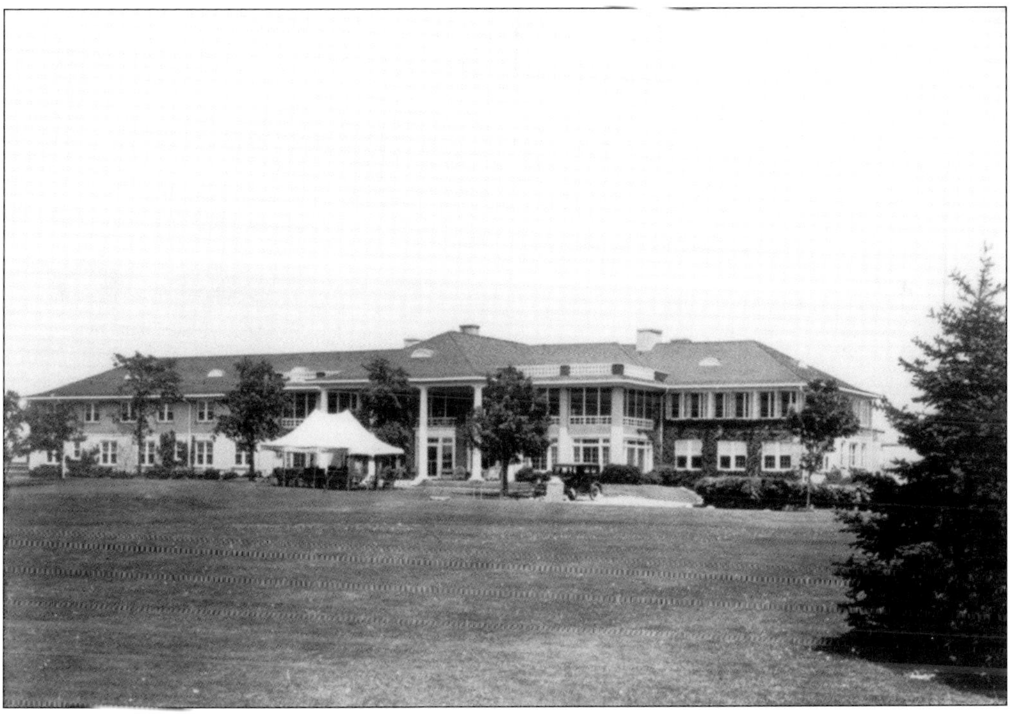

This is the Bloomfield Hills Country Club in 1922. The club was organized in 1909 and its articles of association state: "The purpose of said Club shall be to promote Social Intercourse, Golf and Automobiling." Many prominent automotive industry visionaries were members of the club, including Henry Ford, the Dodge brothers, Frederick Smith (GM), Roy Chapin (Hudson Motor Car Co.), Henry Joy (Packard), and countless others. They had almost as much fun driving the new horseless carriages out to Bloomfield as they did playing a round on their new golf course. (Courtesy of Bloomfield Hills Country Club.)

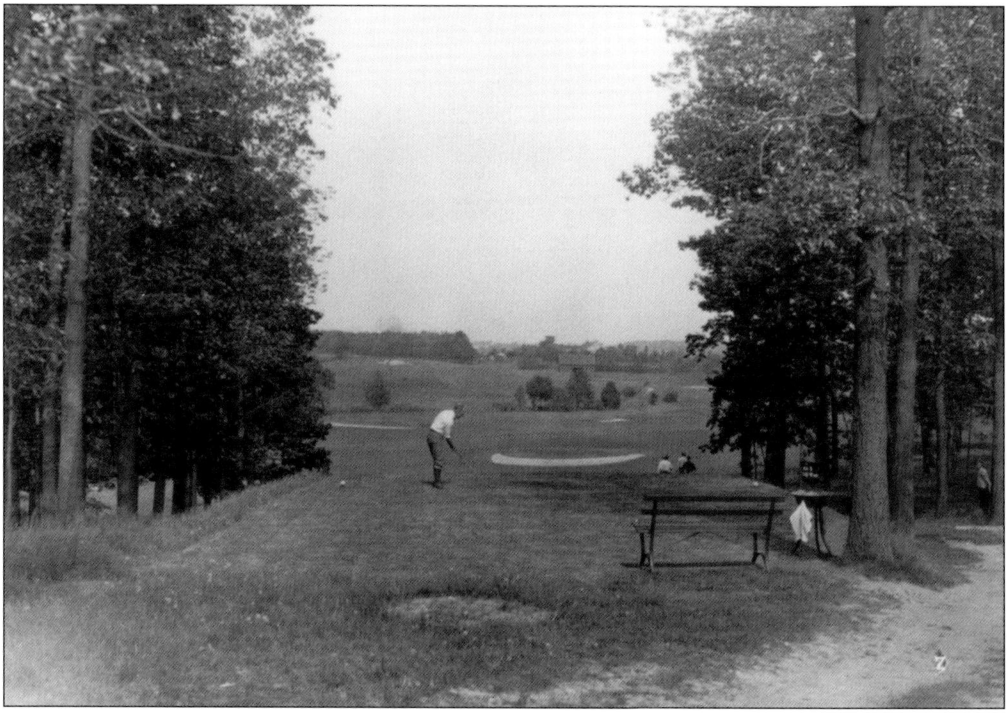

This 1922 photograph taken at the Bloomfield Hills Country Club shows a golfer at Hole Seven, a 287-yard par 4 with the typical Colt cross bunker design in play. In 1909, the original 18-hole golf course was designed by Tom Bendelow and completed in 1912. A year later, renowned English architect H.S. Colt redesigned the golf course, which included 50 additional acres. (Courtesy of Bloomfield Hills Country Club.)

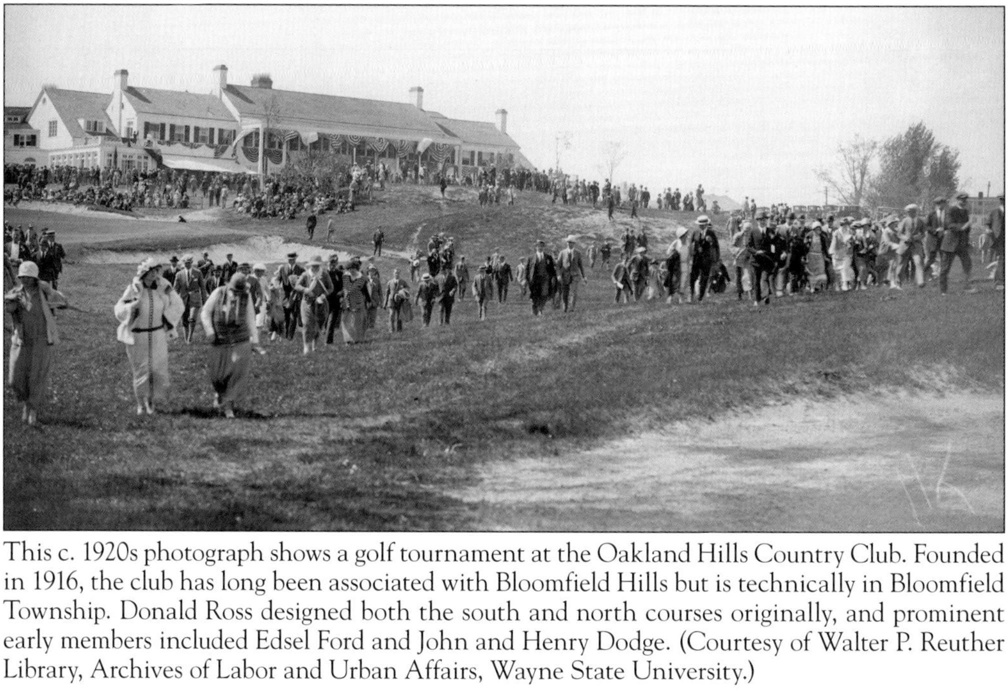

This c. 1920s photograph shows a golf tournament at the Oakland Hills Country Club. Founded in 1916, the club has long been associated with Bloomfield Hills but is technically in Bloomfield Township. Donald Ross designed both the south and north courses originally, and prominent early members included Edsel Ford and John and Henry Dodge. (Courtesy of Walter P. Reuther Library, Archives of Labor and Urban Affairs, Wayne State University.)

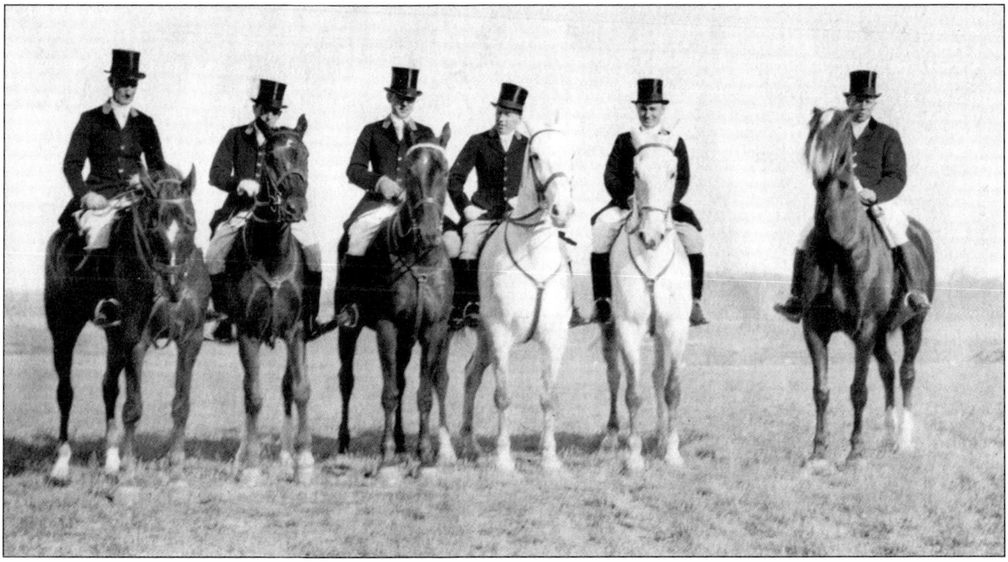

Equestrian sports were popular with many of the residents of Bloomfield Hills during the 1920s. The center of this activity was the Bloomfield Open Hunt Club on Long Lake Road at Kensington Road. These six gentlemen on horses were the patrol judges at a Meander Plate One-Mile Flat Race held there in 1924. (Courtesy of the Burton Historical Collection, Detroit Public Library.)

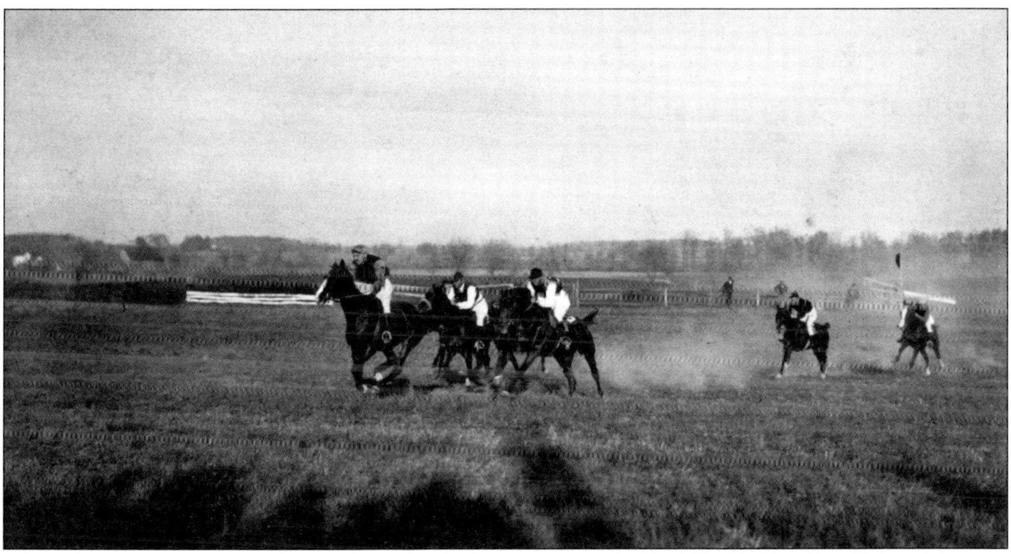

Some racing horses were left in the dust at the November 1, 1924, Meander Plate One-Mile Flat Race. That same day at the Bloomfield Open Hunt Club, riders jumped barriers in their efforts to win the cup race. (Courtesy of the Burton Historical Collection, Detroit Public Library.)

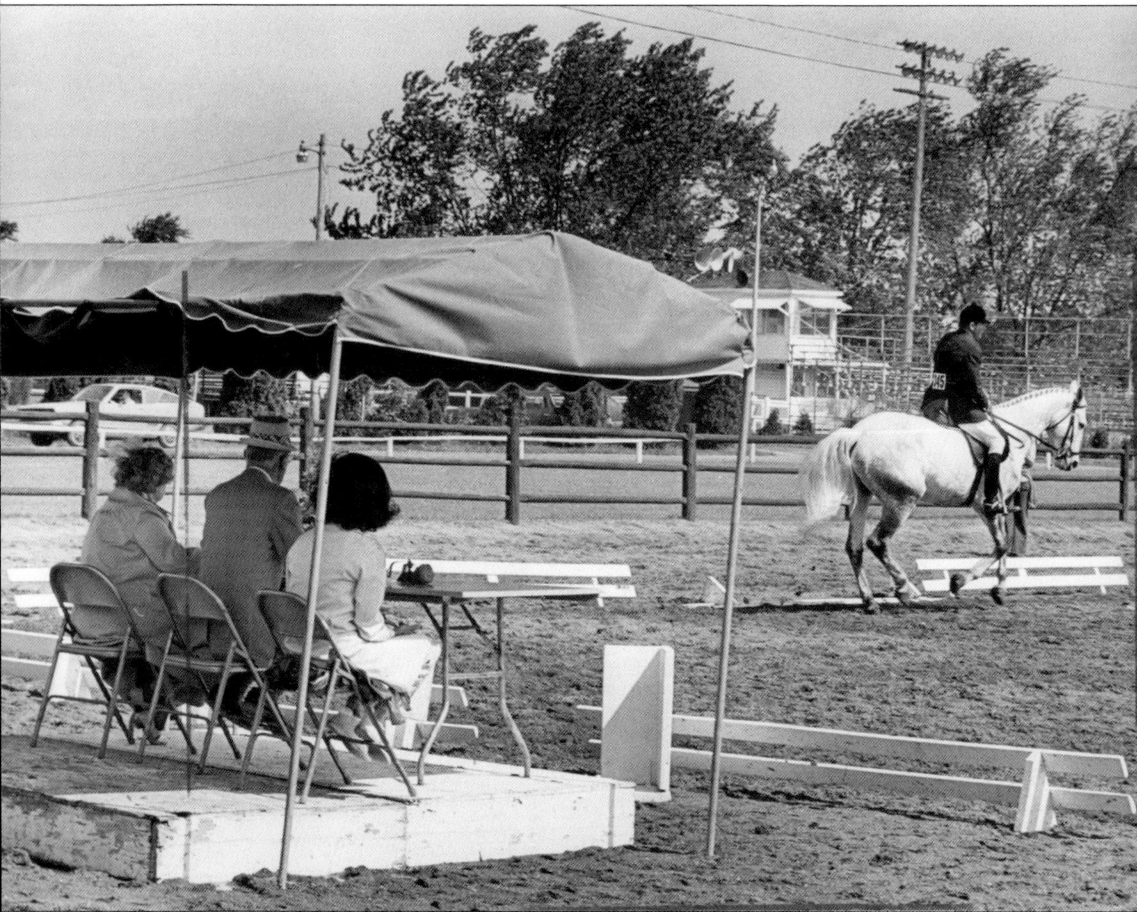

The Bloomfield Open Hunt Club was home to the Detroit/Motor City Horse Show from 1934 to 2000. The club has hosted many other horse shows, races, and equestrian events over the years. In this 1975 photograph, the horse Billiricay and its rider are being judged. The Bloomfield Open Hunt Club was formed in 1917 primarily to provide country space for fox hunting. However, that activity was discontinued in 1965. In its place, the club offers many indoor and outdoor equestrian activities in addition to other recreational activities. The former Hagerman Farmhouse, which served as the original clubhouse, was replaced in 1996 with a 10,000-square-foot deluxe clubhouse. (Courtesy of the Burton Historical Collection, Detroit Public Library.)

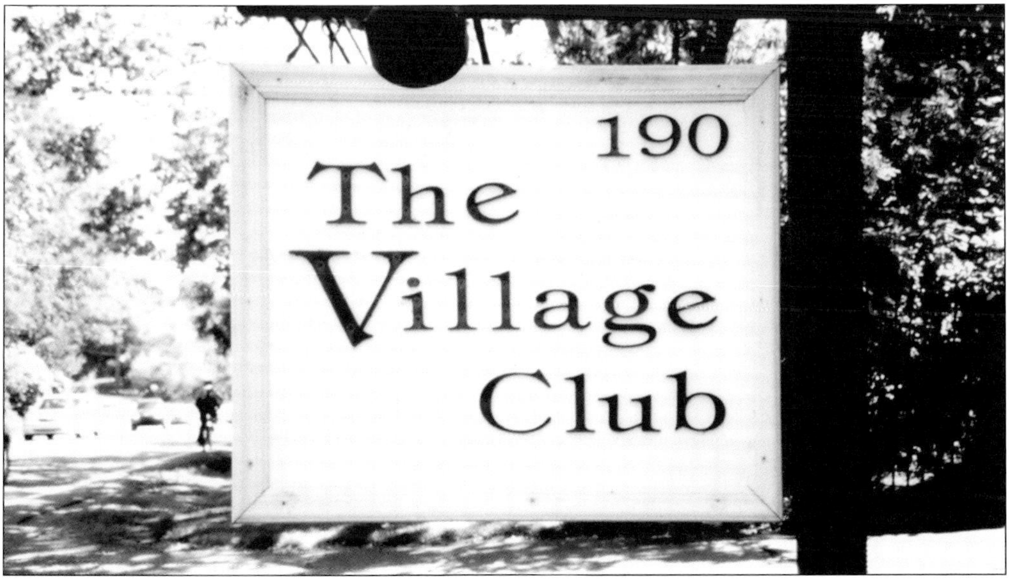

The Village Club sign along East Long Lake Road is one of only a few signs within the city of Bloomfield Hills that is allowed to have black type on a white background. A city ordinance requires that all signs have gold type on a black background. However, this familiar sign was grandfathered because of its historical importance. (Courtesy of the Village Club.)

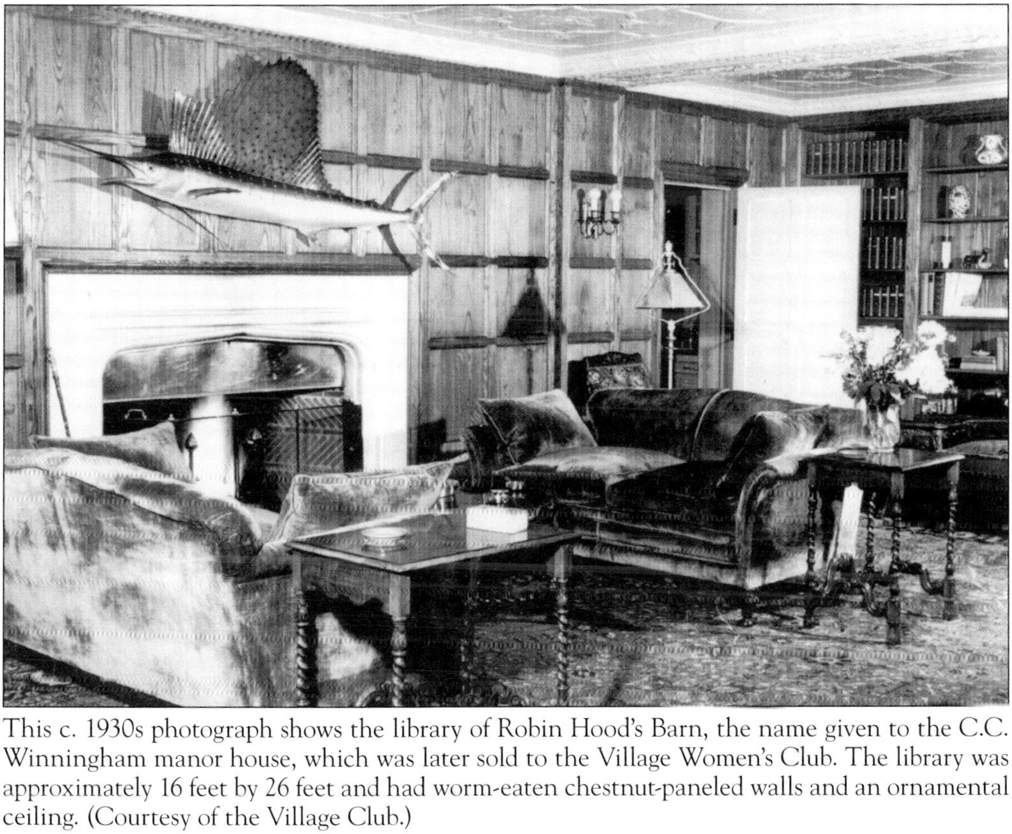

This c. 1930s photograph shows the library of Robin Hood's Barn, the name given to the C.C. Winningham manor house, which was later sold to the Village Women's Club. The library was approximately 16 feet by 26 feet and had worm-eaten chestnut-paneled walls and an ornamental ceiling. (Courtesy of the Village Club.)

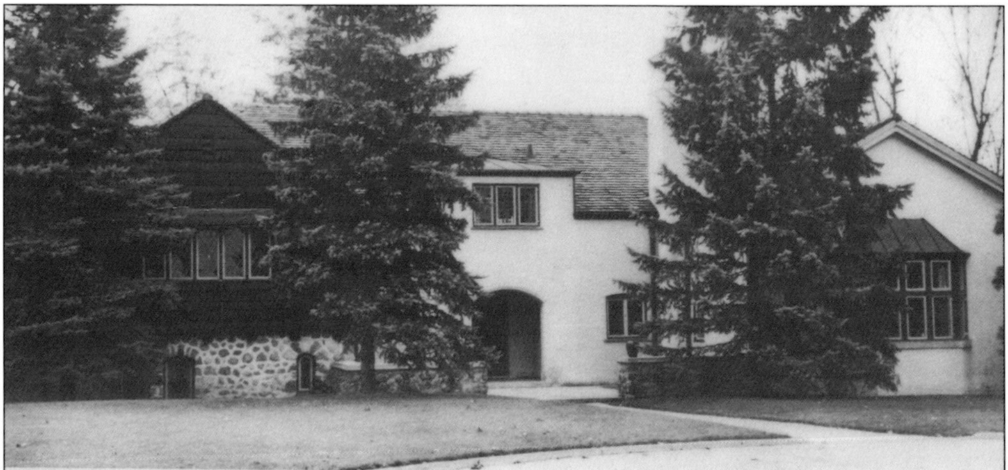

Robin Hood's Barn

Bloomfield Hills, Michigan

A barn that has stood on its present site for nearly ninety years inspired the development of the modern and distinctly beautiful estate known as Robin Hood's Barn.

Paul Honore, the illustrious painter, did the six murals that decorate the walls between the original hand hewn timbers that was once the hay mow and now is the living room of this most interesting house. The murals, regarded as among the finest of Honore's work, depict in rich color and bold figure, incidents from Robin Hood. Thus the place gets its name.

Robin Hood's Barn was remodeled and additions added in 1929 at a cost of $120,000. The finest materials and the most skilled workmen were employed to make it a permanently attractive home.

The character of its enduring quality is manifest in the present condition of every structural and mechanical detail. It is not probable that any private dwelling of such high quality will be built within the next several years.

The charm of the old barn and its rare timbers has been retained, but surrounding it is a modern stucco and stone building with tile roofs, tile floors, equipped with every comfort device and the best of plumbing and electrical appointments.

Built on the side of a hill, there are five main floor levels, which contribute much to the attractiveness of the house. Each floor is accessible to the other by short, easy steps. As approached from the road entrance, the house has the appearance of a small cottage. But immediately on entering the chestnut paneled main hall, one sees beyond the living room with its twenty foot ceiling and mural covered walls, the large sun room overlooking the gardens that extend a thousand feet to the swimming pool; or glances into the library that may be seen at the foot of the short tiled stairs; it is evident that Robin Hood's Barn is a "small house with large and many rooms."

The Village Club first formed as the Village Women's Club in 1956. In 1961, the club purchased Robin Hood's Barn on East Long Lake Road and began converting it into the social club it is today. This highly illustrated eight-page brochure was used in the sale of the property. The home featured a main hall, a huge living room, a library, six master bedrooms, a terrace overlooking a large swimming pool, and a three-car garage, among other amenities. The Village Club extensively renovated the building while retaining some of its best historical qualities. The club is well known for its philanthropic, educational, and social activities, with its foundation awarding grants to nonprofit organizations totalling more than $2 million since 1983. (Courtesy of the Village Club.)

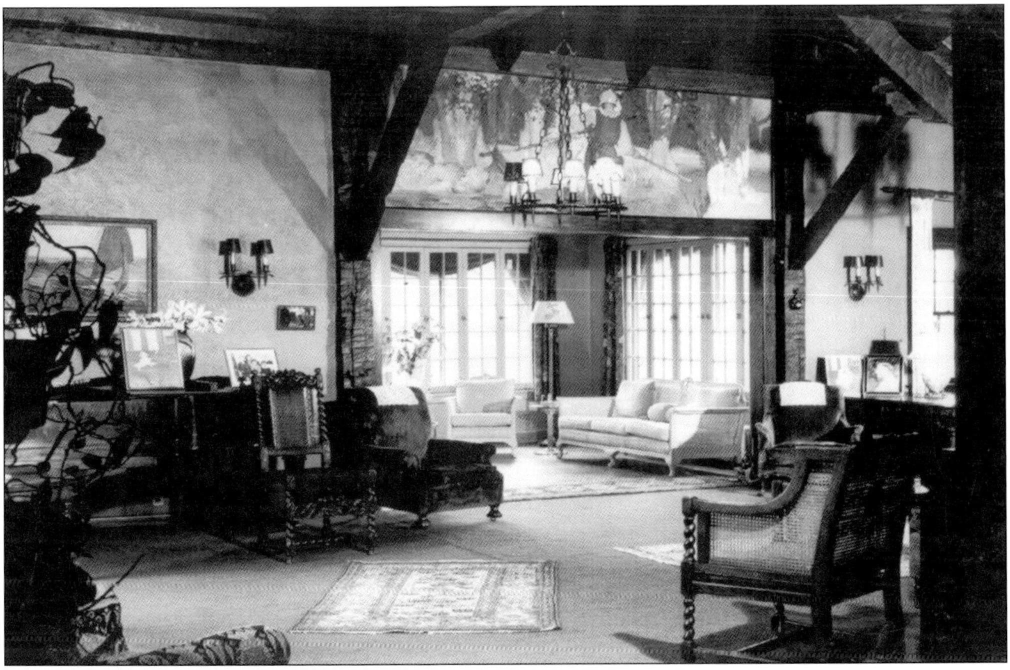

One of six Robin Hood murals painted by Paul Honore decorates the living room wall of Robin Hood's Barn. The murals were considered among Honore's best work. Pictured here are Robin Hood and Little John, who meet and fight and then become friends. The living room was approximately 26 feet by 32 feet. (Courtesy of the Village Club.)

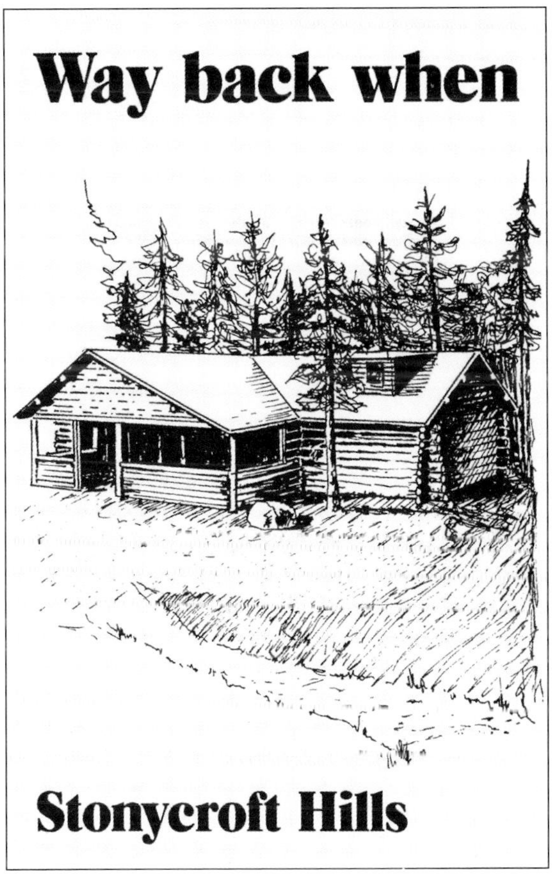

This 1960s pamphlet shows a drawing of the log cabin that served as the Stonycroft Hills Club's first clubhouse. The land on which the club and golf course sit is part of the former Stinchfield Tanglewood Farm, which Theodore MacManus purchased in the 1920s and renamed Stonycroft. The D'Onofrios owned the course next but sold it in 1960. Stonycroft Hills Club was founded that same year. (Courtesy of Stonycroft Hills Club.)

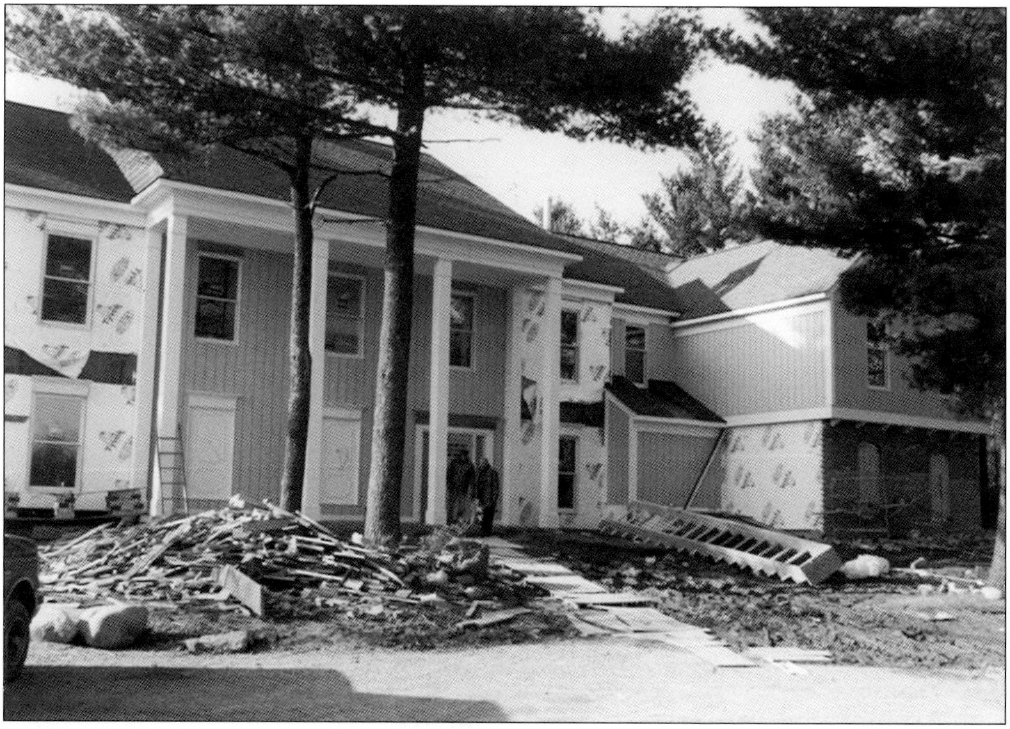

In 1991, the private, nine-hole Stonycroft Hills Club replaced its log cabin clubhouse with a much larger two-story building, shown here under construction. The new clubhouse houses the locker rooms, sitting room, and dining room and overlooks the rolling terrain and gardens. The club is sometimes called Bloomfield Hills' "hidden gem" because its entrance is set far back off of Long Lake Road. (Courtesy of Stonycroft Hills Club.)

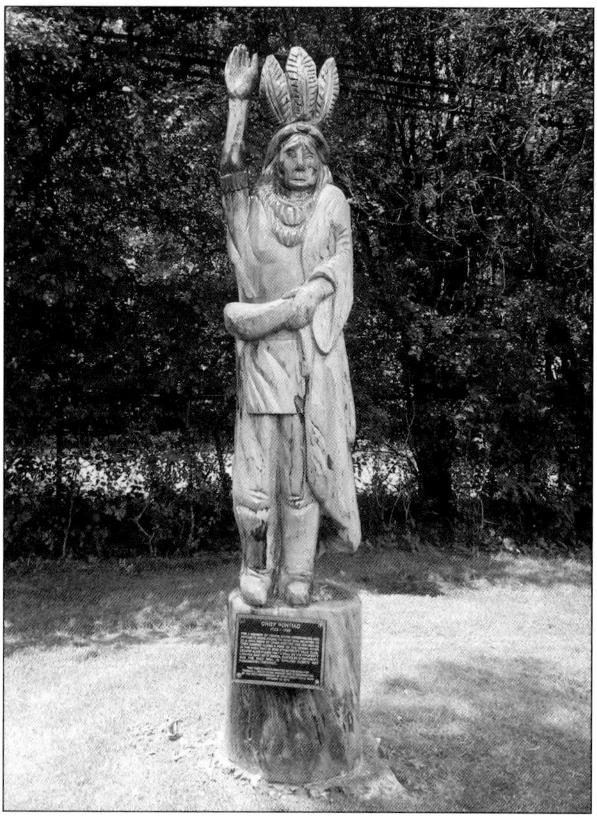

A carving of Chief Pontiac greets golfers on the Stonycroft Hills Club golf course. Stone arrowheads and hatchets discovered over the years led club members to believe that the chief once camped on the property along a fork of the Rouge River. Local legend holds that a well east of the No. 7 green was the only well in Oakland County not poisoned by the chief. (Courtesy of Stonycroft Hills Club.)

Seven

Businesses

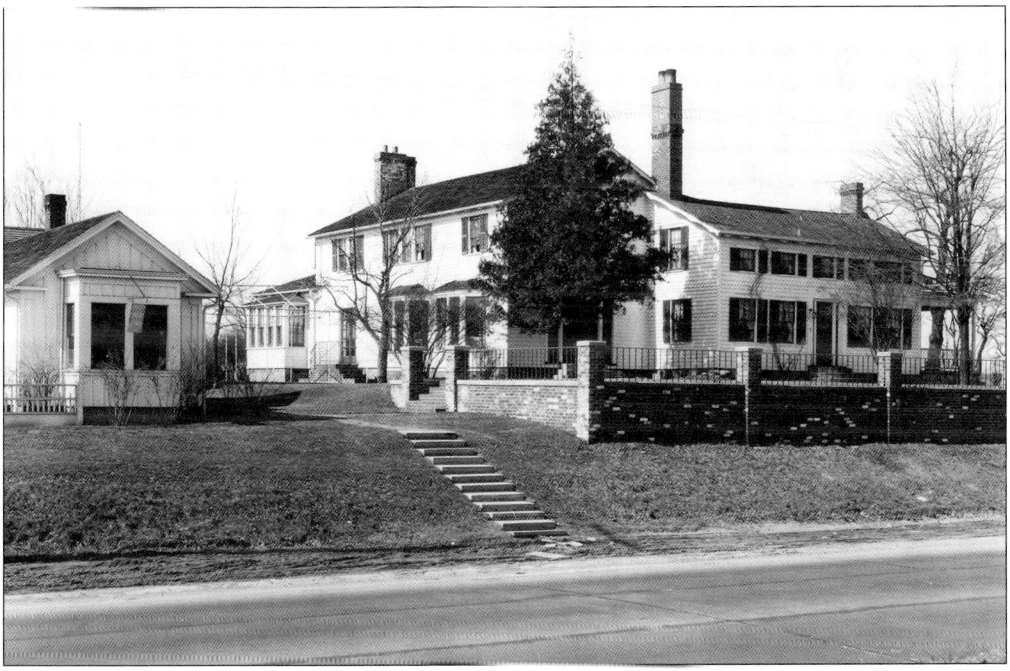

The Lone Pine Inn, on the northwest corner of Lone Pine Road and Woodward Avenue, had an extensive history before it actually became an inn. Ezra Parke, who was the father of Hervey Parke, founder of the Parke-Davis Pharmaceutical Company, built the house as a home for his family in 1872. Parke also operated the area's first post office from the house. In 1910, George Booth bought the house and enlarged it by adding a wing. He also built an Interurban waiting room on the property. Booth used the building for the Bloomfield Hills Seminary, a private day school for local children that operated from 1912 to 1918. After the school closed, Winifred Eastman leased the building and the small former Interurban waiting room from Booth and opened the Lone Pine Inn and Tea House. The inn was later remodeled for use as faculty housing for Cranbrook employees. (Courtesy of Cranbrook Archives.)

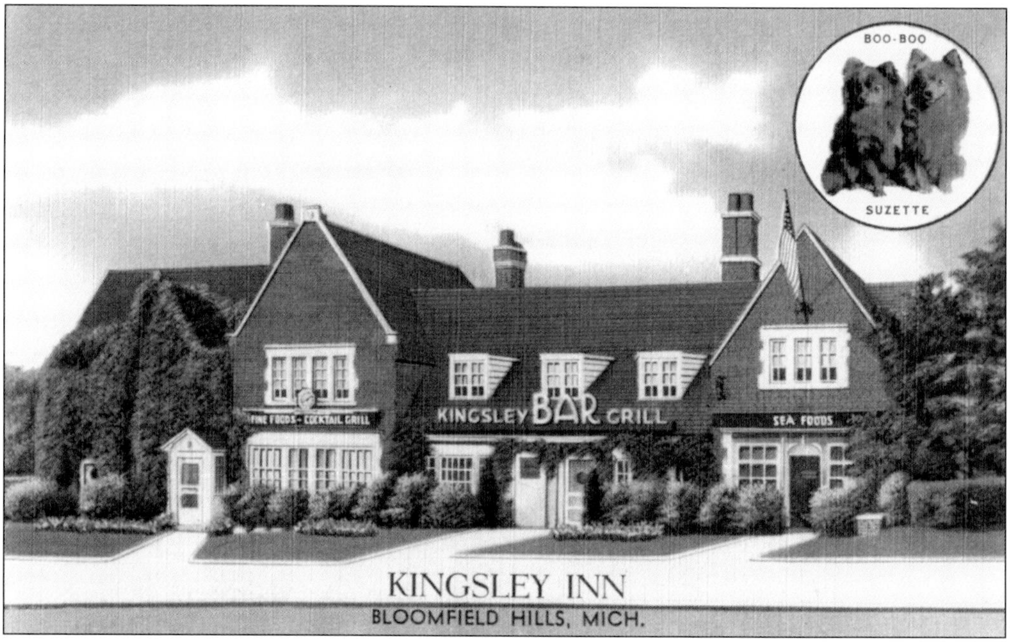

This c. 1930s postcard shows the first Kingsley Inn, which was located at 1312 Woodward Avenue. Fotis "Nick" Takis purchased the former Kingston Inn and renamed it in 1938. In 1970, Nick Takis sold the Kingsley Inn to Curt Terova. The inn has changed owners and names several times since. (Courtesy of Birmingham Historical Museum and Park.)

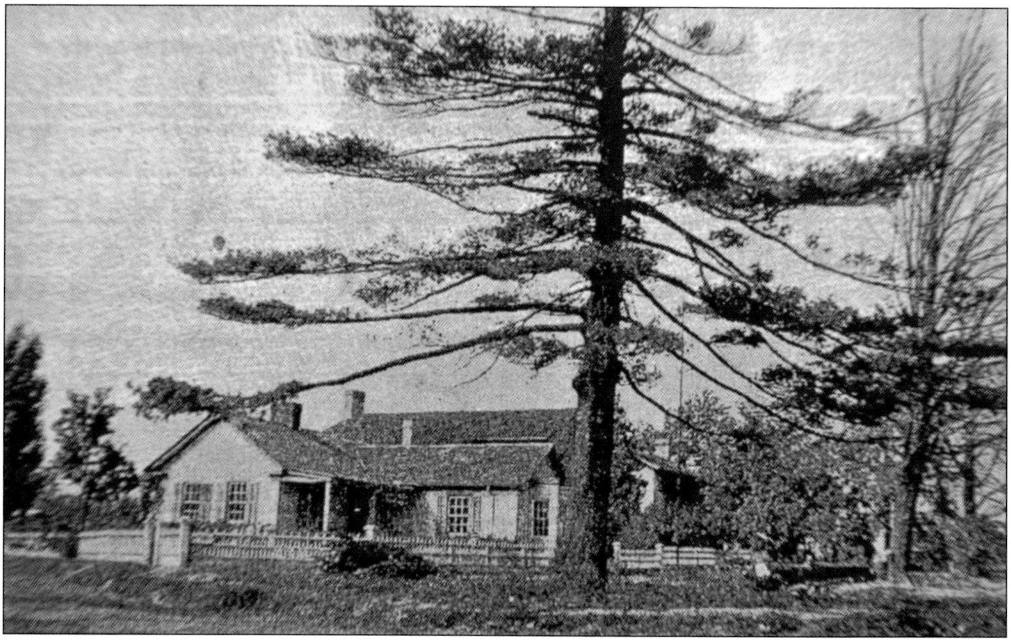

In 1925, a towering lone pine stands near the Lone Pine Treasure Shop, located at Woodward Avenue and Lone Pine Road. Elizabeth Neet and Sarah Fagan lived in and worked out of this little farmhouse. They made and sold their own crafts as well as those of other craftspeople. Pewter and brass pieces, Pewabic and Italian-made pottery, and clothing were some of their wares. (*Afterglow.*)

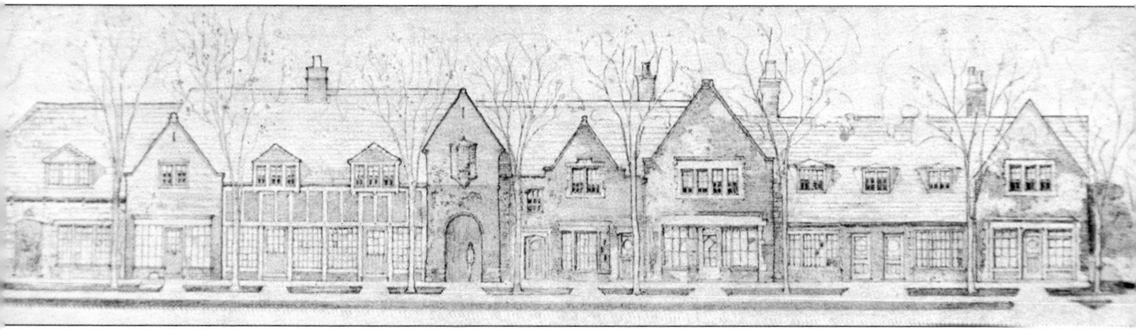

By 1927, William T. Barbour had built a village of commercial buildings and homes on the west side of Woodward Avenue at Long Lake Road in the same English village style that Manley Davis had used for the Fox and Hounds Inn on the east side. Tenants included a post office, an oil station, and the Crown and Blossom Tea Rooms (formerly the Lone Pine Tea House), among others. (*Afterglow.*)

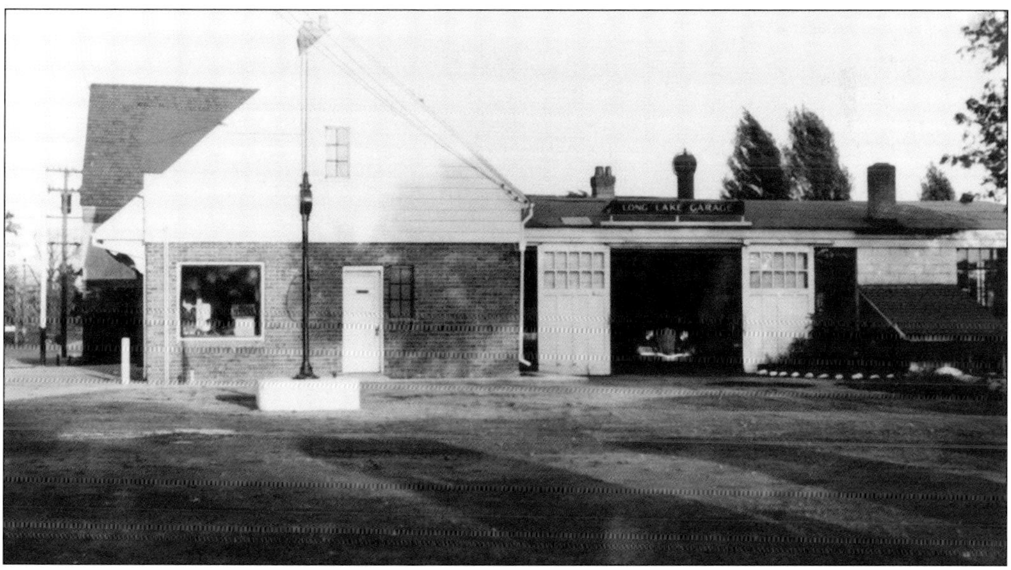

This 1935 photograph shows the Long Lake Garage on the northeast corner of Woodward Avenue and Long Lake Road. The garage also had a fueling pump. A modern Mobil station exists on the same corner today. (Courtesy of Cranbrook Archives.)

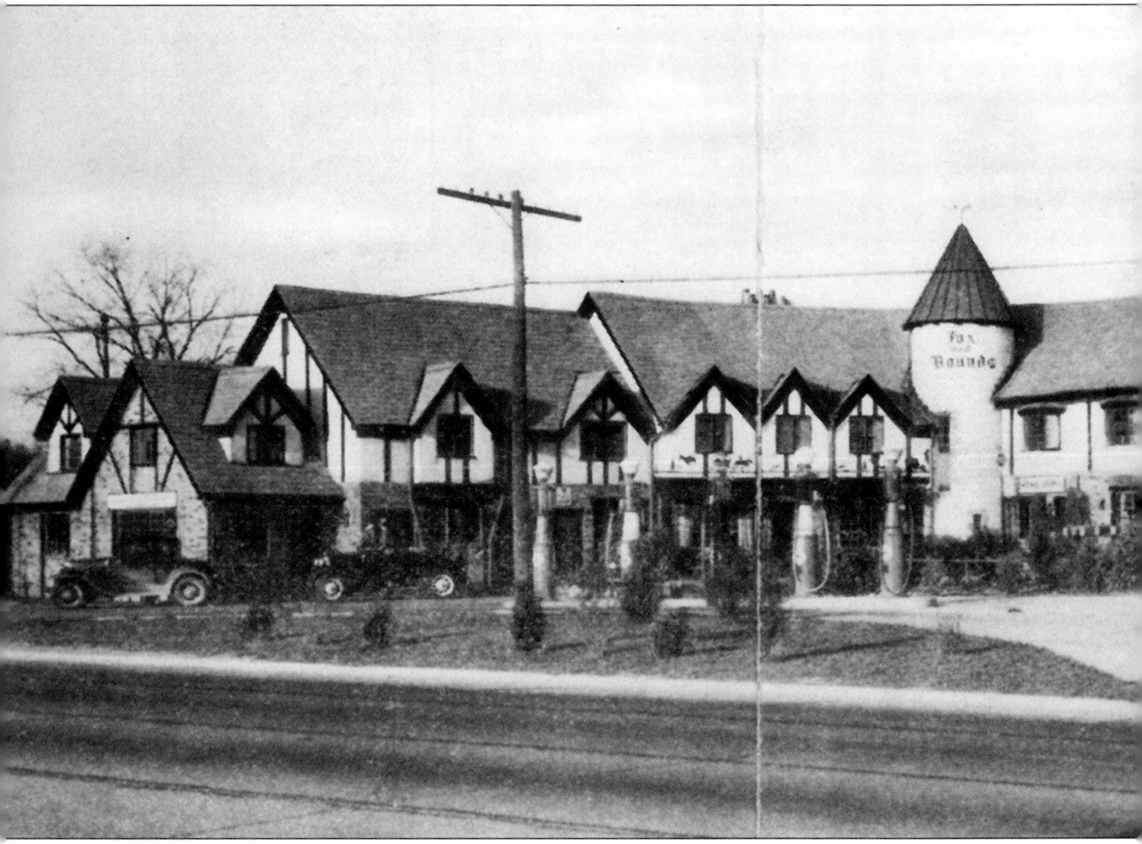

"It is a story-book picture come to life," wrote Theodore H. Millington in 1927 about the Fox and Hounds building that had opened at the southeast corner of Woodward Avenue and Long Lake Road in what was then called Bloomfield Center. Designed by architect J. Robert F. Swanson, the building was developed by Manley Davis. The crescent-shaped structure featured an authentic porte cochere, or "coach port," slate roof, leaded casement windows, timbered walls, and "ancient-

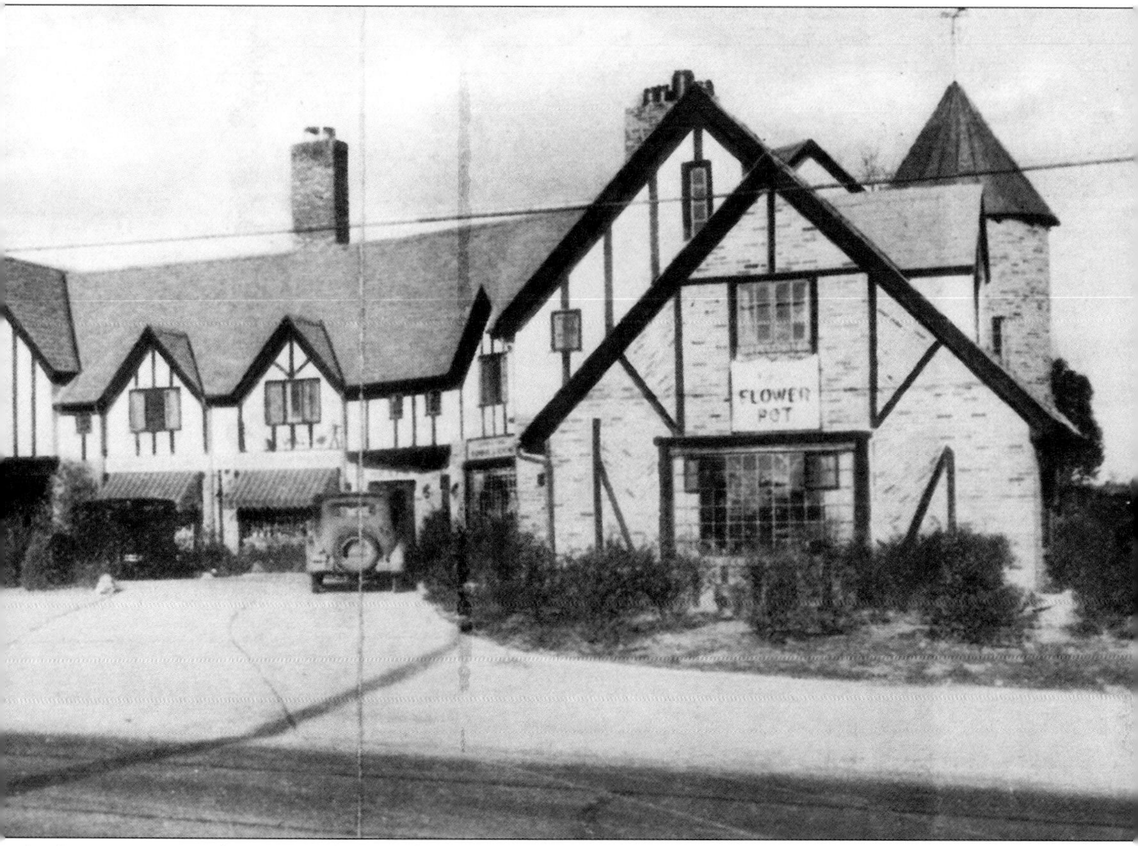

looking" towers. The Fox and Hounds Inn was at the northern end of the building. In addition to a main dining room, the inn had two private dining rooms, a taproom, a ballroom, several fireplaces, and seven bedrooms upstairs. The south end of the building had stores below and apartments above. (Courtesy of Birmingham Historical Museum and Park.)

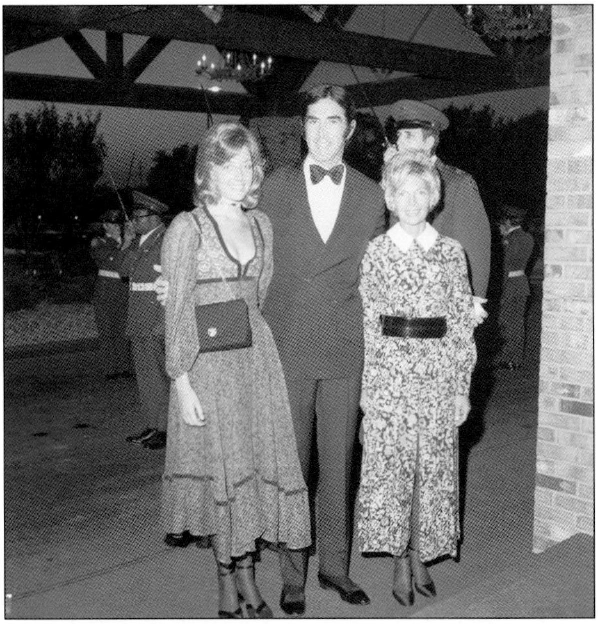

In this 1969 photograph, General Motors executive John Z. DeLorean is about to escort his wife, Kelly Harmon (left), and Harmon's mother, former actress Elyse Knox Harmon, into a local restaurant. DeLorean was a frequent patron at several Bloomfield Hills restaurants, notably the Fox and Hounds Inn. (Courtesy of Walter P. Reuther Library, Archives of Labor and Urban Affairs, Wayne State University.)

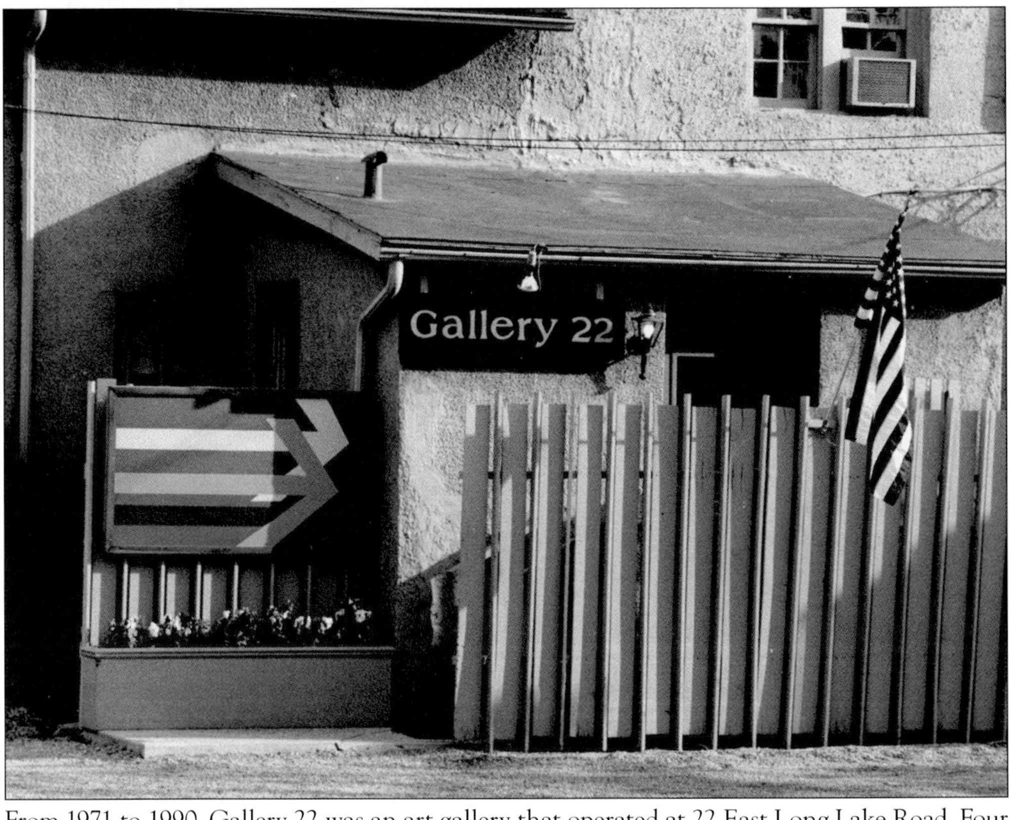

From 1971 to 1990, Gallery 22 was an art gallery that operated at 22 East Long Lake Road. Four two-story townhouses made up the complex, and owner Fred Nordseik occupied three of them. A Shell service station was on the southeast corner, with Deputy Dogs Restaurant next to the Mobil station on the northeast corner. (Courtesy of Mark Wood.)

This is the historic Bagley Inn restored in 1976, but it did not look like this in its early days, nor was it in its present location on Long Lake Road. William Barbour purchased the structure and had it moved around 1920 to its current location. By 1975, the inn was in disrepair. Instead of simply demolishing the inn, owner Dick Miner discovered its history and renovated it in 1976. (Courtesy of Paul DePorre.)

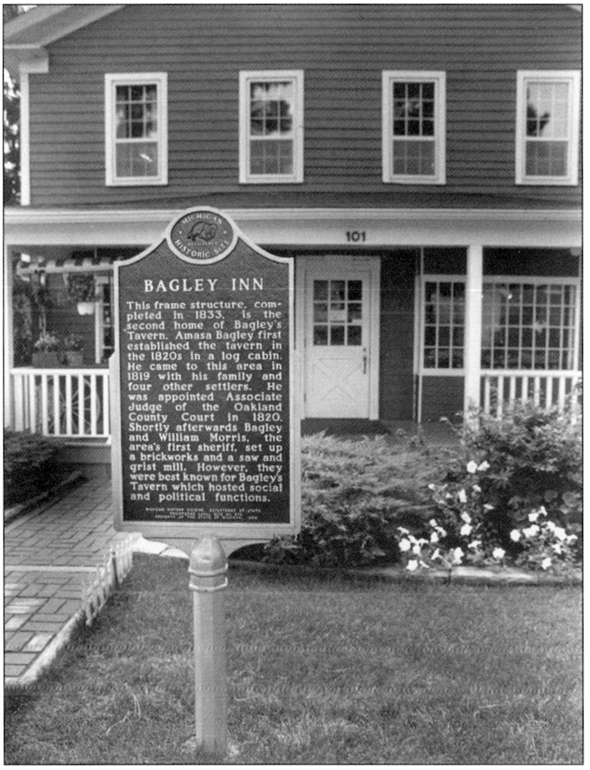

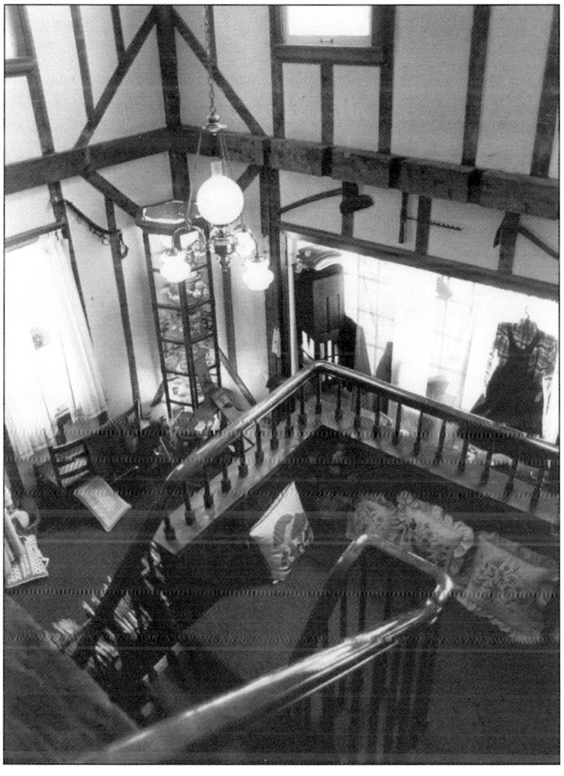

The State of Michigan designated the renovated Bagley Inn a historic site in 1979. It became Miner's Bagley Inn and housed a women's apparel store, shown here, until 1997. Dick and Tom Miner sold the inn to Paul DePorre and Michael Petrucci, who extensively renovated its interior for offices. However, DePorre and Petrucci retained elements of the old interior, such as the hand-hewn oak columns. (Courtesy of Paul DePorre.)

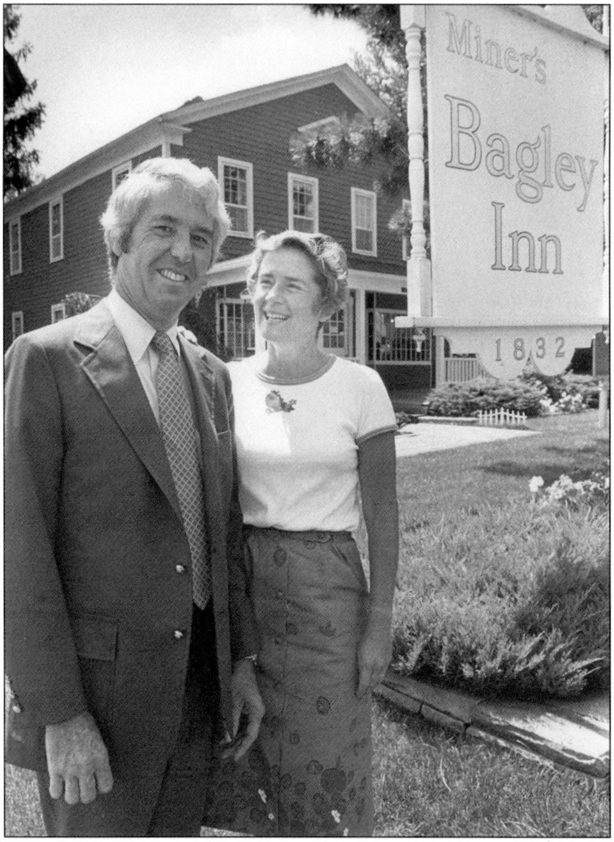

Dick and Susan Miner smile in front of Miner's Bagley Inn, which they ran as a women's sporting apparel store until their retirement in 1997. The Miners also owned and operated Miner's Liquor Store a few doors east. Dick was raised with his brother, Tom, in the old Bagley Inn. His mother, Susan, had purchased the structure in 1943 from William Barbour, her employer. (Courtesy of Paul DePorre.)

This 1960s Kingsley Inn postcard shows a 102-room hotel with three dining rooms, three cocktail lounges, a sauna, a beauty shop, a barbershop, a coffee shop, and a pool. By 1980, the hotel had expanded to 160 rooms, and Trader's Bar and Grill, the hotel's piano bar, was a popular weekend singles hangout. (Courtesy of the Kingsley Inn and Oakland County Pioneer and Historical Society.)

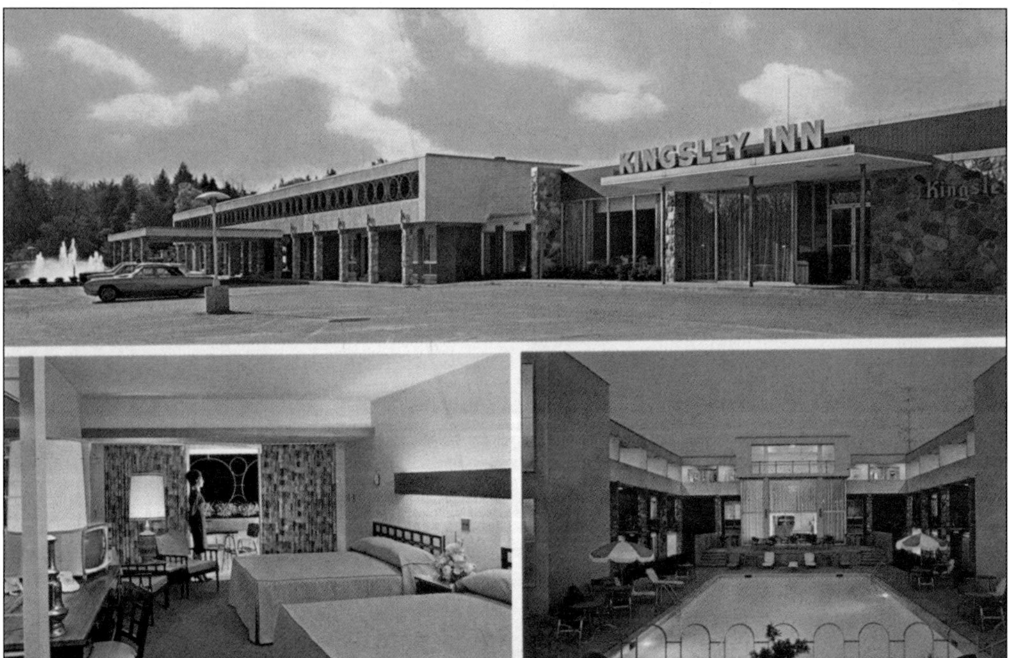

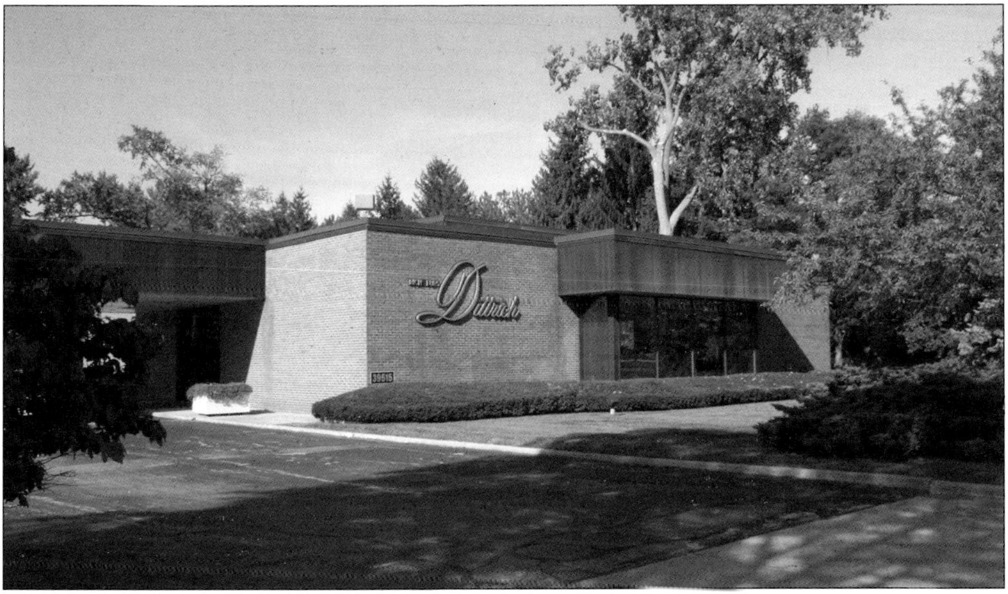

Dittrich Furs, located next to the Kingsley Inn on Woodward Avenue, opened in 1977. The company was founded in 1893 by Emil Dittrich, a furrier from London. Dittrich began his business in Detroit by buying only the finest pelts directly from trappers. Today, Dittrich Furs is the oldest family-owned retail business in Detroit. (Courtesy of Dittrich Furs.)

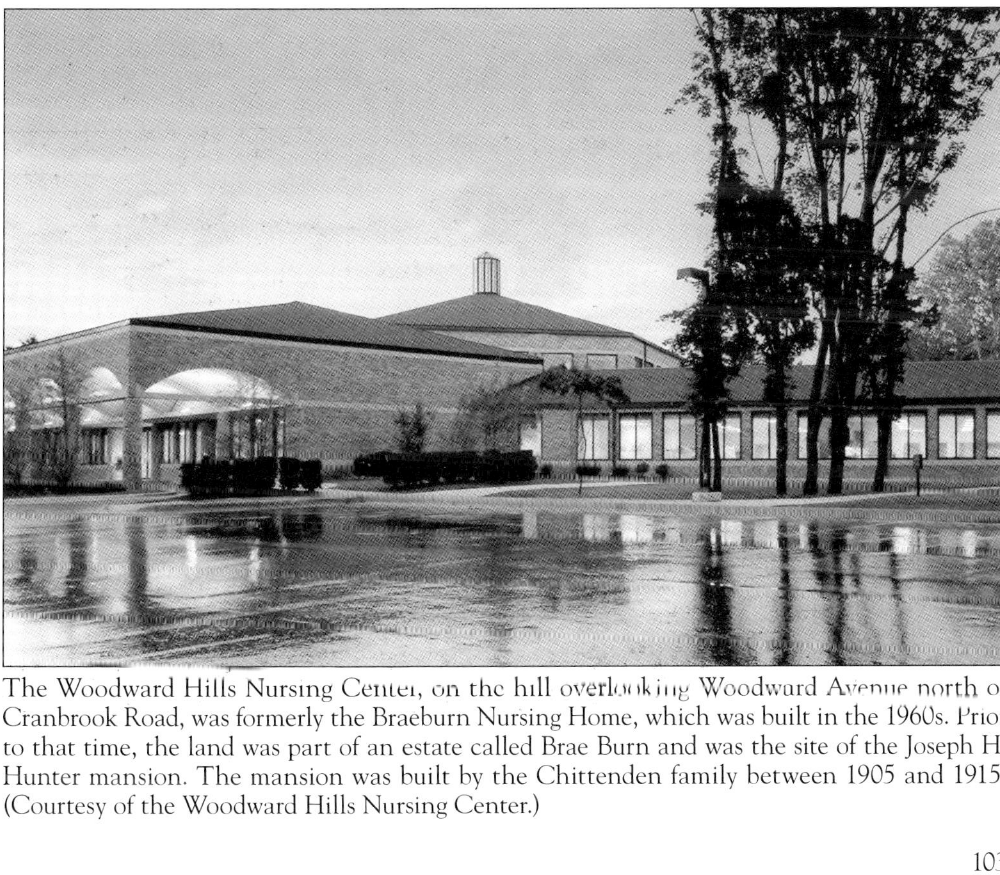

The Woodward Hills Nursing Center, on the hill overlooking Woodward Avenue north of Cranbrook Road, was formerly the Braeburn Nursing Home, which was built in the 1960s. Prior to that time, the land was part of an estate called Brae Burn and was the site of the Joseph H. Hunter mansion. The mansion was built by the Chittenden family between 1905 and 1915. (Courtesy of the Woodward Hills Nursing Center.)

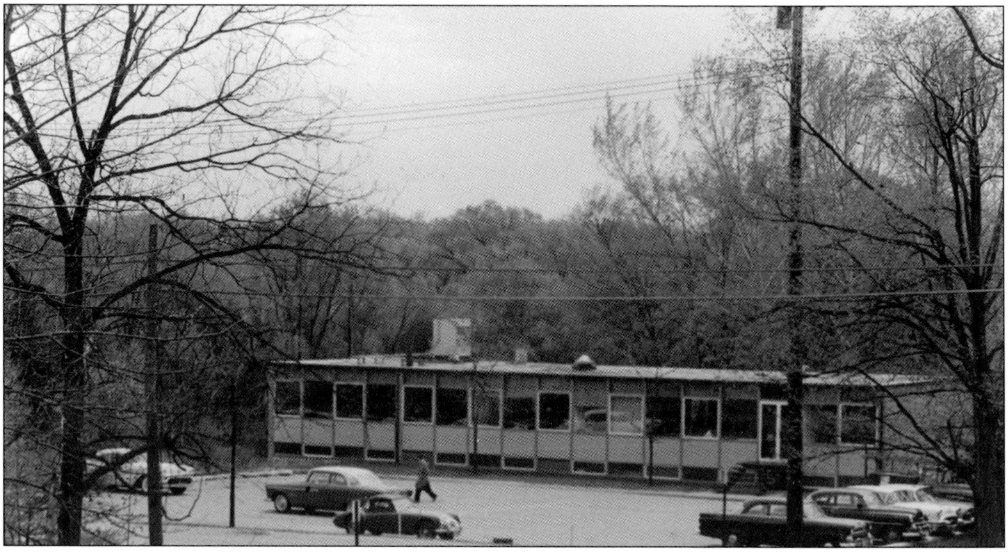

Some of the greatest modern architecture of the 20th century was designed by Eero Saarinen and Associates in this unassuming-looking building at 91 West Long Lake Road. Saarinen's firm had many commissions, and he and his staff developed a reputation for working around the clock to meet schedules. This 1954 photograph shows the building one year after it was constructed into the side of a hill. (Courtesy of Cranbrook Archives.)

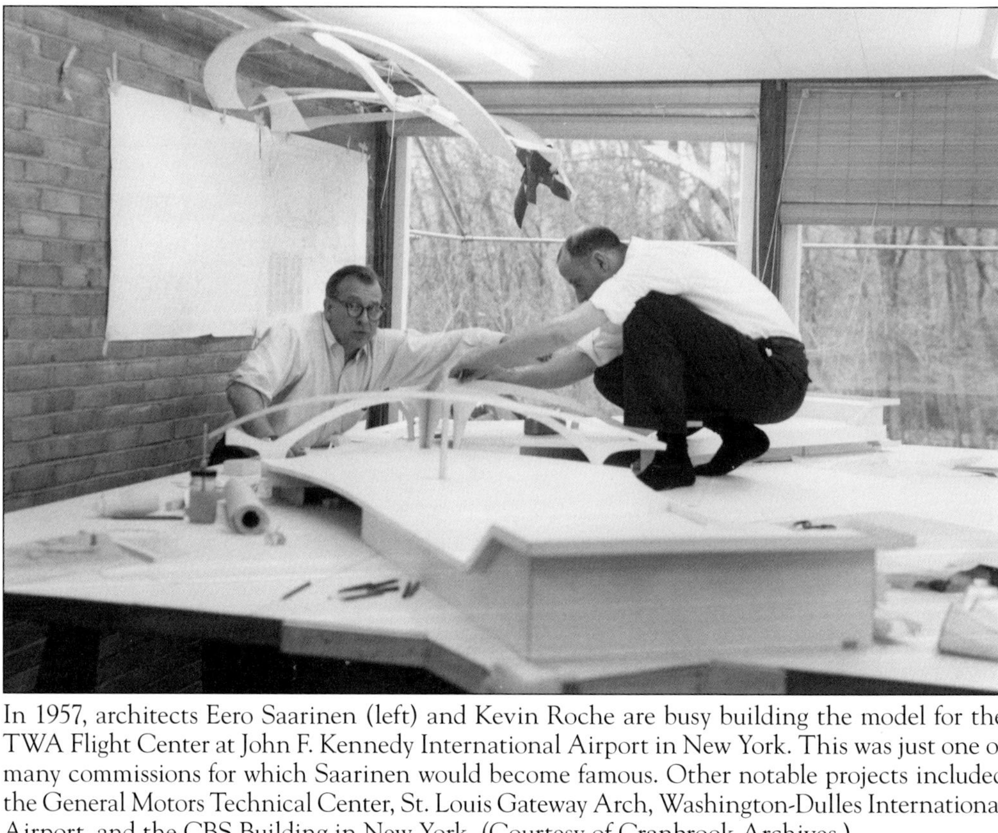

In 1957, architects Eero Saarinen (left) and Kevin Roche are busy building the model for the TWA Flight Center at John F. Kennedy International Airport in New York. This was just one of many commissions for which Saarinen would become famous. Other notable projects included the General Motors Technical Center, St. Louis Gateway Arch, Washington-Dulles International Airport, and the CBS Building in New York. (Courtesy of Cranbrook Archives.)

Eight

Churches

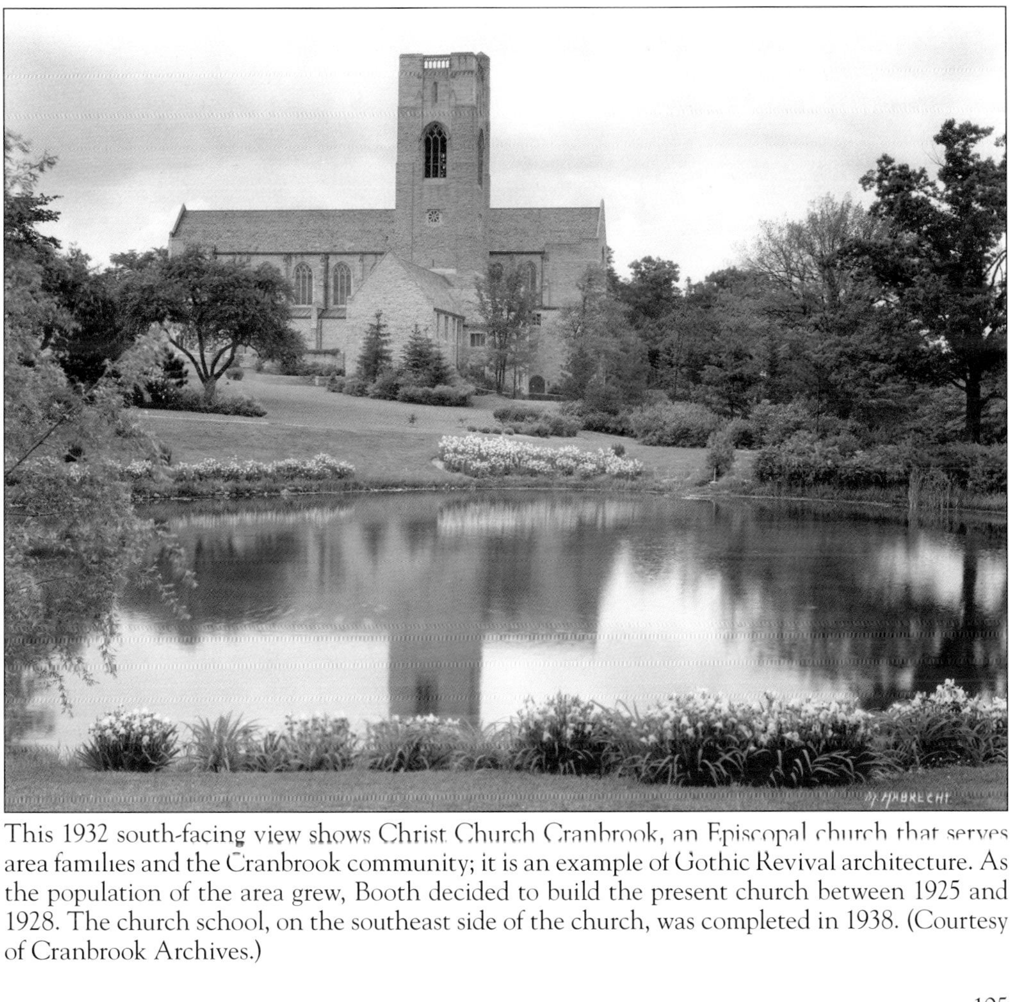

This 1932 south-facing view shows Christ Church Cranbrook, an Episcopal church that serves area families and the Cranbrook community; it is an example of Gothic Revival architecture. As the population of the area grew, Booth decided to build the present church between 1925 and 1928. The church school, on the southeast side of the church, was completed in 1938. (Courtesy of Cranbrook Archives.)

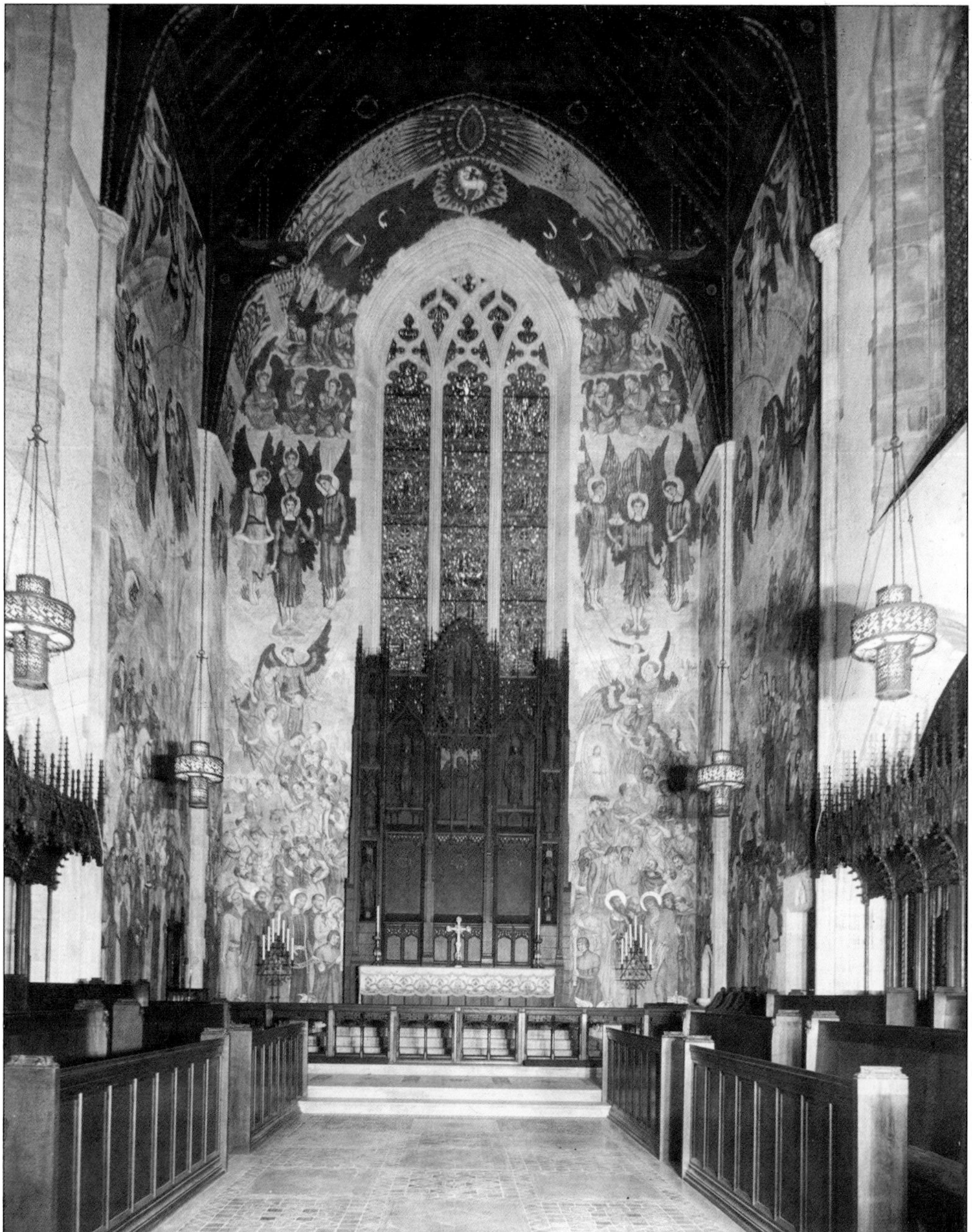

The first service held in the church proper of Christ Church Cranbrook was on Christmas Eve, 1927. This 1957 photograph shows the nave and high altar. Katherine McEwen painted the large fresco surrounding the altar, signing it with a painting of a cat in one corner. The intricate high-relief panel of the reredos above the altar was carved by John Kirchmayer. (Courtesy of Cranbrook Archives.)

This May 1928 photograph shows St. Dunstan's Chapel in Christ Church Cranbrook. The chapel lies beneath the chancel. It includes the stained-glass East Window, which depicts the arts and crafts by showing Jesus, Joseph, and Noah holding tools associated with their earthly lives. The window was made by Wright Goodhue of Boston in 1927. (Courtesy of Walter P. Reuther Library, Archives of Labor and Urban Affairs, Wayne State University.)

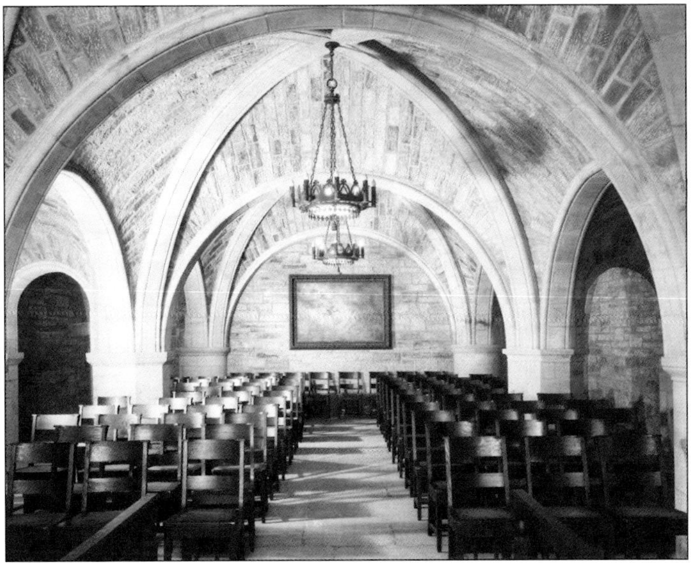

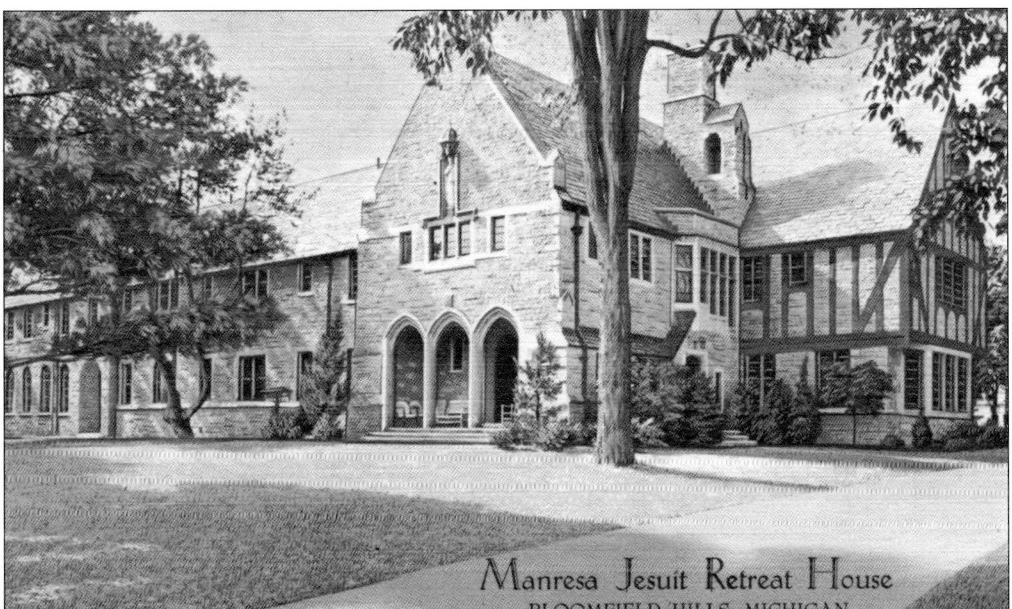

Manresa Jesuit Retreat House is located on parklike grounds at the corner of Quarton Road and Woodward Avenue. The first retreat was held September 23–26, 1926, with 16 retreatants in attendance. The stone front gateway also dates from this period. The 39-acre property was purchased in 1926 from William Murphy, whose country estate was called Deepdale. (Courtesy of Postcard Collection, Bentley Historical Library, University of Michigan.)

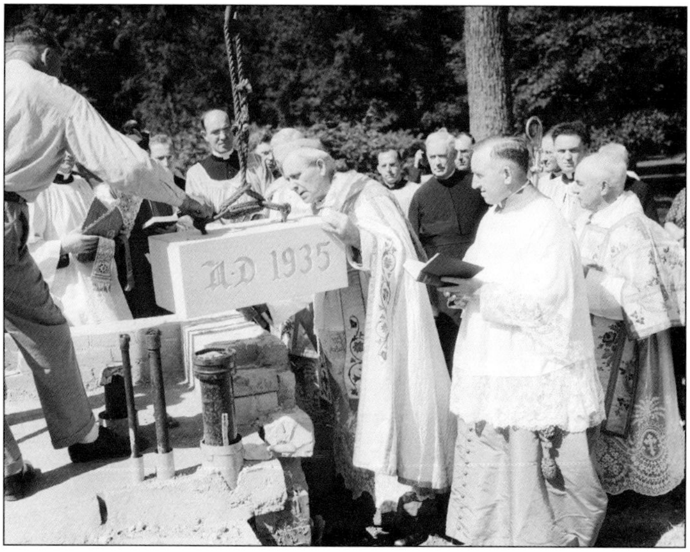

In July 1935, Catholic bishop Michael Gallagher lays the cornerstone for the new building at Manresa Jesuit Retreat House. In 1934, the former manor house had burned to the ground. Despite the Depression, retreatants raised enough money to build a new structure. The new building was completed by August 1936. (Courtesy of Walter P. Reuther Library, Archives of Labor and Urban Affairs, Wayne State University.)

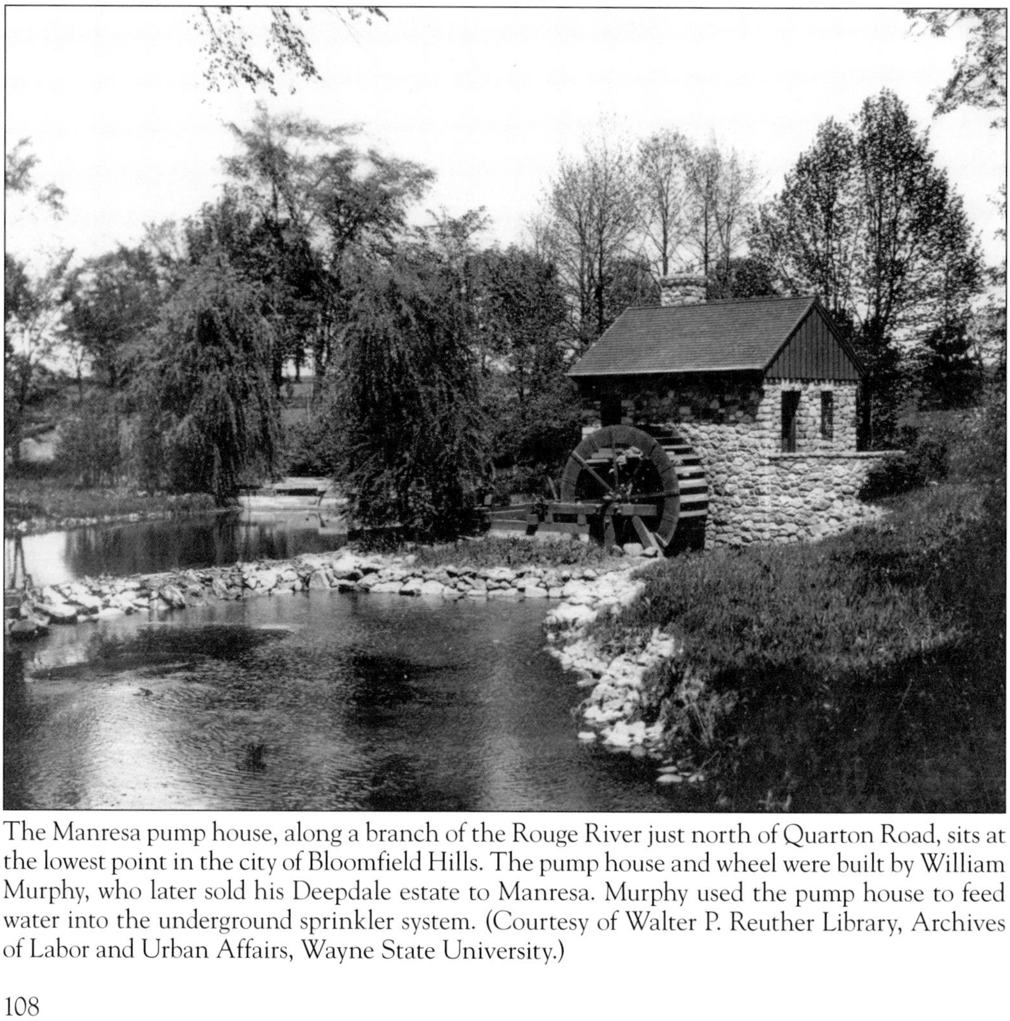

The Manresa pump house, along a branch of the Rouge River just north of Quarton Road, sits at the lowest point in the city of Bloomfield Hills. The pump house and wheel were built by William Murphy, who later sold his Deepdale estate to Manresa. Murphy used the pump house to feed water into the underground sprinkler system. (Courtesy of Walter P. Reuther Library, Archives of Labor and Urban Affairs, Wayne State University.)

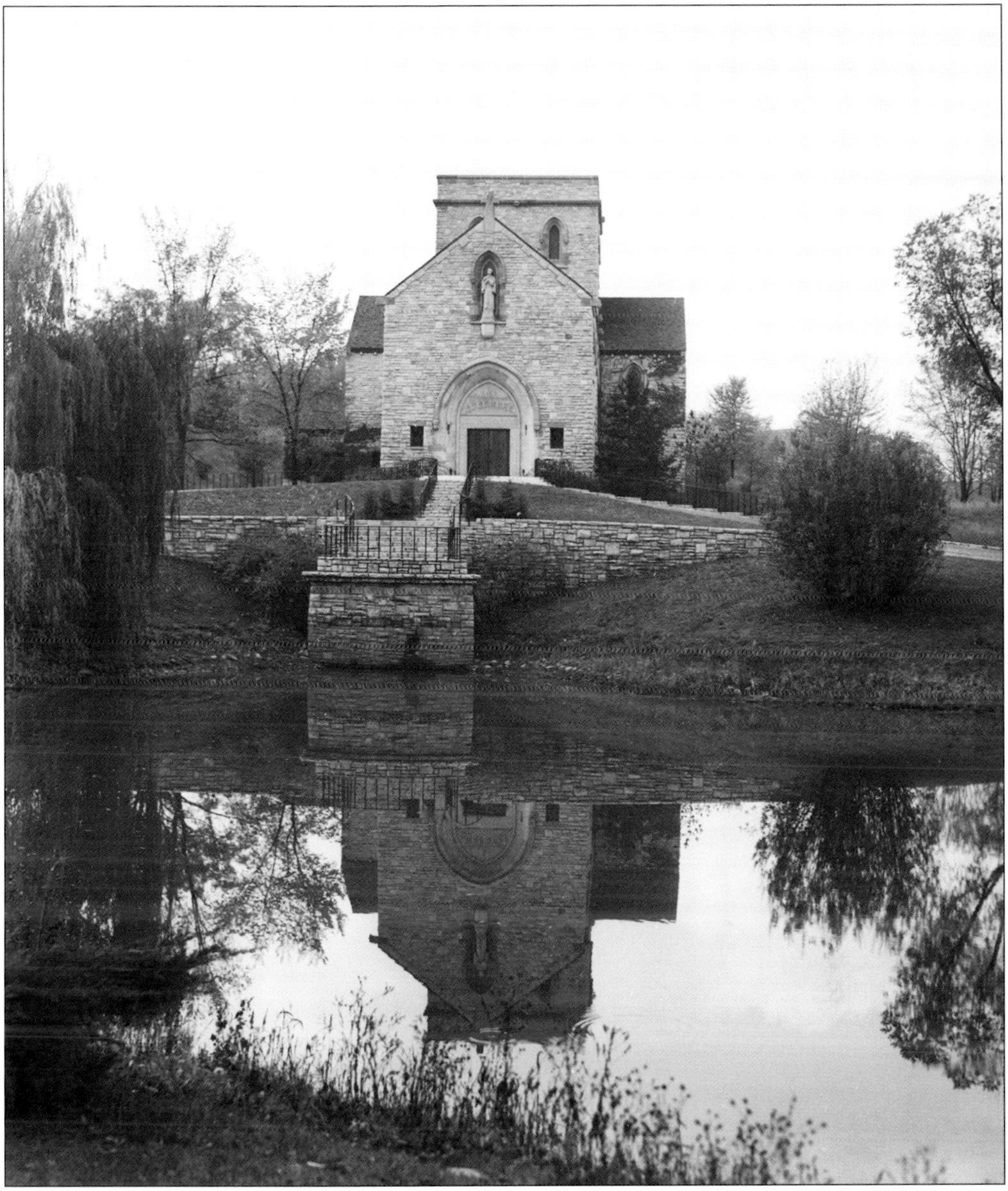

St. Hugo of the Hills was the gift of Mr. and Mrs. Theodore F. MacManus to the Archdiocese of Detroit in memory of their sons, Hugo and Herbert MacManus. The church was dedicated in 1936. In 1937, it was cited as one of the 100 most notable buildings in America by the American Institute of Architects. (Courtesy of Walter P. Reuther Library, Archives of Labor and Urban Affairs, Wayne State University.)

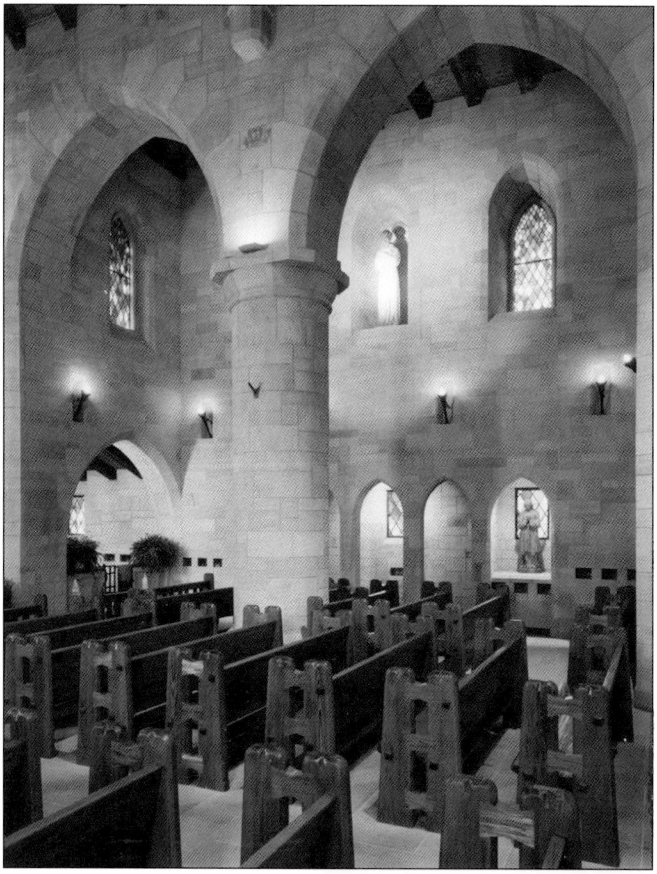

The interior of St. Hugo of the Hills chapel was carefully restored between 1987 and 1989. Air-conditioning was added, which required the building of a new room 20 feet belowground. The renovation cost approximately $3.7 million to complete. (Courtesy of St. Hugo of the Hills.)

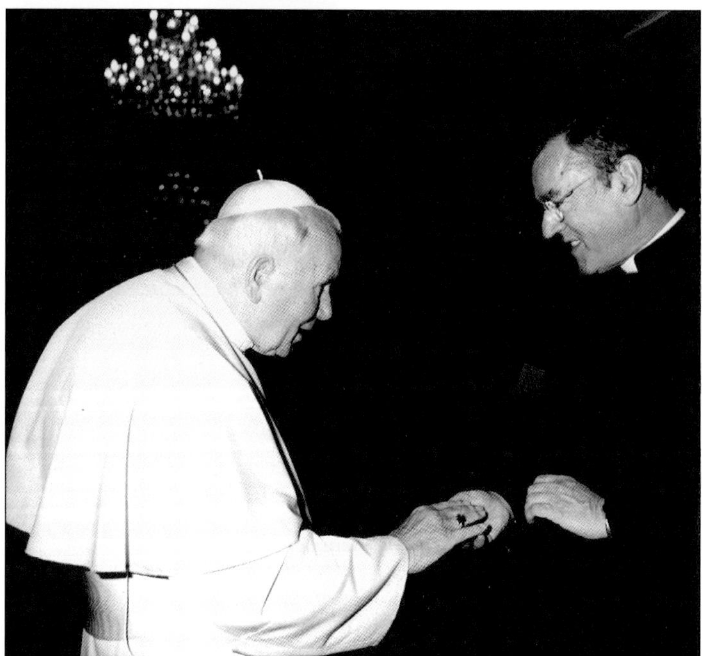

The Reverend Msgr. Anthony M. Tocco (right) is shown here with Pope John Paul II, who elevated him to the prelature of monsignor in 1994. Father Tocco has been the pastor of St. Hugo of the Hills Church since 1985. In addition to attending to his parish community, he has overseen the building of the main church and an extensive restoration of the original chapel. (Courtesy of St. Hugo of the Hills.)

In 1959, the Birmingham Unitarian Church moved to its new location on Woodward Avenue just north of Lone Pine Road in Bloomfield Hills. The new church was designed by Minoru Yamasaki and consisted of several buildings connected by outdoor walkways with periodic gold domes. However, due to budget constraints, the domes were built without the gold. (Courtesy of Birmingham Unitarian Church.)

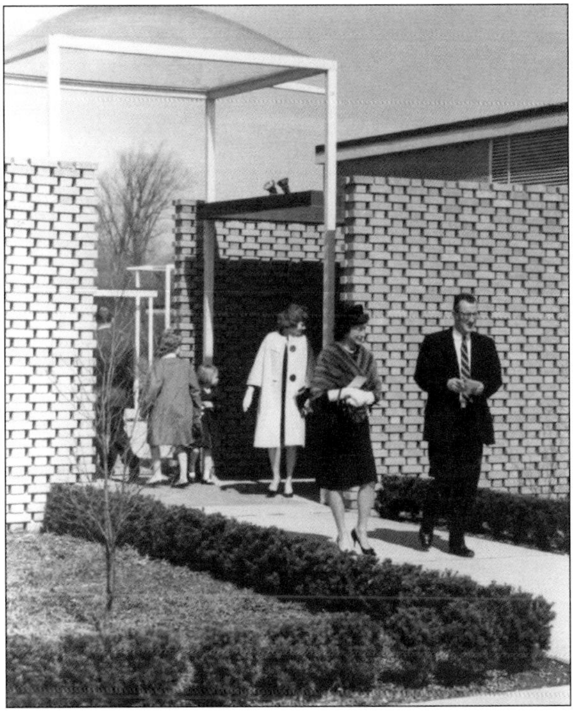

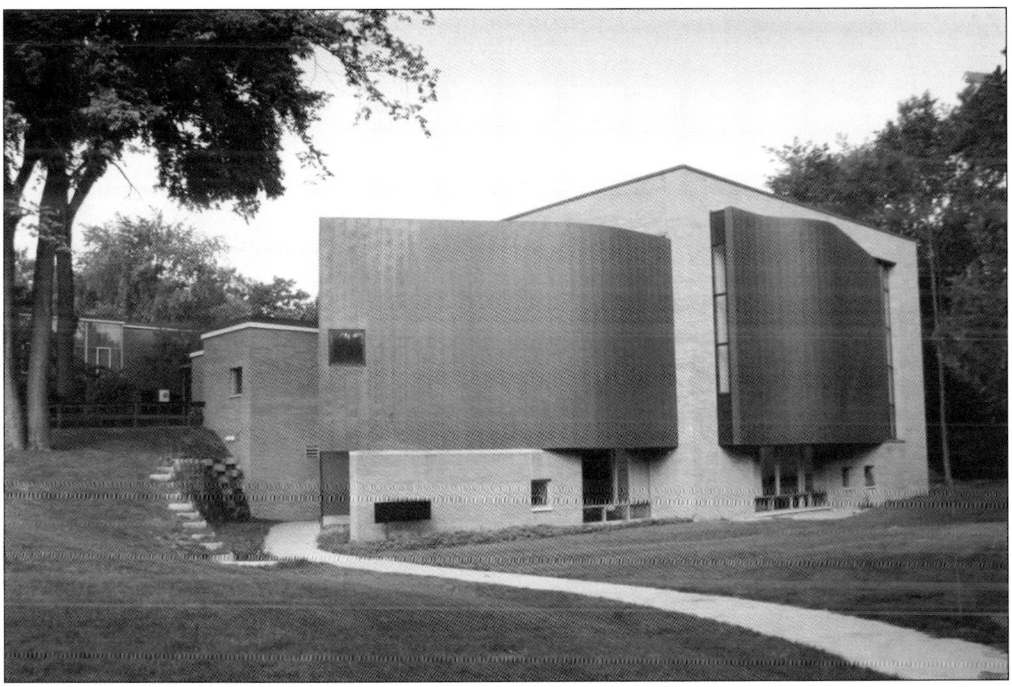

A new, larger sanctuary for the Birmingham Unitarian Church was later built on the eastern side of the church complex, which now fronts Woodward Avenue. An enclosed gallery, additional classrooms, and an elevator were added in one phase. In another phase, church offices were remodeled, the social hall expanded, and conference rooms, a commercial kitchen, and an outdoor family recreation area added. (Courtesy of Birmingham Unitarian Church.)

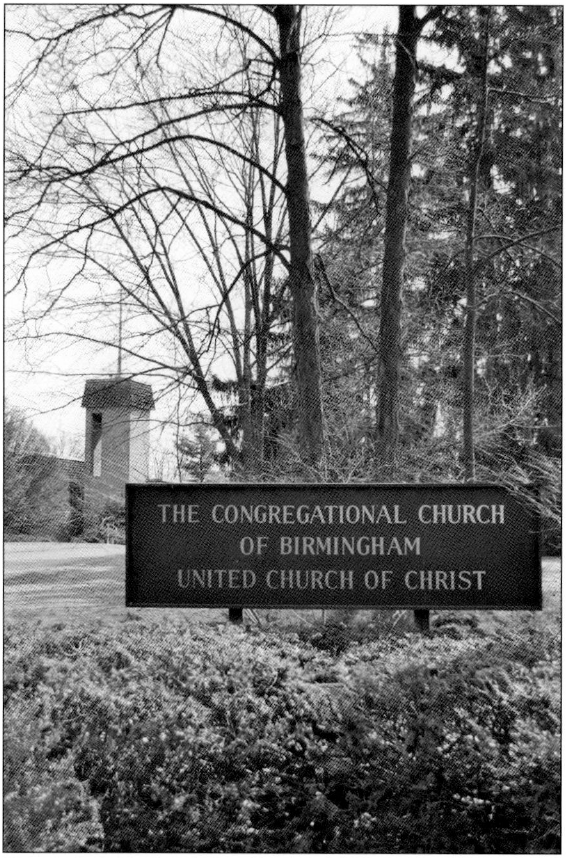

The entrance to the Congregational Church of Birmingham is on Cranbrook Road at the corner of Woodward Avenue. The land the church was built on in 1966 is the former site of Uplands, the Albert Kahn–designed home of the Frank Bromley family. A remnant of that former time is the Bromley garage, which still sits on the western portion of the property. (Courtesy of the Congregational Church of Birmingham.)

This photograph shows the interior of the Congregational Church of Birmingham's sanctuary at Christmas. During the summer, services for the church are sometimes held outdoors in the garden. The church, which is part of the United Church of Christ, also grows produce in plots open to the community. (Courtesy of the Congregational Church of Birmingham.)

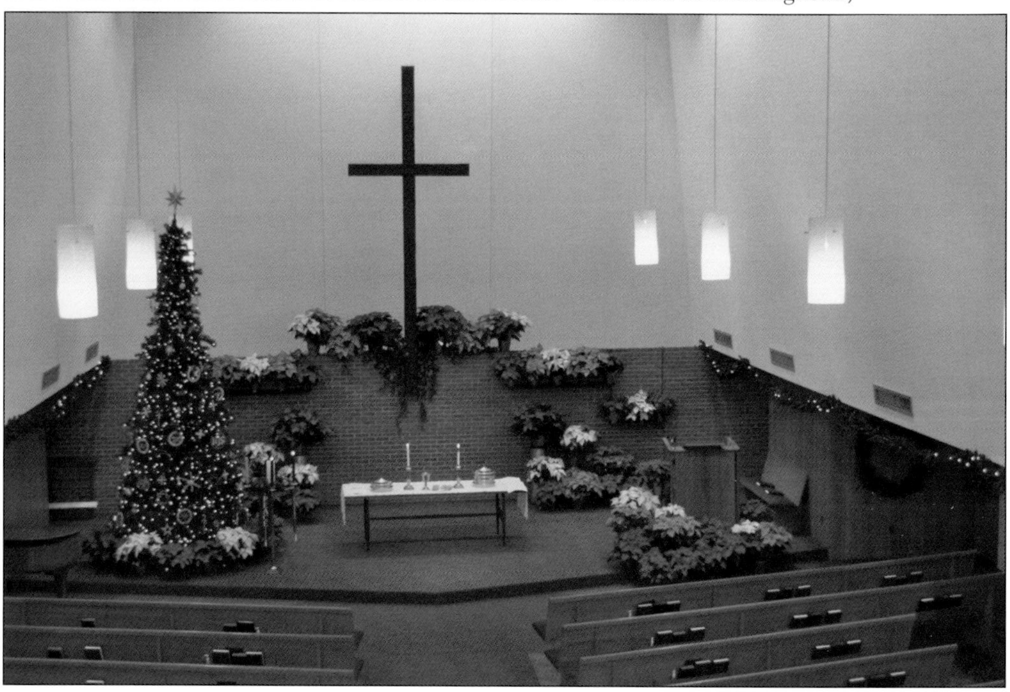

Nine

Some Notable People

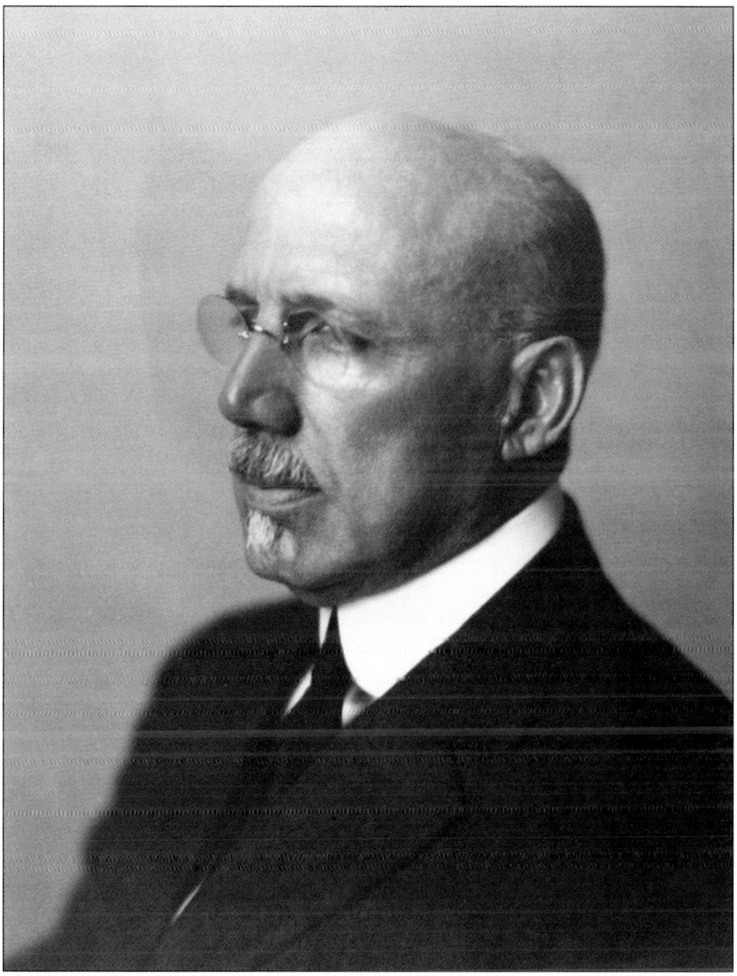

George Gough Booth (1864–1949) and his wife, Ellen Scripps Booth (1863–1948), played such an instrumental role in the development of Bloomfield Hills that the Booth name is almost synonymous with that of the city. In addition to using his entire newspaper fortune of $12 million to build Cranbrook, Booth helped to incorporate the city. (Courtesy of Cranbrook Archives.)

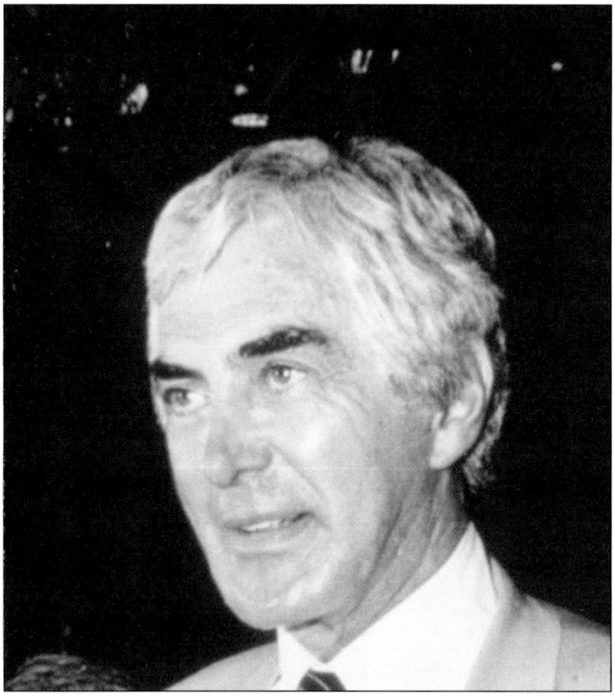

John DeLorean (1925–2005) is perhaps best remembered for his winged-door car, the DMC-12, which is featured in the 1985 movie classic *Back to the Future*. Prior to founding the DeLorean Motor Company, DeLorean was a fast-rising automotive engineer and executive with General Motors Corporation, and he is credited with designing the Pontiac GTO muscle car. (Courtesy of Walter P. Reuther Library, Archives of Labor and Urban Affairs, Wayne State University.)

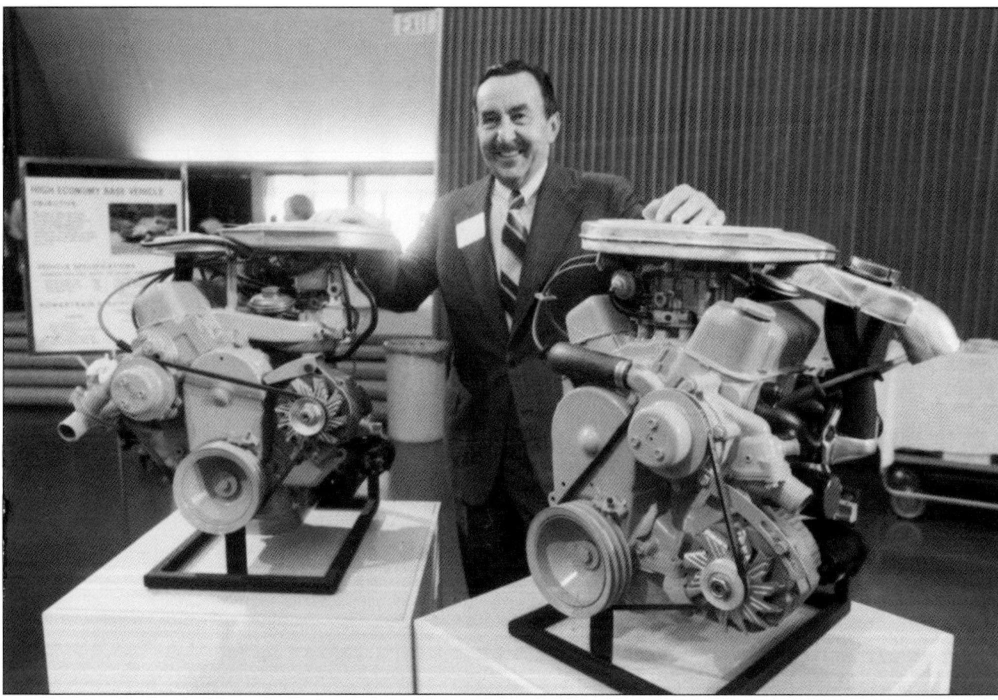

Elliot "Pete" Estes (1916–1988) was an automotive engineer who became the 15th president of General Motors. After a successful stint at Oldsmobile in which he introduced the highly successful Oldsmobile V8 engine, he went on to become the chief engineer at Pontiac and later its division president. He was also president of Chevrolet during the 1960s. (Courtesy of Walter P. Reuther Library, Archives of Labor and Urban Affairs, Wayne State University.)

Aretha Franklin is one of the best-selling female singers and musicians of all time. Often referred to as the "Queen of Soul," she has sold more than 75 million recordings worldwide and is the first female performer to have been inducted into the Rock and Roll Hall of Fame. (Courtesy of the E. Azalia Hackley Collection of African Americans in the Performing Arts, Detroit Public Library.)

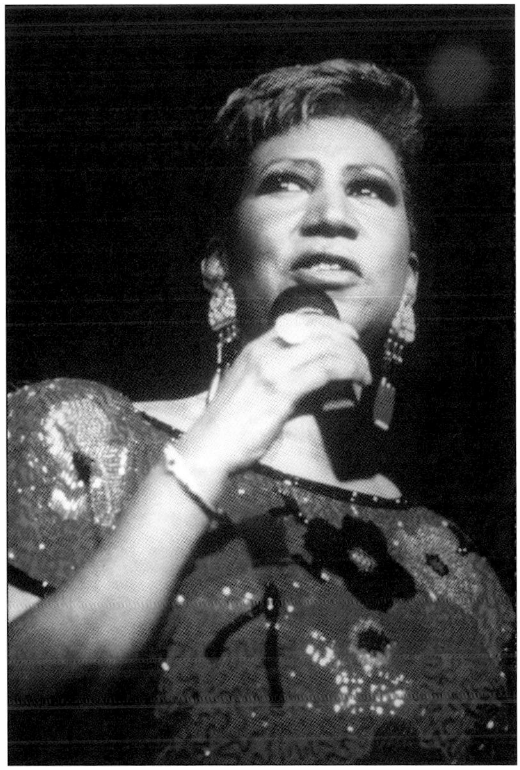

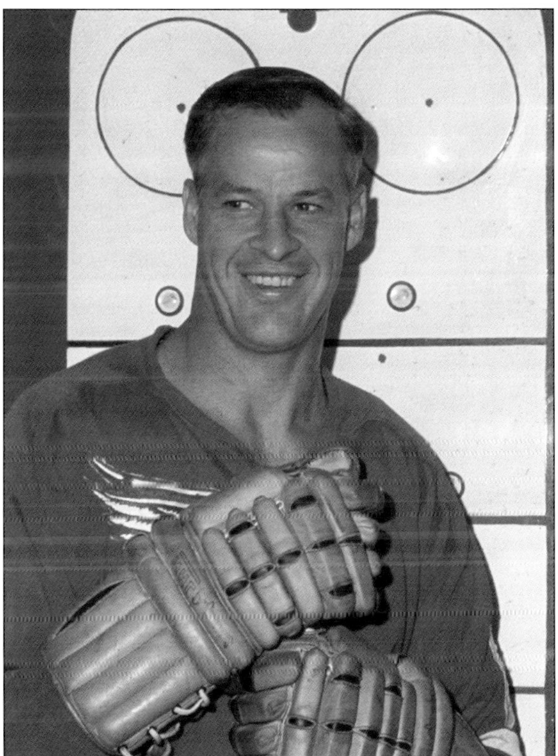

Gordie Howe was recruited by the Detroit Red Wings in 1946 and played 25 seasons with them. He was an NHL All-Star 23 times and held many scoring records. After retiring in 1971, Howe was inducted into the Hockey Hall of Fame. In 2008, he received the NHL Lifetime Achievement Award. (Courtesy of Walter P. Reuther Library, Archives of Labor and Urban Affairs, Wayne State University.)

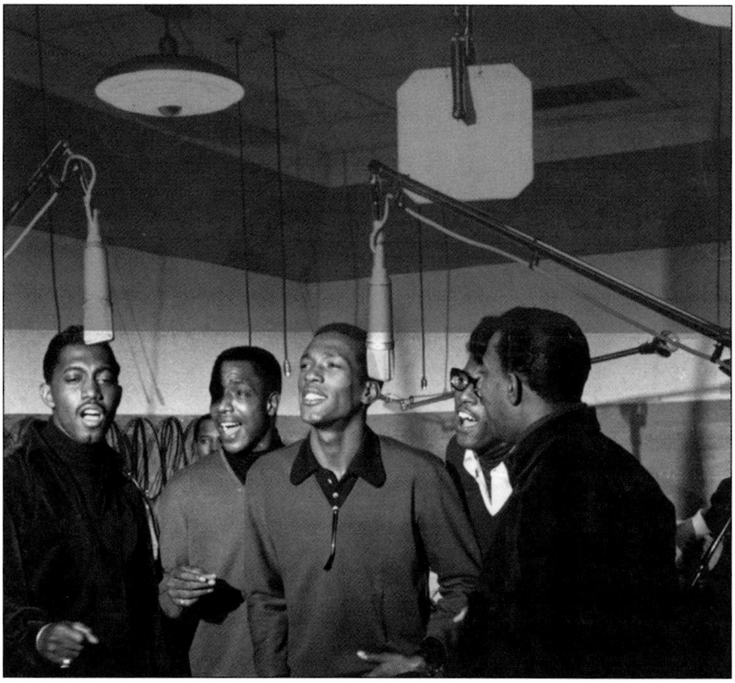

Eddie Kendricks (1939–1992), center, was a singer and songwriter who cofounded the Motown group the Temptations. He became known for his falsetto singing voice and hit songs, including "Keep on Truckin'," which sold more than one million copies. In 1989, Kendricks was inducted into the Rock and Roll Hall of Fame. (Courtesy of the E. Azalia Hackley Collection of African Americans in the Performing Arts, Detroit Public Library.)

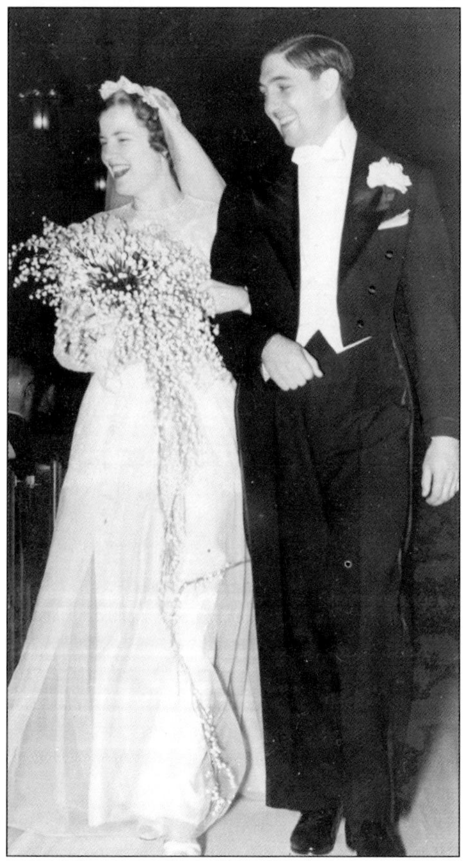

In this 1930s photograph, Semon E. "Bunkie" Knudsen has just wed Frances Anne McConnell, to whom he would be married for 58 years. Knudsen was a high-ranking executive for General Motors, the Ford Motor Company, and White Motors. At General Motors, he improved staid designs for both Pontiac and Chevrolet, increasing sales dramatically. (Courtesy of Walter P. Reuther Library, Archives of Labor and Urban Affairs, Wayne State University.)

Roger S. Penske is chairman of the Penske Corporation, which he founded in 1969. His corporation manages various transportation businesses in excess of $23 billion in more than 3,300 locations. Penske Automotive Group is headquartered in Bloomfield Hills. Penske is also owner of Team Penske, the auto racing team, and an inductee of several motorsports halls of fame. (Courtesy of the Penske Automotive Group.)

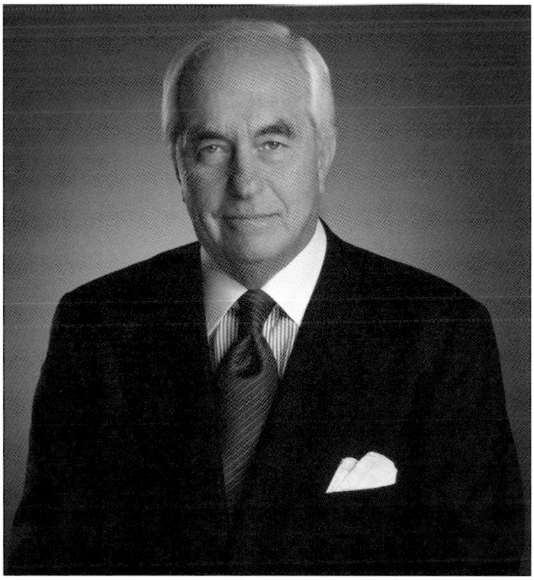

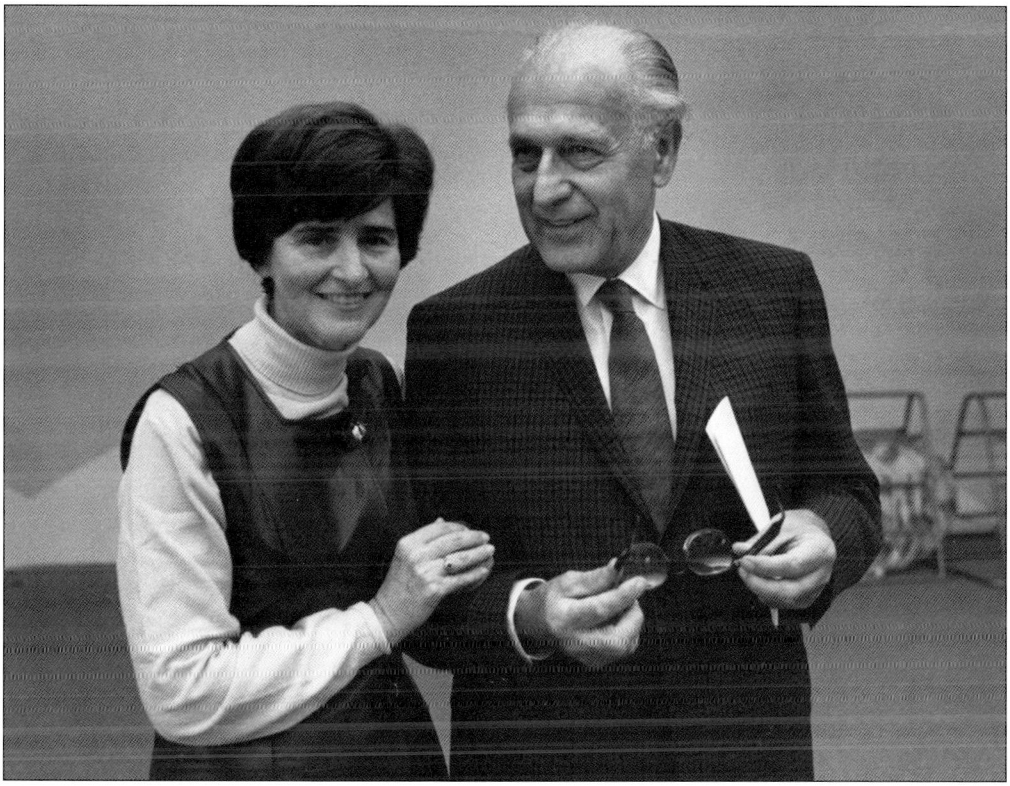

In 1941, George and Annemarie Roeper founded the Roeper School, as it is now called, which was one of the first two institutions in the nation dedicated to the education of gifted students. They also operated the first independent school in Michigan that become integrated. During the 1960s and 1970s, they expanded the campus and facilities considerably, completing the Martin Luther King Jr. Domes in 1969. (Courtesy of the Roeper School Archive, Roeper City and Country School, Inc.)

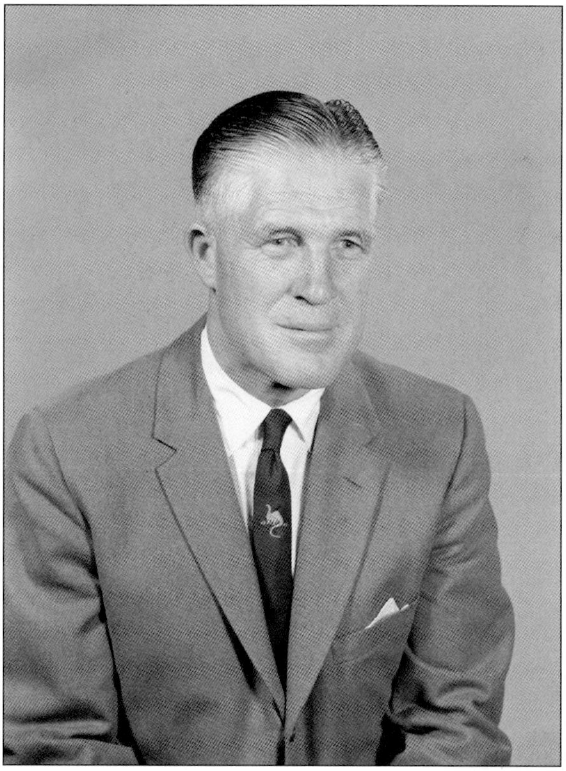

George Romney (1907–1995) was governor of Michigan from 1963 to 1969 as well as secretary of the US Department of Housing and Urban Development from 1969 to 1973. Prior to this, he was president of American Motors Corporation. Romney also presided over the Detroit Stake of the Church of Latter-day Saints, headquartered in Bloomfield Hills. (Courtesy of Walter P. Reuther Library, Archives of Labor and Urban Affairs, Wayne State University.)

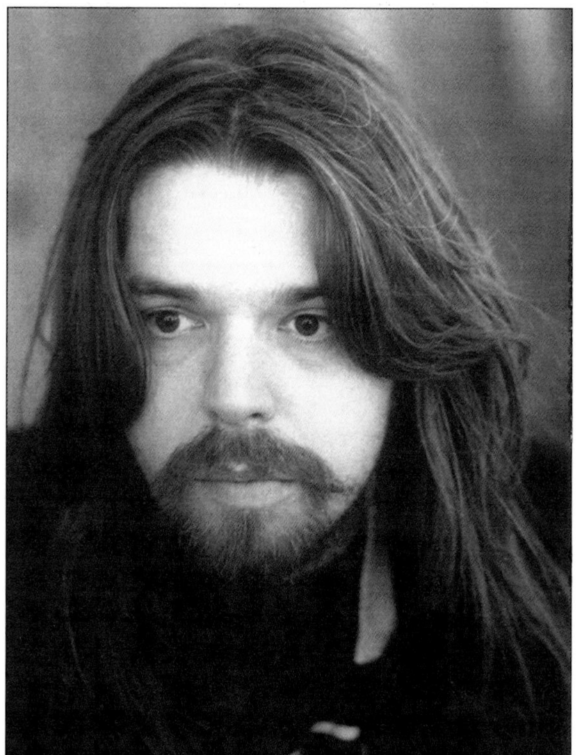

Bob Seger is a famous rock singer, songwriter, and inductee into both the Rock and Roll Hall of Fame and the Songwriters Hall of Fame. Seger owned the Victorian Vaughan House on Vaughan Road during the 1970s and used the Eero Saarinen–designed house on the same property as his recording studio. These homes inspired his song "House Behind a House." (Photograph by and courtesy of Leni Sinclair.)

Chad Smith, world-renowned drummer for the band Red Hot Chili Peppers, grew up in Bloomfield Hills and is a 1980 graduate of Lahser High School. Rated by *Spin* magazine as one of the world's top 10 drummers, Smith is also a member of the Rock and Roll Hall of Fame. He has recorded with many famous musicians and is also known for his charity work. (Photograph by and courtesy of Carroll DeWeese.)

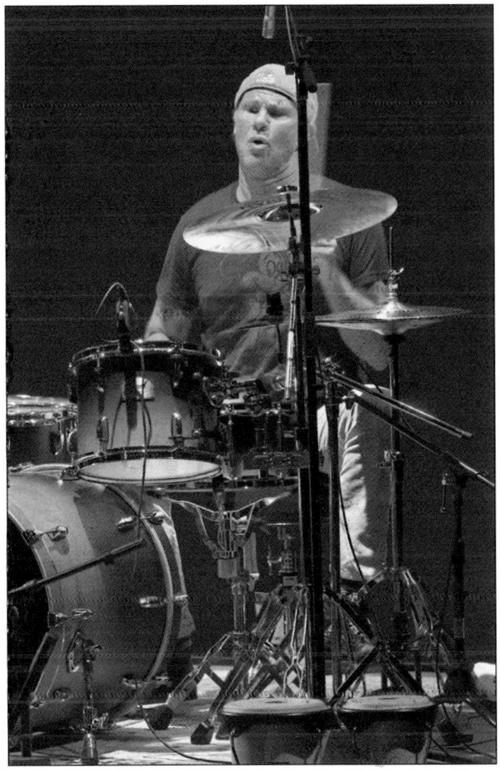

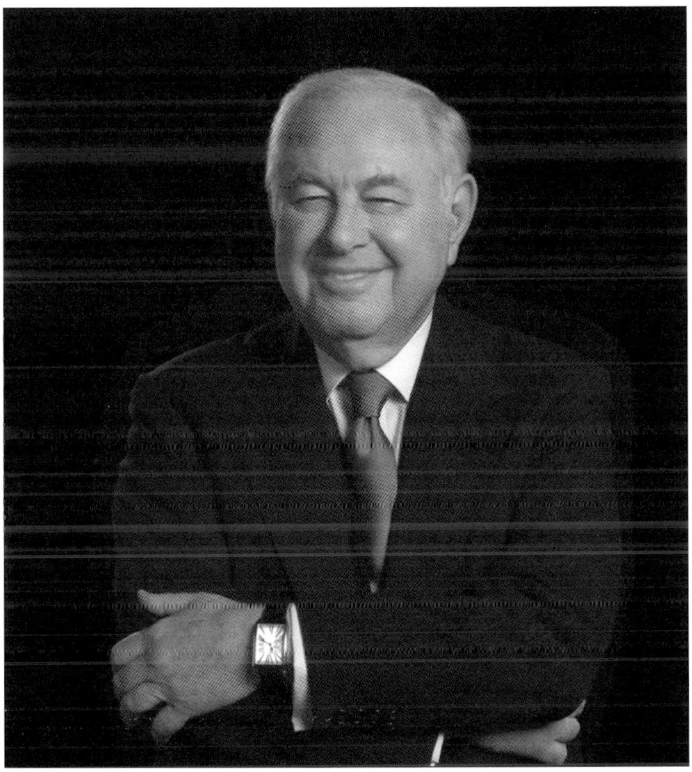

Pioneering shopping mall developer and international entrepreneur A. Alfred Taubman was a Bloomfield Hills resident until his death at age 91. Taubman Centers, Inc., the real estate company he founded in 1950, is headquartered here. The self-made billionaire was a generous supporter of education, art, and health care institutions in Michigan, including the Cranbrook Educational Community, the Detroit Institute of Arts, and the University of Michigan. (Courtesy of Taubman.)

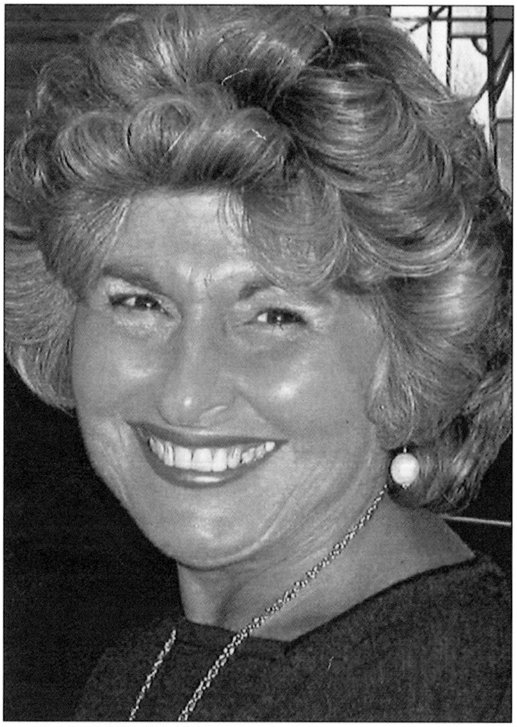

Marilyn Varbedian (1939–2003) served the city of Bloomfield Hills as a commissioner for 22 years and was its mayor four times. She is largely responsible for the ordinance that requires all signage within the city limits to be black and gold. (Courtesy of Pat Hardy.)

Minoru Yamasaki (1912–1986) was an architect famous for his design of the original World Trade Center in New York City. However, he lived and worked here in Michigan, designing the first phase of the Birmingham Unitarian Church on Woodward Avenue in Bloomfield Hills in 1956 and building his residence in Bloomfield Township in 1972. (Courtesy of Walter P. Reuther Library, Archives of Labor and Urban Affairs, Wayne State University.)

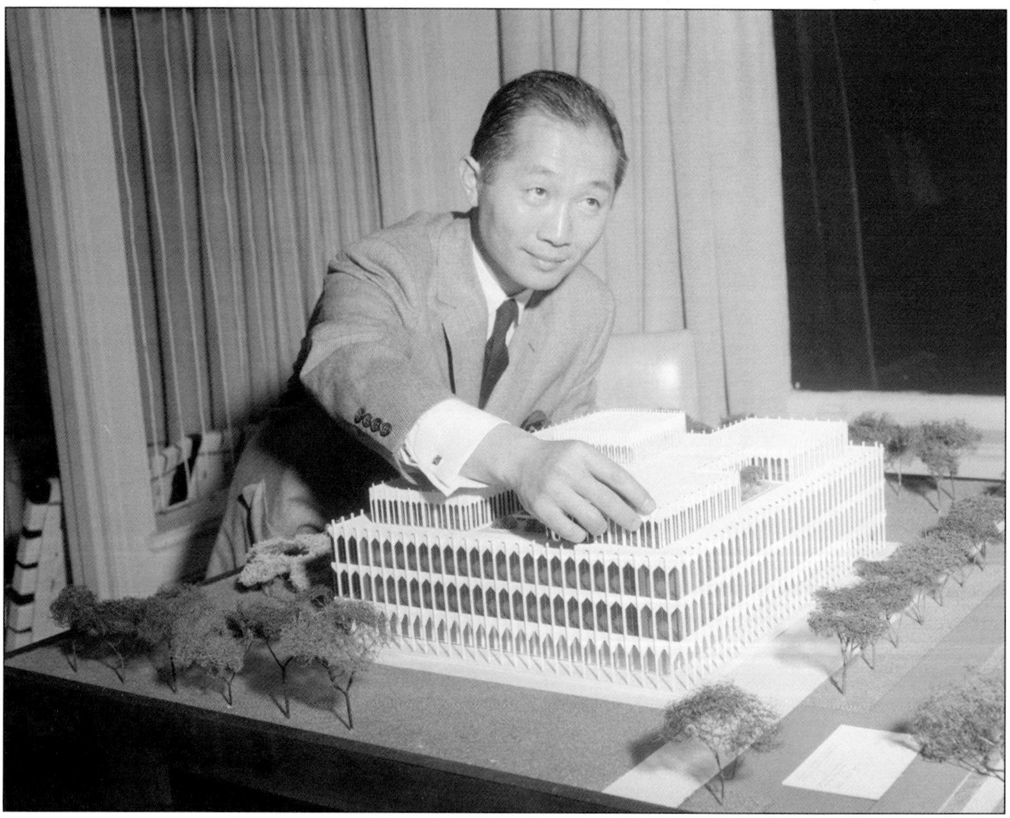

Ten

Greater Bloomfield

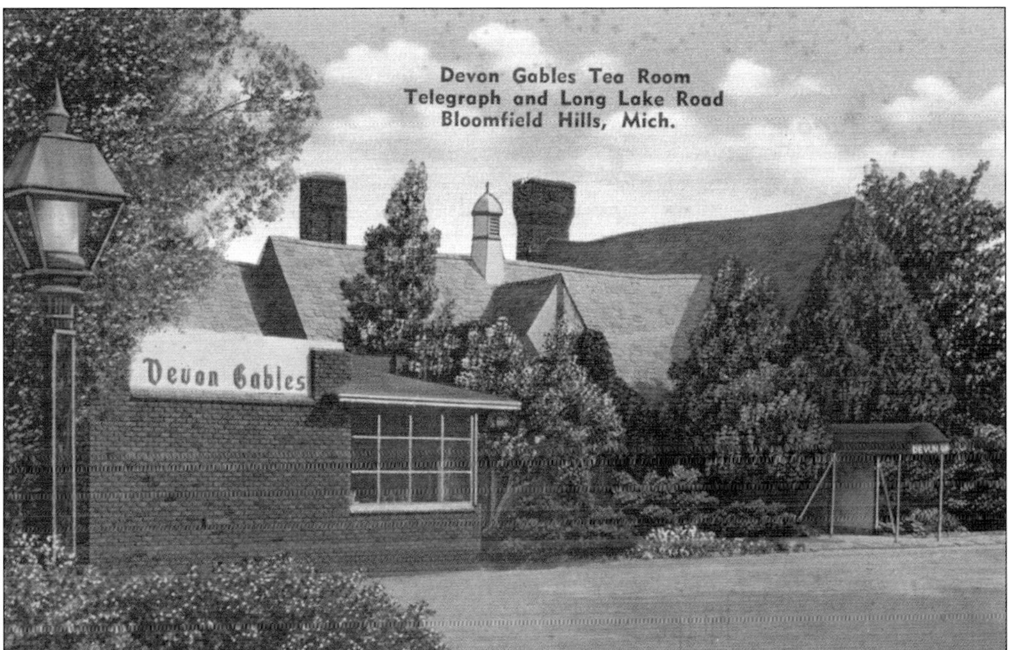

This 1940s–1950s postcard shows Devon Gables, a restaurant and tearoom with an English charm that was located at Telegraph and Long Lake Roads. The restaurant had a gift shop as well as dining areas. (Courtesy of Postcard Collection, Bentley Historical Library, University of Michigan.)

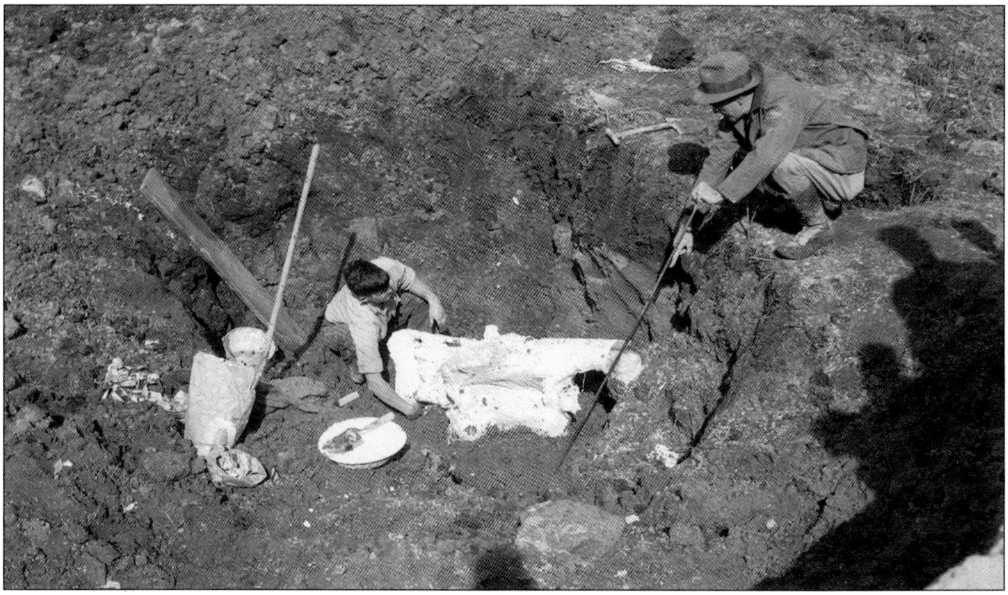

In 1934, bones of "the Bloomfield Hills Mastodon," including its tusks, were discovered in Bloomfield Township on the south side of Charing Cross Road between Woodward Avenue and the Grand Trunk Western Railroad. Some workers had unearthed the bones with a steam shovel while dredging a marl pond. The bones were taken to the Cranbrook Institute of Science for identification. It was determined that this particular mastodon was young when it died more than 250 centuries ago. (Courtesy of Cranbrook Archives.)

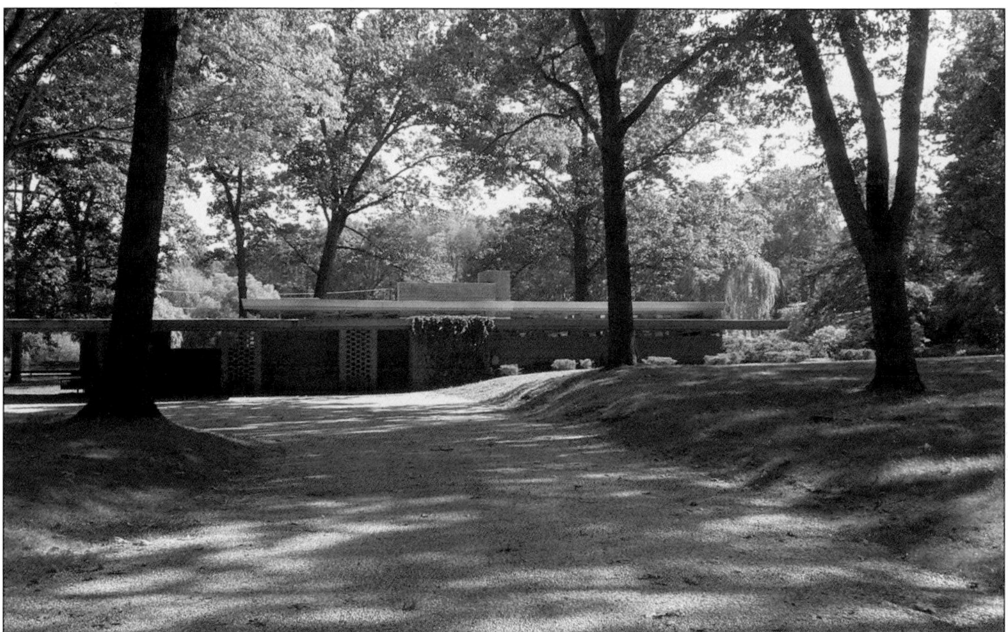

The Melvyn Maxwell and Sara Stein Smith House on Ponvalley Road was designed by Frank Lloyd Wright and constructed in 1949–1950. Called My Haven by its original owners, both schoolteachers, the house is now in the National Register of Historic Places. The Usonian-style house features a dynamic horizontal design with a cantilevered roof. (Author's collection.)

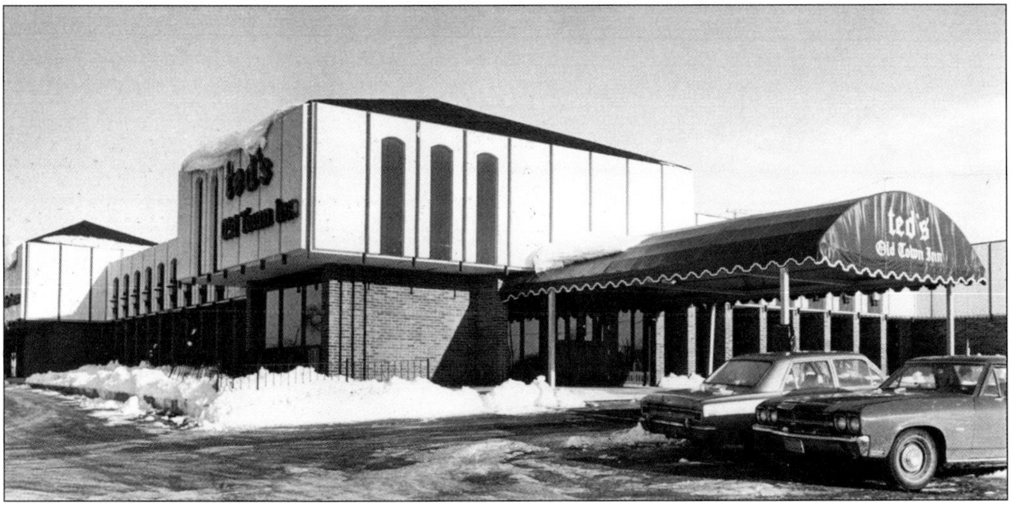

Ted's Old Town Inn is not to be confused with Ted's Drive Inn at Woodward Avenue and Square Lake Road. The latter was a teenage drive-in hangout for Woodward Avenue cruisers that reached its peak of popularity in the 1960s. In this 1974 photograph, Ted's Old Town Inn was an eat-in restaurant that highlighted nightly entertainment and served alcohol. (Courtesy of the Burton Historical Collection, Detroit Public Library.)

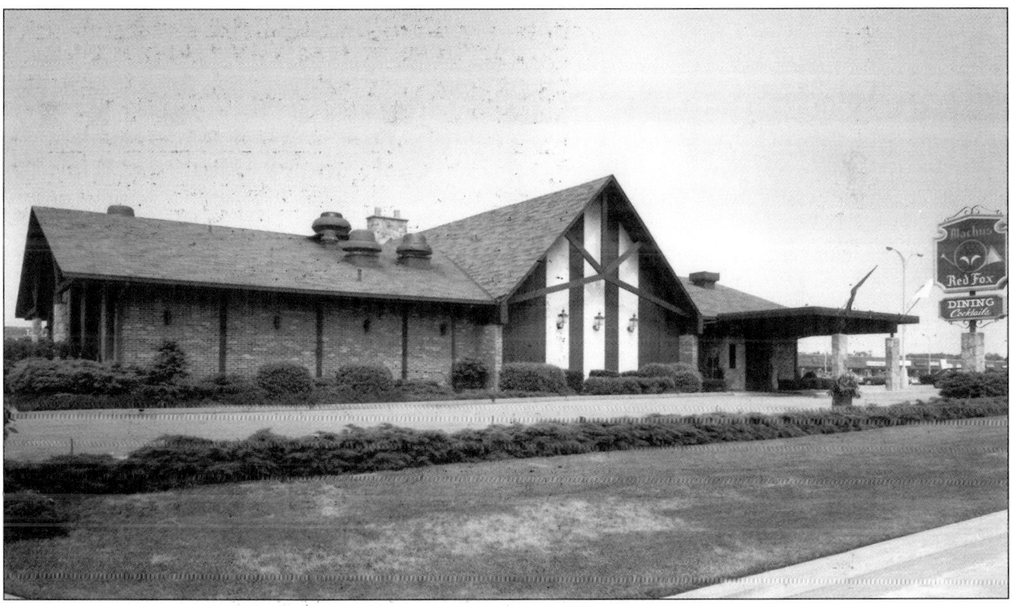

The Machus Red Fox is perhaps best remembered as the place where ex–Teamsters president Jimmy Hoffa was last seen before he disappeared in July 1975. Located on Telegraph Road just south of Maple Road, the upscale restaurant was owned by Harris O. Machus, who operated several other restaurants and bakeries in the Birmingham-Bloomfield area. (Courtesy of Walter P. Reuther Library, Archives of Labor and Urban Affairs, Wayne State University.)

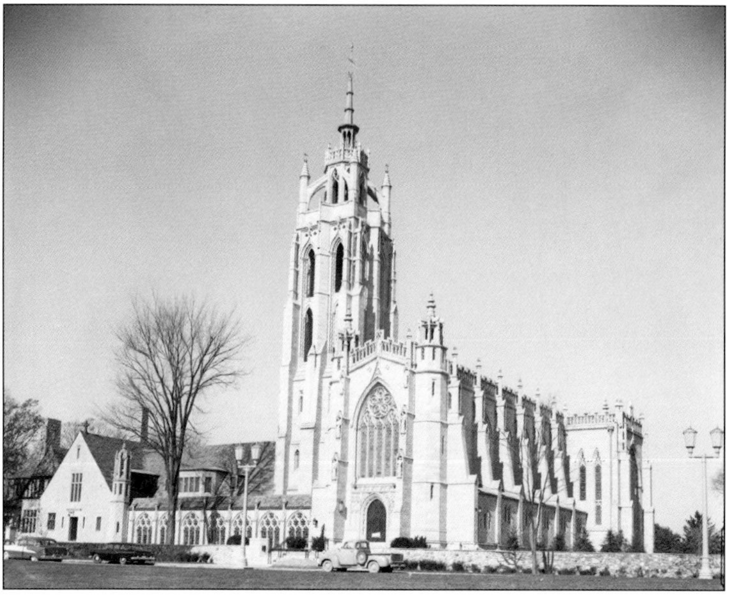

Kirk in the Hills is a majestic Presbyterian church on Long Lake Road that held the first services in its sanctuary in 1958. The neo-Gothic design was modeled on Scotland's Melrose Abbey. In 1947, Col. Edwin S. George donated his home and 40-acre estate, Cedarholm, to build the church. His remains are entombed in the Kirk in the Hills sanctuary. (Courtesy of the Burton Historical Society, Detroit Public Library.)

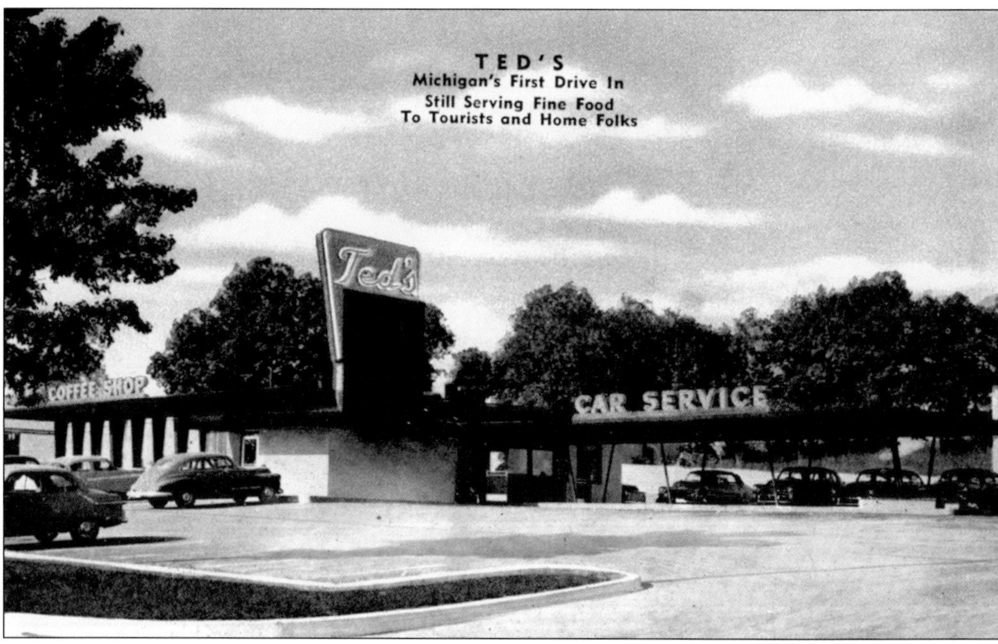

This c. 1950s postcard shows Ted's, "Michigan's first drive-in," on Woodward Avenue and Square Lake Road. This hot spot for teenagers and Woodward cruisers was at the end of a string of drive-ins starting in Ferndale and ending in Bloomfield Hills. Ted's offered year-round curb service as well as indoor meals and advertised itself as the home of the world's largest hot dog. (Author's collection.)

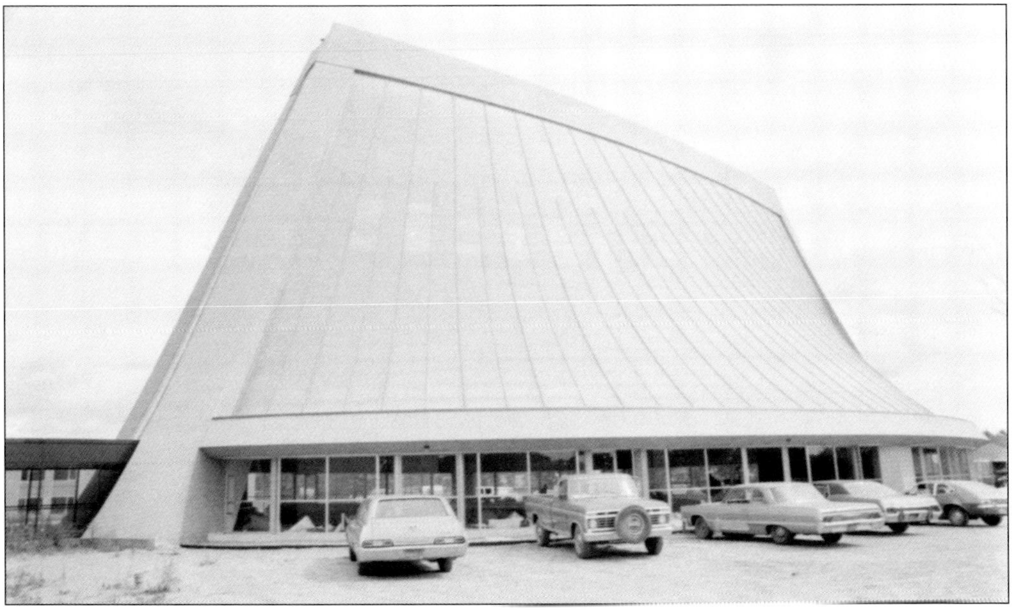

Temple Beth El at the corner of Telegraph Road and 14 Mile Road was designed by architect Minoru Yamasaki and built in 1973. A reform synagogue, Beth El is the oldest Jewish congregation in Michigan. The sanctuary, still under construction here, was modeled to resemble a tent, which recalls the earliest meeting places of the Jewish people. (Courtesy of Walter P. Reuther Library, Archives of Labor and Urban Affairs, Wayne State University.)

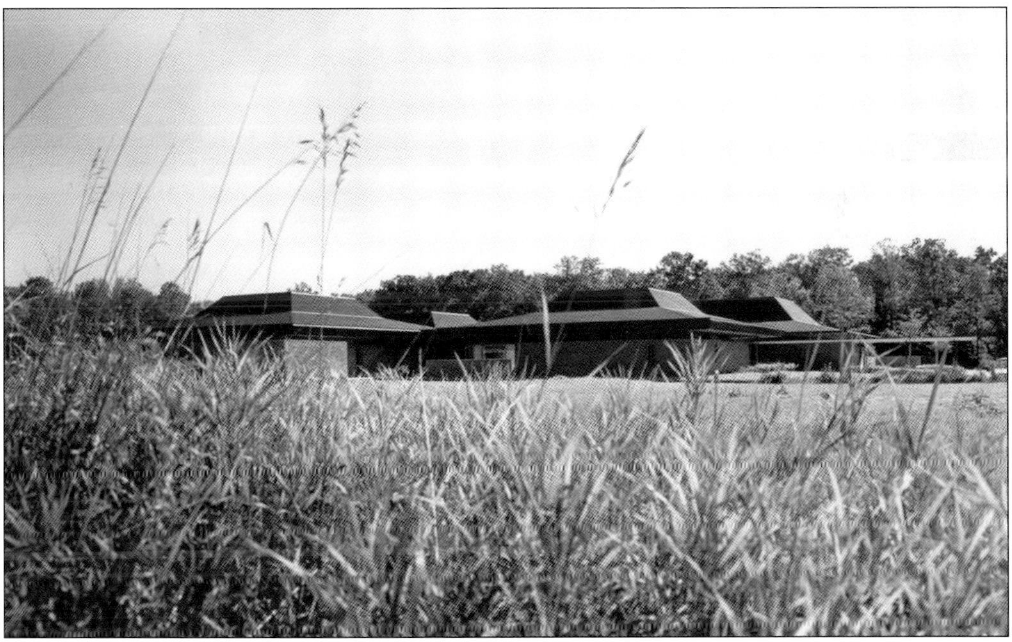

The Bloomfield Township Public Library began service in 1964 in a rented facility on Telegraph Road. In 1969, the library opened in this new building on Lone Pine Road at Telegraph Road. The building was designed by Charles MacMahan and Associates and had four interconnecting pavilions. The library has since been renovated twice and is now connected by 15 pavilions. (Photograph by Balthazar Korab, courtesy of Bloomfield Township Public Library.)

Selected Bibliography

Andrecovich, Mary. *Manresa*. Bloomfield Hills: Manresa Jesuit Retreat House, 2014.

Avery, Lilian Drake, ed. "An Account of Oakland County." In *Historic Michigan*, vol. 3, edited by George N. Fuller. Lansing: National Historical Association, 1924.

Chamberlain, Amylee. *Slates to Computers: A History of the Bloomfield Hills School District*. Bloomfield Hills: Bloomfield Hills School District, 1980.

City of Bloomfield Hills 75th Anniversary Celebration 1932–2007. Bloomfield Hills: City of Bloomfield Hills, 2007.

Clark, Elizabeth C. *Beside a Lake: A History of Kingswood School Cranbrook*. Bloomfield Hills: Cranbrook Press, 2006.

Clark, Robert Judson, et al. *Design in America: The Cranbrook Vision 1925–1950*. New York: Harry N. Abrams, Inc., 1983.

Durant, Samuel W., ed. *The History of Oakland County, 1817–1877*. Philadelphia: L.H. Everts & Co., 1877.

Eckert, Kathryn Bishop. *The Campus Guide: Cranbrook*. New York: Princeton Architectural Press, 2001.

Hagman, Arthur A., ed. *Oakland County Book of History: The Sesqui-Centennial Publication 1820–1970*. Pontiac, MI: Oakland County, 1970.

McMechan, Jervis Bell. *Christ Church Cranbrook*. Bloomfield Hills: Christ Church Cranbrook, 1979.

Pound, Arthur. *The Only Thing Worth Finding*. Detroit: Wayne State University Press, 1964.

Saarinen, Eliel. *The Saarinen Door*. Bloomfield Hills: Cranbrook Academy of Art, 1963.

Smith, Kay. *Bloomfield Blossoms*. Bloomfield Hills: Bloomfield Township Bicentennial Commission, 1976.

Snyder III, Ben M. *Once More with Joy: Perspectives of Cranbrook School for Boys*. Bloomfield Hills: Cranbrook Press, 1997.

INDEX

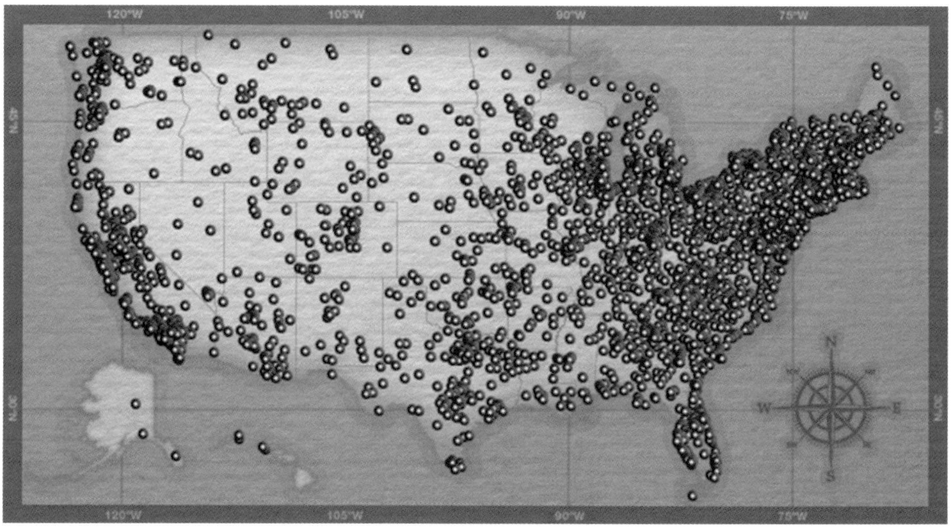